THE COMPLETE GUIDE
TO
NON-DIRECTIONAL TRADING

Heinrich Weber
&
Kermit Zieg

Traders Press Inc.®
703 Laurens Road
Greenville, SC 29607

Phone: 800-927-8222 or 864-298-0222
Fax: 864-298-0221
http://www.traderspress.com

ISBN: 0-934380-71-6
Published by: Traders Press, Inc.®

This publication is designed to provide accurate and authoritative information with regard to the subject matter covered. It is sold with the understanding that the publisher is not engaged in rendering legal, accounting, or other professional advice. If legal advice or other expert assistance is required, the services of a competent professional person should be sought.

EDITING, LAYOUT AND COVER DESIGN
Teresa Darty Alligood
Editor and Graphic Designer
Traders Press, Inc.®

Traders Press Inc.®
703 Laurens Road
Greenville, SC 29607

Phone: 800-927-8222 or 864-298-0222
Fax: 864-298-0221
http://www.traderspress.com

Publisher's Foreword

Ever since becoming conversant with the concept of options and the many strategies which may be employed by using them in various combinations, I've been fascinated with the concept that many of these strategies, if evaluated at expiration, result in the potential of profits over a wide range of prices for the underlying instrument, whether prices move up, down, or sideways. In order to profit, one need not be able to pinpoint the direction or extent of price movement during the time period in question, but merely bracket a wide range of prices outside of which the underlying will NOT move. This book is intended to be a working guide and a comprehensive reference for those traders to whom the non-directional style of trading appeals. It is our hope that it will serve to broaden the awareness of the benefits of non-directional trading to those who have not engaged in it before, and to broaden the knowledge of available strategies for those who have.

An important point to note is that the authors of this book "walk the walk"…it is not written by academic theorists, but by actual practitioners of the principles of which they write. To me, this is a major factor to consider when evaluating the value to a book to potential readers who intend to use the ideas discussed in the "real market"…the advice given is far more valuable when coming from others who have "been there."

Edward Dobson

Edward D. Dobson, President
Traders Press, Inc.®
Greenville, SC
October 12, 2005

Table of Contents

CHAPTER 1

INTRODUCTION

1.1 UP OR DOWN? THAT IS THE QUESTION

What is investing all about? Is it about buying stock and holding it for years as a long-term investor? We don't think so!

Investing is making money in the markets with whatever strategies to reduce risk, while increasing returns. The goal of the investor should be to make the maximum level of profit while controlling the possibility of a catastrophic loss. **Investing should be fun.**

Making money in the markets is possible. But why then do so many investors manage to "screw it up?" They usually fail because they fall into the age-old trap of believing that market successes come from predicting whether a stock will rise or fall. There's no question that accurately predicting the future direction of a stock price movement will make the investor money. The problem is that this is the most difficult task faced by any investor.

> **How do we know that the stock is going to move up or down?**

First, there are the technical tools. These tools focus exclusively on the price and volume action of the stock and are totally unconcerned with anything dealing with the firm as an operating business entity. There are hundreds of technical methods commonly employed by traders and investors alike that reportedly forecast future price directional moves. These would include Point-and-Figure formations, support and resistance lines, moving average penetrations, and a host of other indicators. Most commonly used charting packages have built-in technical formulas for hundreds of such tools. These techniques, when used separately or in some combination, are supposed to telegraph the direction of the next move in the security. Technicians believe that everything known about the company is reflected in the stock price and volume data and the study of these two provides all the information necessary to make highly accurate and intelligent investment decisions.

Then there is always the fundamental analysis approach. A fundamentalist looks at the company as an operating entity. The success or failure of a firm is reflected in numerous financial ratios, competitive market position analysis, review of new products in the pipeline, profit margins, sales growth, earnings trends, free cash flow, and similar data relating to the company's structure, its profitability, market competitive position and related factors. Fundamental analysis is not concerned with stock price action or its trading volume. It only focuses on the business, its past, the current situation, and forecasting how it will perform in the future. Then and only then is the stock price viewed to determine if the current price is too low, too high, or just right based upon the prospects of the economy, the industry in which it operates, and the predictive operating results of the business.

1

Some individuals subscribe to the technical approach, spending their time analyzing charts. Others, the fundamentalists, feel more comfortable reading annual reports, SEC filings, and following the recommendations of security analysts. And then there is the third group, those who combine technical analysis and fundamentals in their stock selection and trading strategies.

Technicians believe their charts hold all the answers. Fundamentalists are convinced that diligent reading of company documents will point them in the correct direction. And those who combine technical and fundamental analysis labor under the belief that they have the best of all approaches for market success.

So the technicians think they're right, the fundamentalists are convinced of their analysis, and those utilizing both fundamental and technical approaches are surely correct in their predictions. If all three have such great strategies, why do so many market participants fail to make money consistently?

Let's view the situation in a slightly different way. Who is wrong in a stock transaction? Remember that all buy orders are offset by sell transactions. When someone buys 100 shares of Microsoft, someone else is selling 100 shares of that stock. The stock buyer is buying because he expects that the security will quickly rise in price. The buyer is buying now in the belief that the security will move up and will do so immediately. If the projected movement date is in the distant future, the buyer would naturally wait to make the purchase until closer to the anticipated starting time of the move. Today's stock buyer has faith in the direction of the stock, up, and in the timing of the move, immediate. But who is this buyer purchasing shares from? The seller's analysis has indicated this stock is going to decline, and will do so immediately. Thus, the buyer thinks the stock is going up immediately and the seller thinks the stock is going down immediately. Both are convinced of the rightness of their predictions, and yet one of them will be wrong. Fifty percent of the shares are incorrectly positioned. Is the buyer dumb? Is the seller ill informed? Absolutely not. Both have strong views, beliefs, and studied convictions. Yet one will be wrong. We're talking about traders and investors who are intelligent, astute, who are wagering real dollars on the accuracy of their predictions. They've done their homework. They have done their analysis. They are making their buy and sell decisions with total confidence and conviction. And yet either the buyer or seller will be wrong. Half the investors are wrong. Making money is not possible when one is wrong, and mighty hard when one is correct on market direction predictions only half the time.

Sometimes we as traders are not totally convinced of our predictive abilities. We look at a stock chart and have no idea as to the future price action. For example, today we have personally examined the charts of 50 stocks. These were technology securities which had risen between 50 and 100% in the last six months. We had absolutely no ability to predict whether the next move for these securities would be a further continuation of the already significant price advance or a market retrenchment from the current seemingly high prices. Our technical analysis yielded confused results. Fundamentally the picture was cloudy. We were baffled. We were unable to predict price direction, either short-term or intermediate term, for these stocks. But we were convinced that whichever direction the price moved, it would be dramatic.

How many traders and investors do you know who are correct at stock price predictions all the time? We know of none. How about most of the time? We know of very few. Our experience has shown that at best most investors can accurately forecast price less than half of the time.

Because half of all investors are wrong on any single transaction, and because it is so difficult to accurately predict the direction of future price movement of a stock, what is an investor to do?

They can cut their losses short and let their profits run. They can also focus on the theory of this book: namely that price direction cannot be accurately predicated, but volatility can.

Most of us have been trained to believe that market profits are derived from predicting which way a stock will move. This is the purpose of security analysts, investment newsletter writers, talking heads, charting packages, and the supposed benefits of technical and/or fundamental analysis. Furthermore, as investors we try to predict more than just the direction of the movement. We also attempt to anticipate the magnitude of the move. It's not enough to forecast that the price will move up from its current level. We also want to know the movement will be significant enough to justify commission costs, opportunity costs, cover the risks associated with the trade, and yield a healthy profit. That is, we want to know the stock will move up, and move up a significant amount.

> **The hard part of investing is predicting which way a stock will move. The premise of this book is that we no longer need to predict the direction of the movement to make money. Price directional predictions can simply not be done with a high degree of accuracy.**

Of the two things that most investors do (attempting to predict the direction of the price movement, and the magnitude of the movement,) the first it is nearly impossible, while the second is relatively simple.

This book will demonstrate how investors can significantly increase returns, while lowering the risks without the need for accurate predictions of price direction. Stock volatility, not price prediction, is the key to success.

This is not to say technical and/or fundamental analysis is not useful. Both will provide some indications of future price direction. The use of either or both technical and fundamental analysis will help in achieving a higher probability of making accurate directional forecasts. Rather than being correct on price directional predictions only 50% of the time, an intelligent user of detailed analysis will have a higher accuracy rate. We strongly encourage the use of both technical and fundamental analysis, yet put greater faith in the technical tools.

Point and Figure is a technical methodology on which we have extensively written. It is one of the simplest and most accurate of technical and charting tools. We will give a full introduction toPoint-and-Figure later on.

Yet no matter how good a technical methodology might be at predicting a future price direction, its accuracy will rather reach 60% than 100%, and this only if you use a very good system. Therefore there is a need to supplement any technical or fundamental analysis with volatility study and then utilize stock options to increase returns and lower risks.

1.2 HOW IS THIS BOOK DIFFERENT?

To fully appreciate this book, it is important to understand how it differs from other books on the market. The ways in which it is different and better are outlined below:

MAKING MONEY

This book is all about making money. It is not a get-rich-quick essay on how to rapidly transform a few thousand dollars into millions. Instead it is a well-documented and painstakingly researched coverage of strategies and techniques to reduce risk while magnifying profits without the need to accurately forecast the direction of price movements. The techniques covered are employed by some of the most successful investors and hedge funds in the world – traders interested in "stacking the deck" in their favor, without the need to guess which way a stock price will move.

The goal of this book is to clearly and concisely outline easy-to-implement trading methodologies that rely upon a stock's volatility— rather than its predicted market direction—to make money. Most investors believe market success requires directional predictions, as well as forecasting the magnitude of the move. Not so. The provable premise of this work is that volatility, not price direction, is the driving force for profit enhancement, and to demonstrate that volatility is far easier to predict accurately than price direction.

The techniques covered do not require accuracy in predicting future price moves. To profit handsomely, one needs only to estimate the magnitude of future price movements, not their direction.

Take for example KLA—Tencor Corp (KLAC). The stock rose from 32 to 60 between March and August 2003. On September 10, 2003 the stock declined $2.23, to close at $55.57. At this point, which way will the next major move in the stock be? That is hard to predict. At its current price, are we able to assess if the stock is overvalued, undervalued or correctly valued?

But think how much easier it is to predict that this stock, which on average has moved more than 6 points, or 12%, each and every month between March and August, will continue to move 12% per month in the foreseeable future.

FIGURE 1: KLAC CHART

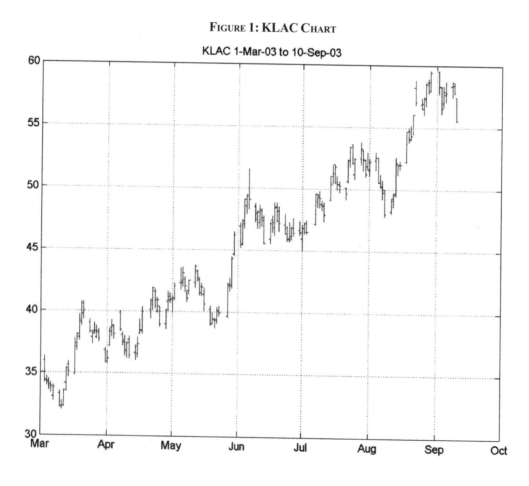

The techniques that will allow you to profit from volatility are presented in a manner easy to understand, always with numerous examples to reinforce the learning of the concept. Research proof of their simplicity and profitability is also presented where it exits.

After completing this book, you will have an arsenal of tried, proven, and profitable market strategies, all designed to increase the profitability of your entire portfolio while at the same time reducing its risk. In other words, this book is all about teaching you, the reader, how to make above average market returns without taking unacceptably high risks. Trading should be fun, profitable, and should allow you to sleep at night. The goal of this book is to teach you a different way to approach the market that will be fun because of its logic, simplicity, and profitability, easy to understand and implement, and that will eliminate a great deal of the uncertainty and risk associated with most market trading approaches.

MAKE IT SIMPLE

Investing is scary and complicated enough to represent a formidable hurdle for many. We know that some are math phobic and/or have limited prior investment experience. We therefore have made this book very simple and user-friendly. All techniques are explained in great detail, numerous examples are provided, and simple arithmetic calculations explain the underlying decision process and the results of the transaction. There are several detailed technical chapters, explaining and providing theoretical proof. But these chapters can be ignored without any loss of continuity in understanding the very practical trading strategies presented.

Our goal is to provide each and every reader with a clear understanding of the strategies presented, and the knowledge to implement them. Further, we want each reader to be at a comfortable level to apply our trading methods. This can only be accomplished by making the material clear, concise, detailed, and understandable. This book is therefore a "how-to book" for trading options utilizing volatility for profitability.

We only succeed with our goal if you understand the concepts, accept them as being logical and valid, and use them. We therefore constantly strive to make all methodologies simple to grasp and easy to implement.

1.3   WHY STOCK OPTIONS?

The purpose of this book is to explain the use of stock options to lessen the need to predict future price movements, while always reaching for high portfolio returns and low risk. The strategies all involve the conservative use of stock options. Why? Because stock options are the perfect investment.

Stock options are the ideal investment media. In buying stock options you have a very small cash outlay in comparison to stock ownership. Through leverage, your profit potential is many times the option cost, and the percentage return on the option investment can far exceed that of a stock investment. Your maximum loss is relatively small in dollars and is known to the penny. Options offer far greater flexibility and more investment strategies than are available in stock. When options are coupled with stock, the return on the portfolio can dramatically increase while individual security and portfolio risk is drastically cut.

As an option seller you are paid money immediately for your willingness to buy your favorite stocks at lower than current market prices in the future, or sell some of your weaker stocks in the future at considerable higher than current market prices.

After studying all types of markets since 1958, writing books and articles on growth stocks, futures, commodity options, and stock options, and investing in, speculating with, and trading stocks, futures, commodity options, index options, and stock options for many years, we have never found a better investment, a more perfect investment or as consistently profitable an investment as options.

If you are not familiar with the terms "puts," "calls," "straddles," "strike price," "intrinsic value," "expiration date," and "time value," then you may be missing out on one of the most interesting and profitable ways to control risks and maximize returns ever developed in the stock market. Everything you need to know about stock option terminology and trading strategies will be covered in detail in this book.

This book is an easy and very user-friendly way to learn the basics of options and their use. It is designed for the average investor, teaching a number of simple, very successful and worry-free strategies to generate large returns while at all times controlling risk to a manageable and comfortable level. It is also designed for the experienced trader who seeks trading techniques with greater probabilities of success. Many other books on options assume advanced investment experience on the part of the reader, or a high level of mathematical skill, or the patience to wade through hundreds of pages of very complex and theoretical examples without ever applying the material to the real world or immediate needs of the student.

This work attempts to change all that, making several basic assumptions, with appropriate responses to each. First, we assume the reader possesses some basic knowledge of the stock market, but has little or no training or experience with stock options. The book is therefore very simple to understand. Strategies are discussed in a very straightforward manner with technical terms omitted whenever possible. And yet the strategies discussed are detailed enough and unique enough that even seasoned investors and traders will be challenged. Second, higher level mathematics and complicated algebraic formulas are of little interest to the reader. No skills above basic arithmetic are needed to fully understand the concepts. Third, theory is not as important as practical examples. We show how things work in the real world, not how they work in the classroom. Fourth, the reader wants to avoid a waste of time. The book gets to the meat of the subject quickly and is not cluttered with fluff or concepts that fill pages but add little to developing a better understanding of the profitable use of options. And lastly, what the reader really wants from an investment book is a very practical, time tested and proven, easy to understand, and quick-to-implement investment strategy that will maximize investment returns while keeping a low and manageable level of risk. So at each step the practical application of the concepts, strategies, and techniques are stressed. It is the ultimate goal of this book to teach in a few hours the basics of options and how to profitably employ them. This is what it is really all about – how can I be a more successful investor?

There is money to be made in options, and plenty of it. This book will provide the reader with everything he needs to get started and succeed in the options markets. Regardless of whether you are a small investor, an inexperienced investor, a trader with years of trade knowledge, or an institutional manager, you will find strategies that are right for you. Most of these techniques actually have lower risk than stock ownership, while offering the investor far greater returns. Profitability and risk management do not require accuracy at forecasting future stock movements.

As a result of the lower risk and greater profit potential of stock options, this book could have been titled *Never Buy Stock Again*. Since some of the strategies do involve the purchase of stock, and the thrust is on volatility and non-directional trading, the title actually selected fits more accurately. This book is not about buying stock for a direct profit on the stock, but using options to avoid the use of stock.

1.4 THE ORGANIZATION OF THE BOOK

First we talk about the opportunity, namely non-directional strategies. Then we explain all you need to know – and even a bit more – about options, the building block of our strategies. We go on to the major brain teaser, volatility. Finally, we put it all together and present the non-directional strategies that will work for you.

1.5 ABOUT COMPUTERS AND ONLINE RESOURCES

A computer with an internet access and nothing more, is required to profit from the content of this book. No expensive Bloomberg or Reuters terminal required!

In the examples we have tried always to use the best value for money resources, especially Yahoo's finance content and PCQuote, which are both available for free at the time of this book's publication.

Then we make reference to two exceptional options sites, namely www.ivolatility.com and www.optionmonitor.com, both of which are inexpensive, but deliver excellent information for a small subscription.

We are not associated with any of those companies and do not get anything in return for recommending them. We recommend them because they are good.

Then you will probably trade through a high quality online broker, such as www.optionsxpress.com, www.interactivebrokers.com, or any internet access services of the major financial institutions. All of those sites, too, have an excellent compilation of information and price quotes.

Of course, when you trade actively, you should invest in fast computers, charting and pricing software. Later in the book, we will give a list of interesting products, with the active private trader in mind.

We often include graphics generated by MatLab because we use it for our own research. But luckily you don't need such a sophisticated product to trade options in its most profitable way! With the few online resources mentioned plus a charting package, you should do great.

CHAPTER 2
OPPORTUNITY IDENTIFIED:
THE THEORY OF NON-DIRECTIONAL TRADING

2.1 MARKETS ARE DIFFICULT TO PREDICT

In the introduction we have outlined the problems surrounding the prediction of future market action. There are still many academics who adhere to the Efficient Market Hypothesis, which basically says that it is impossible to predict markets at all. As we mentioned in the introduction, we use technical analysis for stock price forecasting, but are aware of the frequently experienced ambiguity of the signals. The reasons why markets are difficult to predict have been studied at length, but the common sense reason is this: the actors in the markets are humans driven by their hopes and fears, and the sum total of those human motivations for buying or selling constitute a highly complex system. One trader buys because he has a strong belief in market direction, another sells because he has to reduce his positions, a third transacts in the process of hedging an options portfolio. All these involved parties create the dynamics and the ever-changing prices in a market.

Many reasons could be found why markets are so difficult to predict, and so we would like to give you some examples, throughout the entire book. The examples are very strong changes in market directions. Their abruptness is the proof that the change in direction was not at all foreseen by the market participants, otherwise a trend-change would happen gradually by gradually increasing the number of market-players that believe in, or bet on, the new market direction.

2.2 ABOUT CHARTS AND CRASHES

The graphic representation of price moves over time—charts—are ideal as decision support for trading and investing purposes. Charts allow the use of the human brain's enormous capacity as a pattern-recognizer. Moreover, we know, based on the most recent research, that the performance of our brain in recognizing patterns goes far beyond the one of computers, and therefore we encourage you to use charts as your major source of price-action information.

Thus charts are the tool to visualize the market moves. Since we use them continuously you will find many of them throughout the book. We prefer three types of charts, namely the line chart, the bar chart, and the Point-and-Figure chart. Other charts, such as candlesticks or Kagi are not used by us and we therefore cannot comment on them.

2.2.1 LINE CHARTS

Line charts are the most basic of all charts. They are constructed by drawing a line from closing price to closing price. The closing prices we use are most commonly daily, but they can also be weekly or monthly or of an intraday time segment. Line charts are useful to chart very long price series (cf. first chart), to chart tick-data (cf. second chart) or to compare prices (cf. third chart).

FIGURE 2: DOW JONES LINE CHART LONG

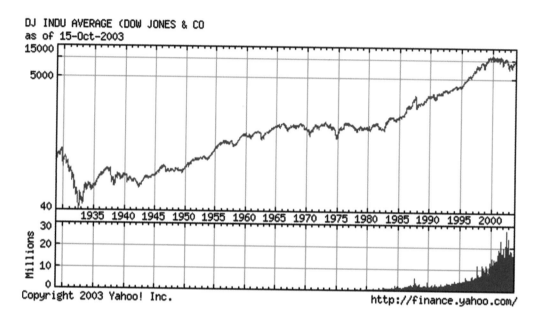

FIGURE 3: DOW JONES INTRADAY LINE CHART

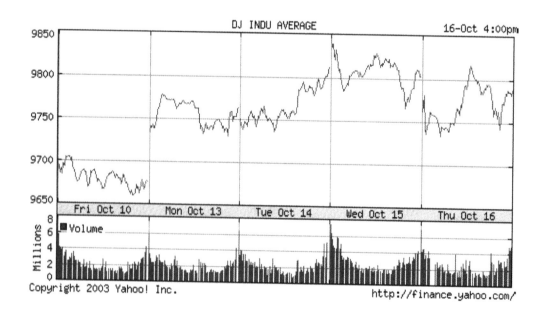

FIGURE 4: LINE CHART FOR COMPARING AMZN AND S&P

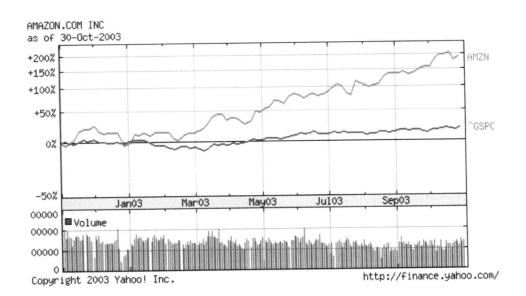

2.2.2 BAR CHARTS

Bar charts consist of bars, representing the high and the low of the price during a chosen time-interval. Additionally they mark with a tick on the left of the bar the open and with a tick to the right the close. Therefore, because they indicate the trading range of the day, they give more information than a daily line chart.

FIGURE 5: DOW DAILY BAR CHART

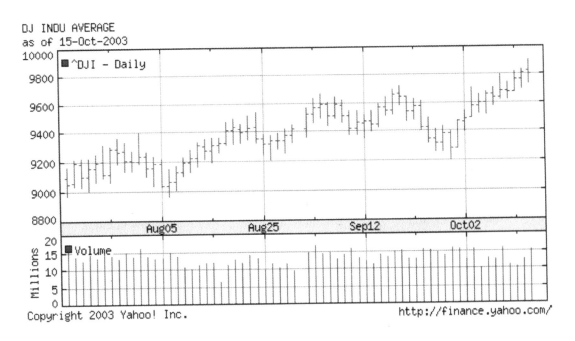

FIGURE 6: DOW 3-DAY BAR CHART

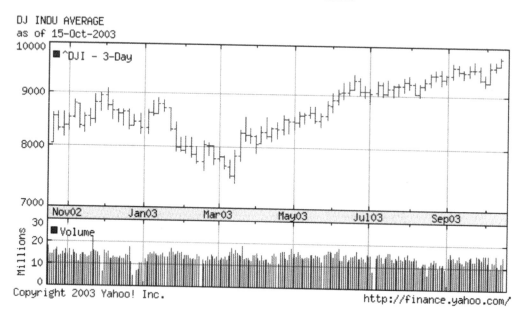

2.2.3   *POINT-AND-FIGURE CHARTS: A FULL INTRODUCTION*

Point-and-Figure (P&F) charts are the least common of the three types. However, they have some significant advantages, especially clarity and inherent trading signals, which means that P&F is a charting and trading system in one. Therefore, we include a short summary on Point-and-Figure charts. However, for further information we recommend our book *The Complete Guide to Point-and-Figure Charting: The New Science of an Old Art*, which was called "BEST FINANCE BOOK OF THE YEAR."

Point-and-Figure is a powerful technical analysis tool. Point-and-Figure charts follow a price axis and not a time axis, and therefore discretize—or divide—price and not time, a method that has significant advantages, most notably **crystal clear signals and absolutely unambiguous trendlines**.

The main reasons why we recommend Point-and-Figure are derived from the interesting fact that **Point-and-Figure is a charting and trading system in one,** as the Point-and-Figure method generates with clarity all necessary trading signals, namely through the charting process itself, so there is no additional manipulation required. The powerful advantages of Point-and-Figure are numerous; we would like to highlight the most important ones:

Point-and-Figure is easy to understand. You can learn it in an hour or so and you don't need any advanced math skills or any other prior knowledge. **The Point-and-Figure signals are easy to detect and they always give exact instructions.** Being a high performance trend following system, Point-and-Figure based trading benefits from all major moves, as entry signals are always generated. Point-and-Figure works for both long and short positions and it clearly indicates the levels where protective stops have to be placed and where positions could pyramid. Moreover, it is universal and can be applied to any asset. A further advantage that we would like to mention is that **Point-and-Figure is straightforward to optimize**. The optimal parameter set is selected from very few combinations. This makes the system safe against the dreaded over-fitting. Last but not least, **Point-and-Figure has been rigorously tested**. Numerous studies have been conducted over decades, all with similar results, namely that **Point-and-Figure charting is a profitable trading technique.**

2.2.3.1   P&F BASICS

BASIC CHARACTERISTICS OF POINT AND FIGURE CHARTS:

* X for rising prices.
* O for falling prices.
* A Column can never include both Xs and Os.
* Columns of Xs alternate with columns of Os.
* Months are marked by substituting the X or O by the month code, 1: January... C: December.
* Reversals occur if no new box in the same direction can be added, but a certain amount of boxes (most often 3) can be filled in the opposite symbol than the last one.
* Trendlines are always drawn with a 45 degree (diagonal) angle.
* Charts are always bullish or bearish, never neutral, never fuzzy.

2.2.3.2   TYPICAL P&F CHART

FIGURE 7: EXPLANATORY P&F CHART

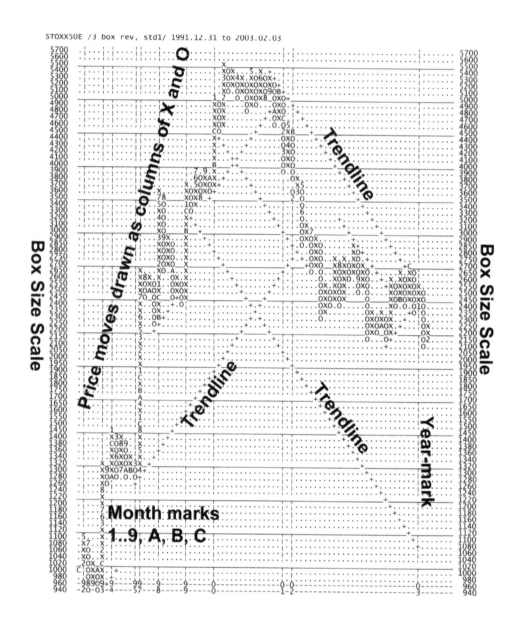

Table ZZ: P&F Month Codes

P&F MONTH CODES	
MONTH	CODE
January	1
February	2
March	3
April	4
May	5
June	6
July	7
August	8
September	9
October	A
November	B
December	C

2.2.3.3 CONCISE INSTRUCTION FOR CREATING POINT-AND-FIGURE CHARTS

If the current column consists of Xs, check if new Xs can be added, or, if the current column consists of Os, can new Os be added? If yes, do so.

If no new identical symbol could be added to the current column, check if a reversal has happened and if so, start a new column with the opposite symbol. If no reversal has happened, look to the next day.

Interpret the chart for new buy or sell signals.

The above can also be represented as a flow chart: see the following page.

FLOW CHART DESCRIBING POINT-AND-FIGURE CHART CONSTRUCTION

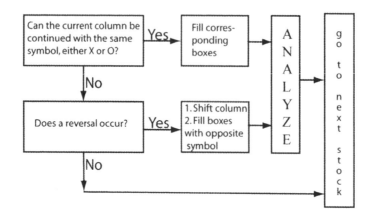

2.2.3.3.1   WHEN CAN THE BOX BE FILLED?

The expression *box* has its origin in the use of a paper with grid-lines for manual charting. The *box-number* refers to the number on the vertical price-scale identifying the box. Testing whether a box can be filled depends on the direction of the price move. Two cases exist, either you're coming from above, testing for Os (falling prices) or you're coming from below, testing for Xs (rising prices). The box can be filled if and only if the price range—defined by the high and low—includes the box-number.

Therefore:
X: the price used in the charting process (normally the high of the day) has to be higher than or equal to the box-number in order to draw the X.

O: the price used in the charting process (normally the low of the day) has to be lower than or equal to the box-number in order to draw the O.

Example: Testing when a box can be filled
Assume we are testing if box 40 can be filled. In the case of:
testing for **rising prices** the X can be drawn if the high is higher or equal to 40; or
testing for **declining prices** the O can be marked if the low is lower or equal to 40.

2.2.3.3.2   WHEN DOES A REVERSAL OCCUR?

The reversal occurs when no new identical symbol can be added to the current column; instead a certain number – traditionally 3 - of boxes can be filled in the opposite direction, starting on a box one higher in the case of a reversal from O to X or one lower in the case of X to O.

Note that in order that the box can be filled the price has to touch or move over the limit of the box. The following graphic serves as an illustration. The dots refer to the boxes that have to be checked.

REVERSAL PATTERNS

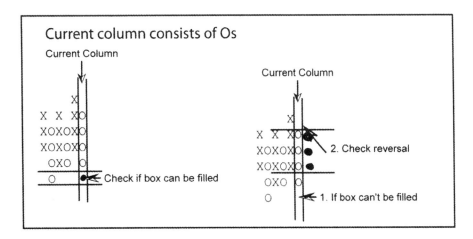

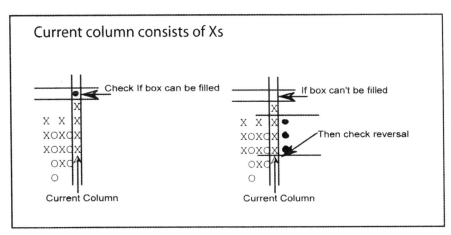

2.2.3.4   *P&F SIGNALS*

2.2.3.4.1   *THE BUY SIGNALS*

We use the same format to picture the eight basic buy signals as we use throughout the book to chart the different stocks. Please note that there are trendlines used in the three last signals. We'll come back to the subject of trendlines in a later chapter. But for the moment keep in mind that trendlines are used to signal certain patterns, such as supports and resistances, and are always drawn in 45 degree angles and marked with '+.'

2.2.3.4.1.1   *B-1: SIMPLE BULLISH BUY SIGNAL (OR, DOUBLE TOP)*

The most basic of all signals is the simple bullish buy signal, sometimes called the double top formation. It is formed by a column of Xs, then a column of Os, then a column of Xs, which rises one box above the prior column of Xs.

FIGURE **B-1**: SIMPLE BULLISH BUY (OR, DOUBLE TOP)

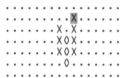

2.2.3.4.1.2   *B-2: SIMPLE BULLISH BUY WITH A RISING BOTTOM*

The second formation, the simple bullish buy with a rising bottom, is similar to the B-1 in that the tops are identical in both cases, meaning that the current column of Xs exceeds the top X of the prior X column by one box. But the bottoms of the B-1 and B-2 differ. In the case of the simple bullish buy signal with a rising bottom (B-2), the bottom O in the most recent column of Os is higher than the lowest O of the preceding O column, a condition not present in the B-1, where the lowest O of the most recent column is horizontal to the lowest O of the prior O column.

Having rising bottoms is significant, it means that support is coming into the market at progressively higher prices with each decline.

FIGURE **B-2**: SIMPLE BULLISH BUY WITH A RISING BOTTOM

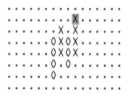

At least one of the simple bullish buy signals, B-1 and B-2, is contained as an element of all of the more complicated buy signals, and when either occurs alone or as an element of a more complex formation, all shorts should be covered. Entries on the long side may be made or the trader may hold off, waiting for a specific and more complex formation to evolve, but *all short positions must be covered*, for the security is now bullish with the degree of bullishness forecast by the type of formation which ultimately evolves. But because the position is bullish, there is absolutely no justification for remaining short.

2.2.3.4.1.3   *B3: BREAKOUT OF A TRIPLE TOP*

The third formation, but the first of the complex formations, is the breakout of a triple top. It is made up of five columns, three of Xs and two of Os. The first two columns of Xs peak at the same level, while the current X column rises one box higher than the tops of the prior two columns.

FIGURE **B-3**: BREAKOUT OF A TRIPLE TOP

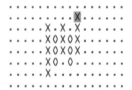

The triple top formation is stronger than either of the simple bullish buy signals, B-1 and B-2, because it represents a breakout of a resistance level which held more times than in the simple formations, and it is considered a complex formation because it contains a simple signal as an element as well as requiring a wider span of columns than either of the simple formations.

2.2.3.4.1.4 B-4: ASCENDING TRIPLE TOP

The fourth buy signal is the ascending triple top, which is nothing more than two simple bullish signals (B-1 and/or B-2) given in succession in five columns. If the bottoms are rising along with the rising tops, the formation is more bullish than if the bottoms are horizontal.

FIGURE B-4: ASCENDING TRIPLE TOP

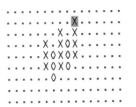

2.2.3.4.1.5   B-5: SPREAD TRIPLE TOP

The spread triple top is the fifth formation. It is similar to the breakout of a triple top (B-3), except that it is spread over seven rather than five columns because one rally failed to match or exceed the highs of the prior X columns, and it thus takes an additional X column to break the horizontal resistance.

FIGURE B-5: SPREAD TRIPLE TOP

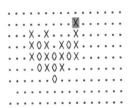

The next three formations deal with the combined relationship of support and resistance lines to the height of the tops of X columns and the bottoms of O columns.

2.2.3.4.1.6   B-6: UPSIDE BREAKOUT ABOVE A BULLISH TRIANGLE

The sixth formation is the upside breakout above a bullish triangle. This formation is created by resistance (supply) coming into the market at progressively lower levels with each rally, thus keeping each succeeding column of Xs from rising as high as the prior column, while support (demand) comes in at progressively higher levels with each decline as revealed by rising bottoms. The formation is completed and a buy signal generated when the upside breakout occurs, meaning that a column of Xs rises one box higher than the high of the preceding X column. The triangle is bullish because the last signal prior to the start of the triangle was a buy signal.

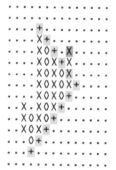

2.2.3.4.1.7   *B-7: UPSIDE BREAKOUT ABOVE A BULLISH RESISTANCE LINE*

The seventh signal is the upside breakout above a bullish resistance line. The resistance line in this case is drawn as a 45 degree line up and to the right, beginning from the lower right hand corner of the lowest box containing an exposed 0, i.e., an 0 not bordered by an X on its right. The longer the resistance line holds, i.e., the more columns of Xs that approach the resistance line but fail to break through, the more bullish is the ultimate breakout. A breakout is defined as a penetration which completely clears the resistance line and not just straddles the box through which it crosses. Chart ZZ provides an example of both a straddled position (not a breakout) and a true breakout.

FIGURE B-7: UPSIDE BREAKOUT ABOVE A BULLISH RESISTANCE LINE

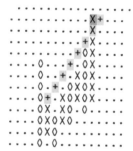

2.2.3.4.1.8   *B-8: UPSIDE BREAKOUT ABOVE A BEARISH RESISTANCE LINE*

In B-7 signals, the security is already bullish and prices have been steadily rising prior to the signal. But in the eighth formation, an upside breakout above a bearish resistance line, the security is in a steady decline, trading within a bearish channel defined by an upper resistance line and a lower support line both moving down at a 45 degree angle as they extend from left to right.

In B-8, the support line may be well defined or almost non-existent, yet there must be a resistance line declining at a 45 degree angle from top left to lower right drawn as the best-fit 45 degree line to the declining tops of the X columns. The buy signal occurs when an X column both breaks through the resistance line and rises one box higher than the highest X of the prior column.

FIGURE B-8: UPSIDE BREAKOUT ABOVE A BEARISH RESISTANCE LINE

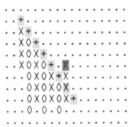

2.2.3.4.1.9 BREAKING OR STRADDLING OF TRENDLINES

In order to illustrate the difference between breaking a trendline and straddling a trendline we use a 2-year chart of British Telecom [B.T.L].

BT [BT.L]: TOUCHING, STRADDLING AND FINALLY BREAKING OF A BEARISH RESISTANCE

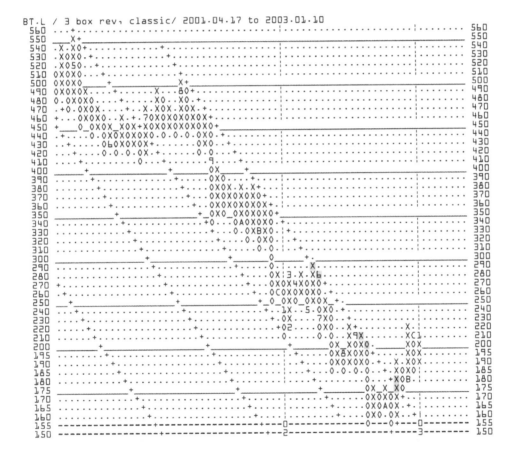

You will see that in the first two instances (June, September 2002) the bearish resistance trendline was only straddled whereas in the third instance (October 2002) the extrapolated trendline was truly broken.

BUY SIGNALS ON THE € / $

```
ECU / standard / 3 box rev / 2001.12.06 to 2003.06.05
```

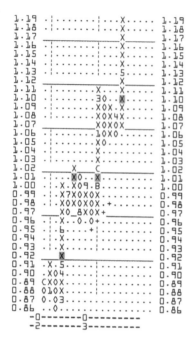

Point-and-Figure detects all major moves, as shown here on the rally of the Euro against the Dollar. The chart is said to be bullish, because the last signal was a buy.

2.2.3.4.1.10   WHEN IS A SUPPORT OR RESISTANCE LINE BROKEN?

The line is broken if an entire box can be filled above (resistance line) or below (support line). If the filled box coincides with the line only, it is said that the X or O straddles the line.

2.2.3.4.1.11   SUMMARY OF BUY SIGNALS

BUY SIGNAL SUMMARY

```
630 B1...B2....B3.....B4.....B5.......B6.........B7.........+B8............ 630
620 .............................+...................+............ 620
610 .............................+...................X+........... 610
600 .............................X+..................X0+.......... 600
590 .X.....X....X.......X........X0+.X.........X+..X0X+........... 590
580 X.X...X.X...X.X...X...X..X...X..X0X+X........X...X0X0+..X...... 580
570 X0X..0X0X..X0X0X..X.X0X..X0X0X.X...X0X0X.+......+X...0X0X+.X.... 570
560 X0X..0X0X..X0X0X..X0X0X0X..X0X0X+.....+0X...0X0X0X....... 560
550 .0...0X0....0.0...X0X0....0X0X0X..X0X0++.0...+0X....0X0X0X+...... 550
540 .....0.......0.....0..0..X.X0X+.....0..+X0X....0.0.0......... 540
530 .....................X0X0+......0.+.0X0X......... 530
520 .................X0X+......0+X0X0X.......... 520
510 ................0+.......0X.X0.0........... 510
500 .................+........0X0X0............ 500
490 ...........................0X0.............. 490
480 ...........................0.0.............. 480
470 .......................................................... 470
```

2.2.3.4.2   THE SELL SIGNALS

Based on Point-and-Figure's symmetry all sell signals are the exact opposite of the buy signals. Therefore the next few paragraphs may be skipped, but the discussion and illustrations that follow will clear up any confusion that may exist as well as serve as an indirect review of the buy signals.

2.2.3.4.2.1 S-1: SIMPLE BEARISH SELL

The simple bearish sell signal occurs when the price falls, rises and falls again with the current decline or current column of Os dropping one box below the lowest O of the prior column of Os.

FIGURE S-1: SIMPLE BEARISH SELL

The occurrence of the simple sell formation calls for two responses. It demands that all long positions be liquidated and also suggests, but does not demand, that consideration be given to a short sale. The trader should never wait around for a more complex sell formation to evolve before closing out his longs, because the occurrence of the S-1 signal immediately indicates a bearish posture. But a short need not be taken if the trader prefers not to be on the short side at all or would prefer to wait for a more bearish formation before shorting.

2.2.3.4.2.2   S-2: SIMPLE BEARISH SELL WITH A DECLINING TOP

The simple bearish sell with a declining top is the second of the sell formations. The S-2 is more bearish than its cousin the S-1, for it has a declining top as evidence that selling pressure is coming in at lower levels with each rally.

FIGURE S-2: SIMPLE BEARISH SELL WITH A DECLINING TOP

The third and remaining sell signals are not really sell signals for the closing out of longs, because this is always done on an S-1 or S-2. Instead, these more complex formations only signal the opportunity for effective short selling. They are considered more complex formations in that they involve at least five columns, three of Os and two of Xs and they all contain within their pattern at least one of the two basic signals, S-1 and S-2.

2.2.3.4.2.3   S-3: BREAKOUT OF A TRIPLE BOTTOM

The third sell signal is called the breakout of a triple bottom regardless of whether the tops are level or declining. Declining tops represent the more bearish pattern.

FIGURE S-3: BREAKOUT OF A TRIPLE BOTTOM

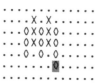

The breakout of a triple bottom evolves from a price decline, an upside reversal, a second decline that meets downside support at the same level as the lowest O of the prior declining column, a second rally which fails to break out on the upside and a third decline which drops one box below the lowest Os of the prior two columns.

Never anticipate the completion of the S-3 before it happens and short in anticipation, for the support which stopped the decline of the first and second columns of Os might hold a third time and be strong enough to send the price up to a top side breakout.

2.2.3.4.2.4 S-4: DESCENDING TRIPLE BOTTOM

The next formation is the descending triple bottom. It is simply two successive S-1 and/or S-2 formations in five consecutive columns. Or defined differently, it is composed of a column of Os, a rally of Xs, a second column of Os which declines one box below the low of the prior declining column followed by a second price rise succeeded by a third decline signaling the sell by falling one box below the low of the prior decline.

FIGURE S-4: DESCENDING TRIPLE BOTTOM

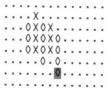

2.2.3.4.2.5   S-5: SPREAD TRIPLE BOTTOM

The fifth sell pattern, the spread triple bottom, has the basic triple bottom design of the S-3, yet the formation is spread over seven rather than five columns.

FIGURE S-5: SPREAD TRIPLE BOTTOM

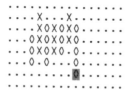

2.2.3.4.2.6   S-6: DOWNSIDE BREAKOUT OF A BEARISH TRIANGLE

The downside breakout of a bearish triangle is the sixth of eight sell signals. This formation originates from an earlier sell signal followed by a major decline.

FIGURE S-6: DOWNSIDE BREAKOUT OF A BEARISH TRIANGLE

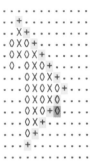

After the decline, support develops and a rally occurs which finally gives way to a new decline that bottoms higher than the low of the prior declining column. The next rally falls short of the high of the preceding rally and the price again declines. This pattern of rising bottoms and falling tops can continue for any number of columns and defines the sides of the triangle. The formation is finally completed and a sell signal generated when an O column declines below the lower support line.

2.2.3.4.2.7   S-7: DOWNSIDE BREAKOUT BELOW A BULLISH SUPPORT LINE

The next formation, the downside breakout below a bullish support line, occurs when there is a downward penetration of a well defined bullish support line. The bullish support line is the 45 degree best-fit line of bottoms and the penetration must completely clear the support line, not just touch or straddle the box through which it crosses from lower left to upper right, as well as decline one box below the lowest O of the prior column.

FIGURE S-7: DOWNSIDE BREAKOUT BELOW A BULLISH SUPPORT LINE

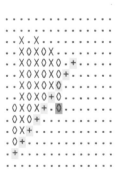

2.2.3.4.2.8   S-8: DOWNSIDE BREAKOUT BELOW A BEARISH SUPPORT LINE

The eighth and last of the sell signals is the downside breakout below a bearish support line. This pattern evolves from a sudden breakout below a bearish support line running from upper left to lower right at a 45 degree angle which has repeatedly held in the past.

FIGURE S-8: DOWNSIDE BREAKOUT BELOW A BEARISH SUPPORT LINE

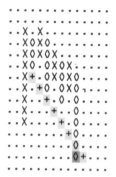

2.2.3.4.2.9   EXAMPLES OF SELL SIGNALS

We can show many great examples for sell signals, especially in the actual market environment. We have included a typical high-tech stock and the Nikkei225 index.

SELL-SIGNALS ON ARM HOLDINGS [ARM.L]: S3 AND S8

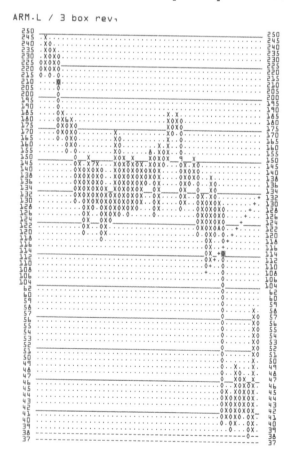

In the example of ARM we see the formation of a base at 215 which is eventually broken, generating a breakout from a triple bottom. Later, not only is a simple sell formed, but also a bullish support is broken. Such a chart shouts: *Sell!* A sell around 110 would nicely be covered at 46, based on a simple buy signal.

NIKKEI-225 AND ITS FIRST SELL SIGNAL: A SIMPLE SELL OR DOUBLE BOTTOM BREAKOUT

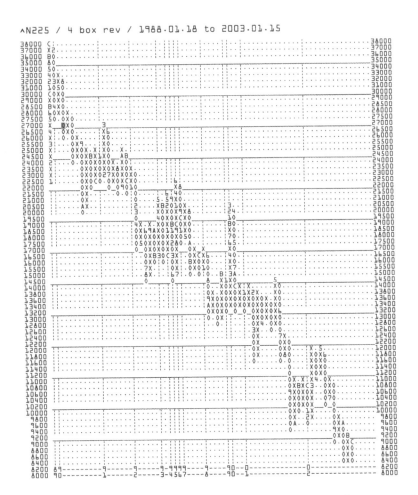

The Nikkei during the period 1990-2002 is a tremendous example

The Nikkei during the period 1990-2002 is a tremendous example of a bear market and should never be forgotten. It shows that bear markets can last for a very long time. Therefore we have included this long-term Nikkei Point-and-Figure chart, where we see a first sell on the fourth column, and thereafter many more sell signals can be detected.

2.2.3.4.2.10   SUMMARY OF SELL SIGNALS

SELL SIGNAL SUMMARY

```
470 S1...S2....S3.....S4......S5......S6...........S7............S8....... 470
460 ...................................+............................ ...... 460
450 ...............................X+......................X.-X...... 450
440 .....X............X.......X...X...OXO+.................XOXO...... 440
430 .X...XOX....X.X...OXOX....XOXOXO..OXOX+.........X.-X........XOXOX..... 430
420 OXO..XOXO..OXOXO..OXOXO..OXOXOXO..O.OXO+........XOXOX.....XO.OXOX... 420
410 OXO..XOXO..OXOXO..OXOXO..OXOX0-O....OXOX+.......XOXOXO.+......X+.OXOXO.. 410
400 0-0..0-0..0-0.....0-0..0-0.0....0..OXOX0+......XOXOX0+......X.+0-OXO.. 400
390 ..0.....0.....0......0.......0...OXOXO......XOXOXO......X.-+.0-0.. 390
380 ................................OXO+0......XOXO+0......X...+..0.. 380
370 ................................OX+......OXOX+.0.......X.....+.0.. 370
360 ................................0+......OXO+...........+0. 360
350 ................................+......OX+.............0. 350
340 ....................................0+..............0+. 340
330 ................................................... 330
```

2.2.3.5   TRENDLINES

Stock prices do not move in totally irregular and unpredictable ways. Instead, their prices tend to rise and fall within channels or trends. Although the use of the buy, sell, and short sell formations can provide excellent returns, it is often wise to view the formations within the context of the current trend as a means of avoiding those signals counter to the trend which have high probabilities of being false.

2.2.3.5.1   THE FOUR BASIC PRICE CHANNELS

ACCUMULATION CHANNEL: marked by an equilibrium position of supply and demand and a horizontal price movement normally following a major decline.

BULLISH CHANNEL: marked by rising demand and thus an increase in price.

DISTRIBUTION CHANNEL: indicated by an equilibrium position of supply and demand and a horizontal price movement normally occurring after a major bullish move.

BEARISH CHANNEL: denoted by supply exceeding demand and thus a declining price.

PRICE CHANNELS

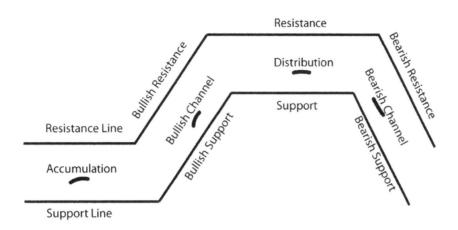

2.2.3.5.2   TRENDLINES DRAWN AT 45 DEGREES

Each channel is defined by trendlines drawn on the Point-and-Figure chart at 45 degrees rising or falling, intersecting the diagonal corners of each square.

You will be amazed how well these simple diagonal 45 degree trendlines actually work at defining price channels. You will experience the significance of such trendlines in almost all charts—especially those over a longer time horizon—again and again. They will become as indispensable a tool in your trading as they are in ours.

The exclusive use of 45 degree trendlines is again an asset to the beauty of Point-and-Figure and which translates into *no ambiguity and no errors of interpretation*. Most importantly, penetrations through Point-and-Figure diagonal trendlines are absolutely clear, either true or false, no guessing as with bar charts or candlesticks.

2.2.3.5.2.1 THE FOUR TYPES OF TRENDLINE

BULLISH SUPPORT: a line upwards and below columns

BULLISH RESISTANCE: a line upwards and above columns

BEARISH SUPPORT: a line downwards and below columns

BEARISH RESISTANCE: a line upwards and below columns

29

2.2.3.5.2.2 ACCUMULATION AND DISTRIBUTION CHANNELS

The horizontal lines defining accumulation and distribution channels are not drawn in a Point-and-Figure chart because they are obvious since Point-and-Figure charts are drawn in a grid structure, and such a grid makes horizontal levels evident.

2.2.3.5.2.3 EXAMPLE OF TRENDLINES

The following chart of the French CAC 40 [.FCHI] includes all of the four types of trendlines. As you can easily detect, they nicely define the channels of the price moves.

PRICE CHANNELS IN THE FRENCH MARKET

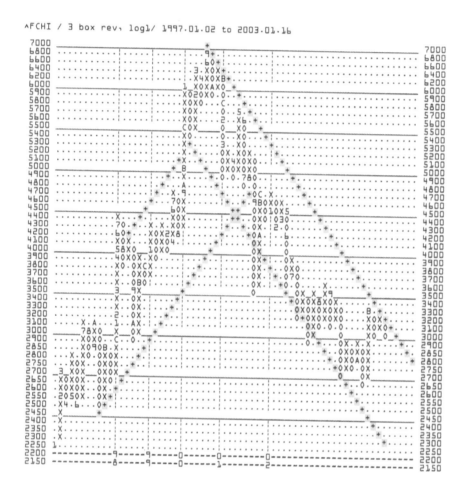

2.2.3.5.2.4 NO AMBIGUITY

Please note how well the trendlines in the above chart work. And don't forget, Point-and-Figure only uses 45 degree trendlines and it is therefore absolutely clear where to trace them. All trendlines in this book are drawn by the computer. That means no guessing and no tinkering, just clearly defined trendlines.

Bullish support lines are drawn from the lower right corner of a low O—or exposed O—at a 45 degree angle from lower left to upper right when the chart has rising bottoms.

The bottom side of a bullish channel is defined by a bullish support line, while the top of the trend is bordered by a bullish resistance line drawn from the lower right corner of the lowest exposed O in a wall (highlighted) of two or more exposed Os at a 45 degree angle from lower left to upper right.

Bearish support lines are drawn on bearish charts from the upper right hand corner of the highest exposed X in a wall of two or more exposed Xs (highlighted) at a 45 degree angle down from upper left to lower right.

A bearish resistance line forms the top of a bearish channel and is drawn from the upper right hand corner of the highest X in a column of abnormally high Xs, down from upper left to lower right at a 45 degree angle.

2.2.3.6   SCALING

Scaling (that is assigning numbers to boxes) is significant. Either we use the Standard Scale or a logarithmic scale.

2.2.3.6.1   WHAT POSSIBILITIES DO I HAVE TO SCALE MY CHART?

ONE: STANDARD: recommended for most stocks and other tradable assets.

TWO: PERCENTAGE LINEAR: flaws charting, to be avoided.

THREE: LOGARITHMIC: recommended for volatile stocks, mathematically sound. (Hint: always first try with 2% for stocks and 5% for volatility.)

Standard Scale		
Price		
From	To	Box Size
6	14	0.2
14	29	0.5
29	60	1
60	140	2
140	290	5
290	600	10
600	1400	20

2.2.3.6.2   WHY DOES LOGARITHMIC SCALING MAKE A LOT OF SENSE?

Logarithmic or standard scaling—which is an approximation to logarithmic scaling—has the property that reversals have the same percentage value irrespectively of the price charted. It is clear that security price moves—or returns—have to be compared on a relative basis. That means a 2% move of Citi with a 2% move of UBS.

Or explained the other way round: a 100 point down move on the Dow at 1,200 is something totally different from a 100 point at 8,500: one represents an 8.3% crash and the other a 1.2% slight correction.

Or a move from 15% volatility to 25% is significant, whereas a move from 70% to 80% is much less so.

2.2.3.6.3   HOW CAN I DRAW A LOGARITHMIC SCALE WITH ONLY A CALCULATOR?

You just need one of the simplest calculators. You take the last closing price of the stock or the last reading of the volatility you want to chart (let's say it was 48.5), round it to the next good looking number (obviously 50). Then you decide what multiplication factor you want to use. For volatility charts use 5%. Then you just take 50, multiply it by 1.05 and get the next box limit. Then you take that number and multiply it again with the same 1.05. That way you get the boxes above 50. For the boxes below 50, you simply divide the number by 1.05, again and again. No logarithm table required!

2.2.3.7   VOLATILITY POINT-AND-FIGURE CHARTS

We explain the charting of volatility using Point-and-Figure in the chapter about volatility. But for the moment keep in mind that for the volatility charts we use a 5% logarithmic scale and we especially use the trendlines as predominant indicators regarding the position of a volatility trade.

2.2.4   CRASHES

A crash is an exceptionally strong down-move, which we would quantify as more than 3% on the S&P 500 index in a single day. In recent history, the worst crash happened on Monday, October 19th, 1987, when the S&P500 lost 20.41%.

The great crash of 1929 was even worse, because the market meltdown stretched over many years and the 1929 levels were only regained two decades later!

FIGURE 8: DOW WITH CRASHES

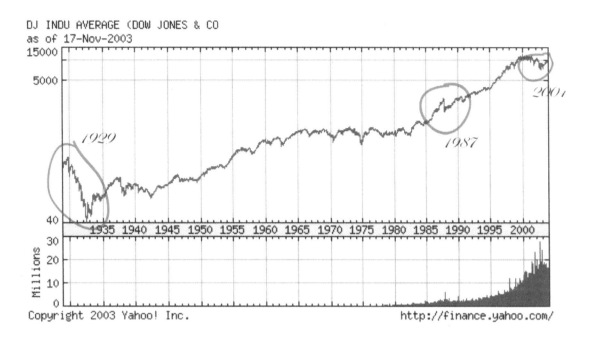

THE QUESTION IS: Can crashes be foreseen? Obviously not! Because otherwise they would not happen, as investors would protect themselves by reducing positions gradually and would therefore generate a bear-trend instead of a crash. They would not happen because the investors would not invest before an anticipated crash and prices would stay on depressed levels, which would as such avoid the possibility of a crash, as crashes are characterized by prior strong price appreciations.

A Summary of Some Financial Turbulences

The most prominent crash was:
1929: Great Crash, leading to great depression.

More recently, the following events allowed us to win or lose money:
1987: October crash
1989: Junk bond market collapse
1990: Japan market crash
1998: Russia defaults, later LTCM bailout
2000: NASDAQ and WWW crash
2001: 9/11, then Andersen and Enron scandals

Crashes always look dramatic; just look at the chart of the 1987 October crash.

FIGURE 9: DOW JONES INDEX OVER THE TIME PERIOD JANUARY UNTIL NOVEMBER 87

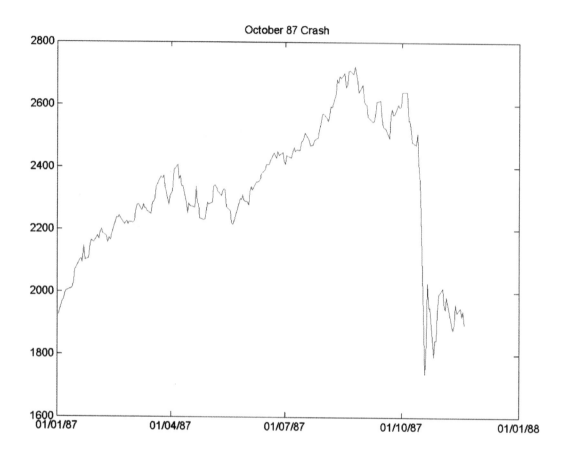

The only thing we know with certainty is that crashes do happen, but we do not know where or when. What one can do is model the frequency of crashes or find some causal relationships with economic data via a neural network, but still the forecasting of a crash is a dream.

We include the paragraph about crashes because they represent the culmination of the problem related to forecasting the direction of the market. The problem inherent to crash anticipation or forecasting should illustrate the point that if even the most violent moves are **not** predictable, how could it be possible to predict minor moves? Please keep this in mind while reading about the proposed non-directional strategies.

2.3   THE BASIC HEDGE-FUND STRATEGIES ARE NON-DIRECTIONAL

Hedge funds are ever increasing in popularity. Over the last ten years they have grown in a number of different funds from 150 to 7500. Most of them are associated with non-directional trading strategies, in the sense that they do not bet on the expectation that their equities will go up in value. Other strategies are based on the idea to take big risks in companies where a special event is likely to happen or has already been announced, like a take-over. Other hedge fund strategies are based on the idea that one can arbitrage between similar financial instruments.

The non-directional strategies used by the hedge-funds consist of buying equities which are believed to have upside potential and of selling equities which are believed to be overvalued. This is called 'market-neutral,' which refers to the fact that their profit does not depend on whether the market as a whole goes up or down. The risk profile of such strategies is very similar to a portfolio of straddles, and that is exactly one of the two ideas we present in this book.

We strongly believe that hedge funds make a lot of sense. Traditional stock funds are based on stock picking. They work fine during boom-times and badly during sideways or down markets. Moreover, they are all highly correlated during crashes and are therefore far more risky than one would generally assume. Such funds are long only, therefore directional, thus they consist of equities and offer no protection against a crash.

Even traditional Swiss private banks understand the benefits of using hedge funds to overcome long only or correlation risk and are thus allocating more and more of their clients' money to such alternative investments. e.g., to date the highly respected Swiss private banks UBP and Pictet in Geneva have each invested more than US $5 billion of their clients' money in hedge funds.

As this book is aimed toward the active private investor or screen trader and not the institutional hedge fund manager, we will not explore hedge fund strategies that are not possible to run for the typical reader of our book.

It is fair to say that the risk profiles of the common hedge fund strategies can be summarized by two strategies we cover extensively, namely the selling of uncovered options (puts in most cases) and trading straddles. In addition, those strategies can easily be implemented by the private or screen trader.

Most importantly, implementing the strategies yourself, you avoid paying the so often exaggerated management fees.

2.4 SUMMARY

In this chapter, we have shown many examples of crashes, which surprised the entire financial market. These extraordinary market moves are charted with different methods and we take the opportunity to explain our preferred chart: the Point-and-Figure. Then, based on the obvious difficulty of knowing if the stock price will go up or down, in this book we suggest strategies that benefit from the stock move as such, but are not dependent on the direction; therefore they are called non-directional strategies. Obviously, for the professional trader there are many ways to set up such positions. However, the private trader does best concentrating on straddle-type strategies and covered-calls. Both of those are based on standard—or so called "plain vanilla"—exchange traded options. In the coming chapters we explain first the basics of options, then option valuation, and then we continue with the money making non-directional strategies.

CHAPTER 3
THE TOOLS FOR NON-DIRECTIONAL TRADING: OPTIONS

3.1 OPTIONS: THE BASICS FOR BEGINNERS

When investors buy shares of common stock, they are becoming the owners of the securities, and as such are owners of the corporation and are entitled to all the rights and privileges the ownership involves. These include the right to get dividends if any are paid and the right to vote through a proxy on major corporate issues. Neither dividends nor voting rights are important to most investors. Dividends if paid at all generally represent an insignificant yield on the investment, and voting normally involves relatively unexciting issues such as reappointing the firm's current auditor for another year, and the continuation of the existing management stock option plan. Thus, the rights and privileges represent a big YAWN!

Stock is normally not bought because of the rights and privileges associated with ownership, but because we expect it to rise in price. When we buy stock today at $50 a share, we are buying because we expect its value to rise dramatically and to do so soon. If we do not believe its price will rise, we do not buy it. And if we believe it will not rise immediately, we wait to buy until closer to the time of the anticipated price increase. We make money through purchasing at one price ($50) and selling at a higher price ($80). If in the interim, the company pays a dividend (25 cents) and we can vote for the retention of Price Waterhouse Coopers as the firm's auditors for another year, fine, but far more important is making $30 on the price advance. Over the decades, the average Standard and Poor 500 stock has annually appreciated nearly 10 times more than the value of the yearly dividend paid.

> *Option Wisdom: Having options is always great: paying too much for them is not!*

In contrast to stock ownership that involves an ownership interest in the corporation and the benefits of ownership, options are totally independent from corporate ownership. Investors who buy options acquire nothing more than the right to buy or sell stock in the future. That means that an option gives its holder the right to buy or sell a certain amount of an underlying security at a specified price over a specified time period. Or stated differently, options are contractual instruments, whereby two parties enter into a binding agreement (the option contract) to give something of value to the other. Specifically, the option contract gives the buyer the right to buy or sell a certain amount of shares for a given period of time, at a price that is fixed at the time of the contract. The option seller stands obligated to buy or sell the number of shares specified for which the seller is paid a certain amount of money. Thus, as in all contracts, each party grants something of value to the other. The option buyer pays the seller a fee (the option price or premium), in return for which the seller grants the buyer the right (but not the obligation) to buy or sell a certain number of shares at a fixed price.

37

CHARACTERISTICS OF OPTIONS: All stock options have certain basic and fixed characteristics:

TYPE: Stock options are either **puts** or **calls**. The put allows the holder to sell a certain number of shares of stock at a certain price for a certain period of time. A call is the opposite of a put. The call gives the holder the right to buy a certain number of shares of stock at a certain price for a certain period of time.

SECURITY: The option is on a specific stock. It could be on Microsoft, General Motors, Qualcomm, Federal Express, or on any one of hundreds of other optionable stocks.

QUANTITY: Stock options are for 100 shares of stock. If you buy one call you have the right to buy 100 shares of the designated stock. Buying 7 calls allows you to purchase 700 shares.

EXPIRATION: Stock options have a limited life. They all expire on the third Friday of a specified month. Technically, they expire on the third Saturday, but they can only be traded through the third Friday. The expiration month can be any month with the closest month called the near month. Expiration dates can go out several years (leaps). As of September 2003, certainly options have expiration dates as far out as January 2006. In September 2003, you could buy a call option on Microsoft to expire in September 2003, October 2003, January 2004, and even January 2006.

STRIKE PRICE: A stock option gives the holder the right to buy the shares of stock at a specified price. This price is the strike price and once specified it remains constant throughout the life of the option.

The fixed characteristics of a stock option remain fixed throughout its entire life with several exceptions. A **stock split** adjusts the number of shares to hold the relative value the same and the option price is adjusted appropriately. For example, if Microsoft were to split 2 for 1, a Microsoft option for 100 shares of stock at 50 would become an option for 200 shares at 25. In this way, the relative value of the old option for 100 shares at $50 and the adjusted option for 200 shares at $25 remains the same $5,000. If the company undergoes a **takeover**, there will also be an adjustment to maintain the relative value.

There are really only two sorts of option types that matter—put and call. Three other terms are occasionally used when referring to options – straddle, spread, and leap. A straddle is nothing more than the combination of a put and a call with identical strike prices and maturities. If the maturity date or strike prices are different, the straddle is called a spread. And leaps—formally known as Long-term Equity AnticiPation Securities—are really nothing more than puts and calls with longer maturity dates. Leaps can have maturities as far into the future as two years and they expire in January. When the maturity of the leap is relatively close, it becomes a regular option.

In addition to the five fixed characteristics of type, security, quantity, strike price, and expiration date defined in the option contract between the buyer and seller, and that remain constant for the entire life of the contract, there are two variable factors determined by the market.

You will come across a myriad of terms specifying so called exotic options, like Asian, Bermudian, knock-in, knock-out, quantos, multi-asset and many more. But don't bother, our strategies hinge on puts and calls, which are (in contrast to exotic options) liquid and represent thus a huge advantage as liquidity minimizes transaction costs.

PREMIUM: The price excluding commissions that a buyer pays for the option and the amount the seller receives for the option is the premium. The premium is quoted in dollars and cents per share of stock. The actual cost of the option is the quoted figure multiplied by the 100 shares covered by the option. Thus a quote of $1.10 means the total cost of the option is $1.10 per share times 100 shares of stock or $110. This is the cost the buyer will have to pay to buy the option and he will have to pay a commission as well, thus increasing the premium cost above $110. The seller will receive $110 and the commission is deducted. Assuming a commission of $10, the seller pays $110 plus the $10 commission for a total charge of $120, and the seller of the option receives $110 less the $10 commission, or $100 net. It is market determined and can and does change from minute to minute. When you get a stock option quote from a broker or from a quote service you will receive a bid price, an ask price, and the last trade price. The bid price is always lower than the ask price and represents the price that a buyer is willing to pay for an option. The ask price is the price the seller wants to receive, and the last trade price is the latest agreed upon price for the trading of an option contract.

MONEYNESS (INTRINSIC VALUE AND TIME VALUE): Options are said to be out-of-the-money, at-the-money, or in-the-money, based upon the relationship of the stock price in the market and the option strike price. Since a call option gives the purchaser the right to purchase 100 shares of stock at the strike price, a call is in-the-money when the market price of the underlying stock is above the strike price. Thus if the strike price of the call is 50 and the stock is trading at 54, the call is 4 points in-the-money. The call is out-of-the-money when the market price is below the strike price. With the stock trading at 47, a call with a 50-strike price is 3 points out-of-the-money. The call is on-the-money (or sometimes called "at-the-money") when the market price is exactly at the call's strike price, or at least near the strike price. The strike price nearest the market price of the stock is the option on-the-money. If the stock is trading at 50, the call is on-the-money.

Since puts are the opposite of calls, and the put purchaser has the right to sell 100 shares of stock at the strike price, the "money" concept must be reversed. Thus when the stock is trading below the strike price of the put, the put is in-the-money. For example, if the market price of the stock is 66 and the put has a strike price of 70, the put is 4 points in-the money. When the stock is trading above the Put's strike price, the put is out-of-the-money. In our example with the 70-strike price put, if the stock is trading at 72, the put is 2 points out-of-the-money. In addition, if the stock is trading at or near 70, the put is on-the-money.

The intrinsic value of an option is the points-in-the-money of the option, excluding commissions. This is the value of the option if it were to expire immediately and therefore have no time value.

Time Value is the cost to the option buyer to control 100 shares for a certain length of time, removing the intrinsic value. And because an option is a wasting asset, the time value declines as the option gets closer to the expiration date. An option with a maturity date 3 months in the future will have a higher time value than an option identical in all terms except for maturity date and which expires in one month.

The premium or cost of an option is composed of the intrinsic value (points-in-the-money) plus the time value. For example, a call with a strike price of 50, expiring in 3 months, and the stock trading at 54 would have an intrinsic value of 4 points and a time value (let's assume 2 points), for a premium cost of 6 points – or $600 – in the market.

SUMMARY OF BASIC TERMS USING TWO EXAMPLES: Microsoft stock is trading at $28.00 on September 11, 2003. Consider a Microsoft (MSFT) October 2003 put at 30 quoted at $2.45. The put buyer pays $245 plus a commission to buy this put. The put allows the buyer (holder of the contract) the right to sell 100 shares of Microsoft at $30 a share at any time up to and including the expiration date of October 15, 2003 (third Friday of the month). The buyer can, but need not, sell Microsoft and would do so only if the stock price is trading for less than $30 a share. The put buyer has the right, but not the obligation to sell stock. The seller (writer) of this put has the obligation to buy 100 shares of Microsoft at $30 should the buyer desire to sell the stock. The seller (writer) has the obligation rather than a right.

TAKE ANOTHER EXAMPLE: Dell Computer (DELL) is trading at 33.77. The November 2003 call at 35 has a premium of $1.25. The buyer of this call, who pays $125 plus a commission, has the right (never the obligation) to buy 100 shares of DELL at any time up to the third Friday of November 2003 at a price of $35 a share. To take this risk, the call seller is paid a premium of $125 less a commission.

ADVANTAGES OF OPTIONS:

The advantages of options will be covered extensively and thoroughly in later chapters, and we will painstakingly demonstrate that "you should never buy stock again," or as a minimum, always use options in conjunction with options. In this Basics chapter it is appropriate to cover many of the traditional advantages of options for both buyers and sellers (writers) in an abbreviated manner.

ADVANTAGES TO OPTION BUYERS:

PREDETERMINED AND LIMITED RISK: When you buy an option, be it a put or a call, the absolute maximum you can lose is limited to the cost (premium) of the option plus the commission paid for its purchase. This amount is known to the penny at the time the option is purchased. If you purchase a call on Yahoo, Inc. (YHOO) for 3 points ($300), your maximum possible loss is $300 plus the purchase commission paid to the broker. The following example will demonstrate this point. Let's assume you purchased 100 shares of stock for $35 a share. You are investing $3,500 plus a commission. Should the stock drop to $25, you have a loss of $10 a share or $1,000. Even though you might decide not to sell the stock at 25, and thus not realize the loss, you have the loss nevertheless. A paper loss, not a realized loss, but a loss exists. Alternatively, rather than purchasing the 100 shares of the stock at 35, you could have purchased a January 2003 call option with a 35 strike price for $300. Since the stock declined to 25, your loss is only $300, not the $1,000 suffered by the stock investor. Thus the risk in purchasing an option is always predetermined and limited to the cost of the premium plus commission. The maximum loss from the option purchase is not known to the penny. It is also often less than the loss that would have been sustained had the stock been purchased and then experienced a decline.

UNLIMITED PROFIT POTENTIAL: The buyer of an option can make many times the premium cost, but can never lose more than the cost of the option. This limited risk coupled with an unlimited profit potential is one of the major advantages of buying options. In the example above, had the stock not declined, but risen in price from 35 to 45, the call buyer would have made $1,000 less the option cost of $300, for a profit of $700 on a $300 investment. This represents a 233% return on invested funds, yet the option buyer never risked more than $300.

LEVERAGE: Leverage means that a relatively small amount of money controls a much more valuable asset, and returns are magnified. Stock purchased in a cash account has no leverage. If you purchase 100 shares of a $60 stock in a cash account, you pay $6,000, and you make $100 for each dollar the stock rises, but you have had to invest $6,000 to do so. If the stock rises to $80, the cash stock investor makes $2,000 or 33% on the investment. Had the stock been purchased in a margin account, you would have been required to invest only 50% of the cost ($3,000) and the brokerage firm advances the other 50% and charges interest on their loan. As the stock rises, the margin investor earns $100 for each point rise, yet has invested only $3,000. At $80, the profit is $2,000, but because the investment was only $3,000, the return is 66%. Had you purchased a call option with a 60-strike price for $400, you would control the same 100 shares of stock for a minor fraction of the investment of the cash or margin stock buyer. If the stock rises to $80, you make $2,000 less the option cost of $400, for a profit of $1,600, but the investment was only $400, and the percentage return is 400%. For option buyers, even a small movement in the underlying shares can yield a huge percentage gain on the investment. This is the benefit of leverage.

ALTERNATIVE TO A STOP LOSS ORDER: A stock investor needs to protect against significant price declines in the security while seeking price appreciation. When you purchase the stock at $80, you are buying it because you are expecting its price to rise by a significant amount and to rise soon. However, there is always the possibility that the price will decline. A small decline can be tolerated in the pursuit of the big gain, while a major price drop cannot. To avoid the loss from a significant price decline, investors often make use of a stop loss order. A stop loss might be placed at $70. If the price goes down to $70, the stock is sold with a $1,000 loss. Unfortunately what so often happens is that the price drops, the stock is sold and the price then immediately does what was originally expected, advancing dramatically, but we no longer own the stock since it was "stopped out" (sold). Had a put been purchased with a strike price of 80 for a cost of $500, there would be no need to worry about the price falling since we can always sell the shares at $80 through the exercise of the put. The stock could go down to 60, 50, 40, or even to 0 and we can still exercise the put and thus sell the stock at 80. No matter how low the stock drops, we have the assurance that we can get our $80 a share and the only cost of the insurance which in this case is the $500 premium. In addition, if the stock rises above $80 at any time during the life of the option, we participate in the rise of the stock, and disregard the put contract. In summary, the purchase of a put in conjunction with a stock position insures for a small premium against suffering from a price decline for the entire life of the option while allowing additional profits if the stock rises.

ADVANTAGES TO OPTION SELLERS:

RECEIVE IMMEDIATE INCOME: Option writers (sellers) receive immediate income credited to their brokerage account when they sell an option. The credit is the option premium less the commission paid to the broker for executing the sell order. Therefore, if a call is sold (written) that carries a premium of 5, the seller receives a credit of $500 immediately to his account. The credit actually appears the day following the sale. This is real money received by the writer for bearing the risk in the transaction. Remember that the option buyer has the right, but not the obligation, under the contract. The option writer has the obligation. The buyer of a call at 50 for $500 pays $500 (plus commission) to the broker. If the stock rises, he has the right to buy the stock at $50. If it declines, he simply throws the option away. The writer of this call has received the $500 (less the commission) from the broker, and has an absolute requirement to deliver 100 shares of stock to the option buyer should the buyer request it. If the stock falls below 50 and stays there, that obligation expires with the option. But should the stock rise to 50½, to 60, or even to 100, the writer will be required to deliver 100 shares of stock at 50. The risk of this obligation can be eliminated by repurchasing the option.

BUY STOCK CHEAPER LATER: One of the greatest advantages of writing a put is that we have the potential opportunity to purchase the stock at a future point in time, at a price lower than currently trading, and we receive a premium for bearing the obligation. If we like a company, and believe the stock is well priced at $53, we could sell a put with a 50-strike price and receive a premium of $400. We are now obligated to buy the stock at 50 until the option expires. But we were willing to purchase it today at $53. So if we are forced to buy the stock, we are buying it in the future at a price lower than today, and the premium of $400 makes our real purchase cost $46 a share (50 strike price less 4 premium). Even if we are never forced to buy the shares, we have still earned $400.

SELL STOCK HIGHER LATER: As an owner of shares of a stock, we might like to sell it at a price higher than currently exists in the market. By selling a call on the stock at a strike price higher than the current market price, we receive immediate income (the premium) and have obligated ourselves to sell the stock at the higher price at any time until the option expires. If we are forced to sell the stock, we have received the higher price for the stock than the one existing when the call was sold, and we have the premium as an additional profit. If we are never forced to deliver the stock, we continue to own the shares and have the premium as a return for the obligation. For example, if the stock is trading at 70, and we want at least $75, we would sell a call with a 75-strike price. We receive a premium ($300). If the option is exercised, we sell our shares at $75, thereby making $5 a share more than today's price and an additional $3 as premium. This means we have actually sold the stock at $78 (75-strike price plus the 3 premium). If the stock fails to reach a price greater than $75, our obligation dies, we have $300 for our risk; we continue to own the stock and can sell another call for additional income.

MARGIN:

Stock can be purchased in a cash account with the buyer paying for the purchase in full. It can also be bought on margin in a margin account, meaning the purchaser need only put up 50% of the purchase price with the broker. Even though stock is purchased in a margin account, the buyer has the choice of how much money to deposit for the stock acquisition, from 100% down to just 50%. The broker pays that portion of the cost of the stock not covered by the buyer and the investor has an interest-bearing loan to the broker.

Options are different. An option buyer must pay the full purchase price of the option. Long option positions are not marginable, with the exception of leaps with nine or more months to maturity. Leaps are marginable with the buyer depositing at least 75% of the leap value and the broker pays the remaining amount up to 25%.

A writer (seller) of an option has more flexibility. The writer can be either naked or covered. Naked means there is no offsetting stock position. If you sell a call on a stock in which you have no position, you are naked. If you sell a put and have no short position on the stock, you are also naked. If you have an appropriate position, long 100 shares of the stock on which you are writing a call, or short 100 shares and sell a put, you are covered. There must be 100 shares long for each call option written and 100 shares short for each put written to be covered and the stock must be identical to the option stock. The margin calculation is different for naked and covered positions. If you write a naked option, you must immediately place money with the broker. These funds are referred to as margin. The amount of the deposit is controlled by a formula and is at least 20% of the price of the stock minus the points out of the money plus the premium, but not less than 10% of the stock value.

The following examples should help clarify this calculation. Assume the option stock is trading at 50 and a put is written with a strike price of 45 for a premium of $300. The put is 5 points out-of-the-money. The formula takes 20% of the value of the optioned stock ($50 times 100 shares or $5,000). The 20% of the stock value is $1,000 ($5,000 times 20%). The points out-of-the-money ($5 times 100 shares or $500) are subtracted from the 20% calculation ($1,000), yielding $500. The premium ($300) is then added, giving a required margin deposit of $800. Of this amount, the writer has received $300 as premium income, and therefore need only deposit another $500. If the calculation results in a margin requirement of less than 10% of the stock value, the writer must have on deposit the 10% of the option's stock value. If the option is at or in-the-money, there is no reduction from the 20%, and the required margin is simply 20% of the value of the optioned stock plus the premium. If the stock were trading at $55 with the strike of the call 50, and the selling premium were $700, the calculation would be 20% of $5,500 ($55 market price of the stock times 100 shares) or $1,100 plus the premium ($700), for a total requirement of $1,800. Of this required figure, $700 was just received for writing the call, and the writer must deposit an additional $1,100. Put margin is calculated in the same manner using the same formula.

The 20% of the value of the stock in the formula is currently the absolute minimum percentage, referred to as the minimum exchange margin. Brokerage firms cannot require less than this percentage adjusted for points out-of-the-money plus premium, but they can and often do charge more. Most firms charge 25% or 30%.

If the option is written as covered, with long stock in the account to cover the call or a short position in the stock to cover the put, no additional margin is required to write the option. The only money the writer need deposit are the funds needed for the long or short equity position. For example, if the investor buys 100 shares of a $50 stock, at least 50% of the $5,000 purchase cost, or $2,500, must be deposited. When a call is sold on the stock, the premium is received as a cash credit to the account and no additional funds are required. Only one call can be written as a covered option against each 100 shares held long and one covered put written against each 100 shares short. If more Calls or Puts are written than can be covered by the stock position, they are considered uncovered or naked and must be margined like any other naked option using the formula discussed above.

In addition to the initial margin that must be deposited for each naked option written, the broker may require additional funds if the option moves significantly into-the-money. Assume a naked call is written with a strike price of 50 with the stock selling at $50 for a premium of $400. The initial margin requirement would be 20% of the $5,000 stock value plus the $400 premium value, or $1,400. Of the $1,400, $400 is perceived premium, so only $1,000 in new money must be deposited. Should the stock now rise to $55 a share, the premium would be at least the intrinsic value ($500) and the broker would recalculate the margin as 20% of the new stock value ($5,500) plus the premium ($500), giving a margin requirement of $1,600. Since only $1,400 is in the account to cover the option, the broker may request $200 in additional funds. Should this occur, the option writer could simply repurchase the option written, thereby eliminating the option obligation and the requirement to deposit additional funds. Alternatively, the writer could make a deposit of funds into the account. The choice of which method of meeting the margin call (repurchasing the option and thereby closing the obligation, or sending the broker additional funds) is solely a decision of the option writer.

Should the option go out-of-the-money, the writer will have a lower margin requirement, and the excess money can be removed from the account, or used to margin another option write. If the stock in our last example declines to $45 rather than rising to $55, the margin calculation is 20% of $4,500 ($900), minus the points out-of-the-money (5 points times 100 shares, or $500), plus the premium of $200 (the premium has declined because the option is less valuable as it is so far out-of-the-money). The margin requirement is thus $600 ($900 minus $500 plus $200), and since the writer has $1,400 on deposit, but only $600 is required, $800 is released.

READING OPTION QUOTES:

Reading option quotes is quite straightforward nowadays. On whatever online service you search for option quotes, they are indicated explicitly. We can be happy that the days are gone where options were solely indicated with confusing letters for underlying strike, type, and month!

If you look at an online quote service you will get the information explicitly and well presented, but the old-fashioned ticker codes are still included.

FIGURE 10: OPTION QUOTES FROM PCQUOTE

MICROSOFT CORP(MSFT)   26.9900 ▼ -0.07

Symbol	Last	Time	Net	Bid	Ask	Reference price	Div freq	Div amt	Historical Volatility	
MSFT	26.9900	11:24	-0.07	26.9900	26.9900	27.0400	27.0700	26.8800	27.0600	16155499

		Calls					Dec 2003			Puts				
Ticker	Last	Net	Bid	Ask	Vol	Open Interest	Strike	Ticker	Last	Net	Bid	Ask	Vol	Open Interest
.MQFLN	16.90		16.90	17.00		223	10	.MQFXN	0.05		0.00	0.05		1
.MQFLV	13.80		14.40	14.50		572	12.5	.MQFXV	0.00		0.00	0.05		
.MQFLC	11.30		11.90	12.00		989	15	.MQFXC	0.00		0.00	0.05		
.MQFLW	9.00		9.40	9.50		743	17.5	.MQFXW	0.05		0.00	0.05		100
.MQFLD	7.10		6.90	7.00		1312	20	.MQFXD	0.05		0.00	0.05		187
.MQFLX	4.60		4.40	4.50		3608	22.5	.MQFXX	0.05		0.00	0.05		8653
.MSQLE	1.95	-0.05	1.95	2.00	53	40188	25	.MSQXE	0.05		0.00	0.05		62057
.MSQLY	0.05	-0.05	0.05	0.10	246	96737	27.5	.MSQXY	0.60	+0.05	0.55	0.60	316	22414
.MSQLF	0.05		0.00	0.05		42685	30	.MSQXF	3.00	+0.05	3.00	3.10	75	4987
.MSQLZ	0.05		0.00	0.05		2915	32.5	.MSQXZ	6.00		5.50	5.60		258
.MSQLG	0.05		0.00	0.05		235	35	.MSQXG	9.30		8.00	8.10		211
.MSQLU	0.00		0.00	0.05			37.5	.MSQXU	11.70		10.50	10.60		1
.MSQLH	0.00		0.00	0.05			40	.MSQXH	13.10		13.00	13.10		10
.MSQLS	0.00		0.00	0.05			42.5	.MSQXS	17.40		15.50	15.60		
.MSQLI	0.00		0.00	0.05			45	.MSQXI	19.90		18.00	18.10		
.MSQLT	0.00		0.00	0.05			47.5	.MSQXT	20.50		20.50	20.60		10
.MSQLJ	0.00		0.00	0.05			50	.MSQXJ	24.30		23.00	23.10		100

> **Option ticker symbol = root + month code (distinguished puts and calls) + strike price code**

Unfortunately, the root is not the same as the stock ticker. In the above case, the stock ticker symbol for Microsoft is MSFT, whereas the root is MSQ or MQF, the month code is a single letter from A to X, and the strike a single letter from A to Z. If you would like to get the exact coding, please refer to one of the quote services or the exchange.

But again, you don't have to bother any longer with those archaic symbols, because options are also listed explicitly. It is so much easier to read and grasp Microsoft December 03 30 put than MSQXF!

SUMMARY:

In summary, an option can be either a **put** or a **call**.

*The **buyer** of an option:*

- **pays** *the full premium price of the option,*
- *can **never receive a margin call**,*
- *can **only lose the money paid**,*
- *has the **opportunity to make many times his investment**,*
- *and **has total flexibility** of what is done with the contract, including exercising the option, letting it expire worthless, or reselling it.*

*The **writer/seller** of an option:*

- **receives** *the premium immediately,*
- *has to place **margin** funds with the broker unless the option is covered,*
- *can have **margin calls** if the option is naked,*
- *has an **unlimited loss potential**, yet has the premium income to cushion against potential losses,*
- *and has the **obligation to perform** at anytime during the option's life.*

Neither the buying of options nor the writing of contracts is necessarily the better strategy, for each offer unique advantages, having different potential risks and different profit opportunities. The uses of both buying and writing will be covered in great detail later in the book, as will proof positive that options are superior to stock.

3.2 PAYOFF DIAGRAMS

3.2.1 BASICS

In the jargon an option payoff is the amount of money the option pays or costs given certain circumstances. For example: if you own an option that increases in price by the amount of 150, then your payoff of that position is 150.

Normally payoffs are calculated and drawn in dependence of the underlying price, because the underlying price is the most important driver for the value of an option. Referring to the example illustrated below, we have bought a call-option with a strike-price of 100 for 5. That means our loss is limited to 5, and in the worst case the option expires worthless.

It will have a moneyness of 10 if the underlying moves to 110, because the option has to have at least a value of 10, as the option could be immediately exercised and the stock purchased at the strike of 100 and sold in the market for 110. Considering the purchase price—or premium—of the call of 5, then the payoff is 5 at this level of 110, calculated by the moneyness (110-100 or stock minus strike) minus the premium of 5.

Moving your index finger horizontally, from left to right, along the payoff line means that you simulate an increase of the price of the stock or underlying, and you will be able to read on the vertical P&L scale, on the left, the amount of money your option position would make or lose.

FIGURE 11: PAYOFF OF CALL 100

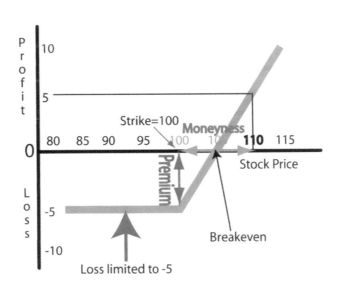

The payoff diagrams show those relationships between underlying price and payoff graphically. The underlying price is drawn as the horizontal axis (X) and the profit & loss of the option on the left vertical axis (Y). The horizontal line in the middle is the break-even line, meaning that at this level the option has a payoff equal to the premium, meaning that no money is made or lost.

3.2.1.1.1 PAYOFF OF A STOCK (LONG/SHORT)

The stock long position is linear. That means its payoff diagram is simply a line. That such a position has such a profile is clear, e.g., if you own 1000 Intel stocks and the price of Intel moves a certain number of points, your portfolio's value changes by the amount of points times the 1000 stocks.

If you are short stocks it is the relationship between P&L and stock price is still linear, but inversed in the sense that you lose if the stock goes up.

FIGURE 12: PAYOFF STOCK LONG

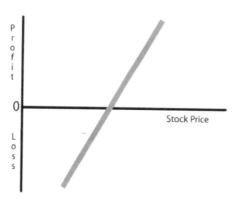

FIGURE 13: PAYOFF STOCK SHORT

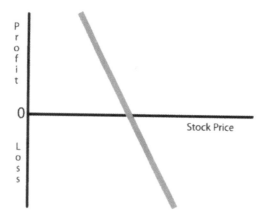

3.2.1.1.2   PAYOFF OF A CALL (LONG/SHORT)

We know that we cannot lose more than the premium being long a call. That means that there is a level on the downside where the call value stops to decrease. This level is the option premium, as on a long position no more money can be lost than the paid premium.

FIGURE 14: PAYOFF CALL LONG

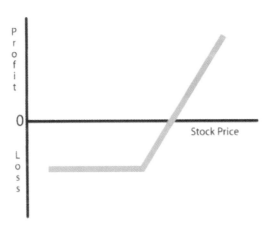

On the short call payoff diagram below, you can see that the profit potential is limited, namely to the received premium; however, the potential loss is unlimited. It is also easy to see that the short call payoff is a mirror image of the long call.

Remember the example in the introduction: call with a strike of 100 bought for 5 and the underlying trading at 110.

FIGURE 15: PAYOFF CALL SHORT

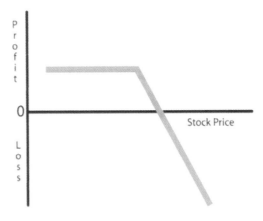

FIGURE 16: PAYOFF PUT LONG

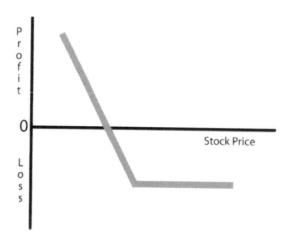

Above we can clearly see that the profit is created if the stock price moves to the left, that is down.

FIGURE 17: PAYOFF PUT SHORT

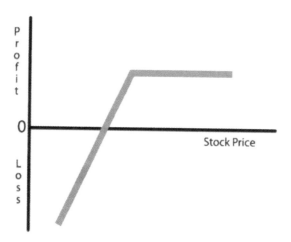

One can see that the long positions are symmetric to short positions. As mentioned before, they are mirror images, whereby the mirror is placed along the horizontal axis. Additionally, Puts are symmetric to Calls according to a vertical mirror. Summarizing:

LONG - SHORT: horizontal symmetry
PUT - CALL: vertical symmetry.

3.2.2 OPTION ALGEBRA

You can easily construct payoff diagrams for combined option strategies, just by adding them to each other, like building blocks. The rules are very simple, namely:

> Adding a 45% diagonal upwards line with a 45% diagonal downwards line results in a horizontal line.
>
> Adding a diagonal line with a horizontal line results in a diagonal line in the same direction, however shifted vertically by the amount of the combined profit and loss.

We mention this algebra of payoff diagrams because you will see it in many publications.

For example, our favorite, the straddle, is the combination of a put and a call. These examples should well illustrate the above-mentioned rules.

FIGURE 18: OPTION ALGEBRA: THE STRADDLE

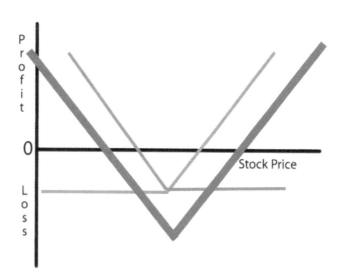

The covered call is a combination of long stock plus short call.

FIGURE 19: OPTION ALGEBRA: THE COVERED CALL

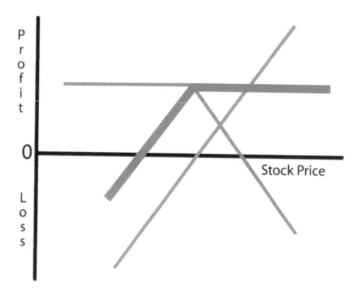

One often sees option algebra based on the put / call parity, which says, simplified:

Pay off of call equals payoff of long stock plus pay off of put or call = stock + put

And therefore

Put = - Stock + Call

And

Stock = Call – Put, or *Synthetic* Stock equals call long, put short.

The expression "synthetic" is used for describing stock positions that are established with options or any position that is created with a multiple of other instruments.

The above formulae are for the risk profile; if you need to calculate the values, the formulas become
Put = Call – Stock + PresentValue (Strike)

The present value function is Strike / 1+RiskFreeRate ^ TimeTilExpiration, and it deducts the interest beforehand.

In the context of options pricing the interest is deducted with the risk free rate, i.e. T-Bills.

The put/call parity relationships are fine for European options, as they can only be exercised at expiration. American options, however, have to be treated more cautiously, as they can be exercised at any time and can therefore ruin a well-meant synthetic position.

3.3 OVERVIEW OF OPTIONS MARKETS

An option market is a service provider to the investor: therefore, it has to assure the hassle-free purchasing and selling of options, and for a good price, too, both in terms of transaction costs and bid-ask spreads. Moreover, the option contracts should be attractive in themselves, by having high-volume stocks or well designed indices as underlyings.

With the advance of computer technology, it has been possible to reduce substantially the transaction costs and the hassle factor. The bid and ask spreads are more difficult to influence, because they are related to the risk that the market makers are willing to take. This risk again is dependent on liquidity, because a high liquidity allows efficient hedging.

Therefore the aim of the different markets is to attract as much volume as possible. This is done by servicing the interests of all market participants in order that they use the specific.

It is actually more difficult to give an overview of the different options markets than one might think. The reason for this difficulty is that options markets have moved from open outcry to electronic systems. Those electronic systems are interconnected computers, whereby the traders can access the market from wherever they want; they just need a fast communication line.

This development has given headway to the possibility that electronic options markets merge. Every week you will see a news release regarding the opening of a new exchange, the closing of a superfluous one and most often the news is about link-ups and mergers between exchanges.

We forecast that within 10 years we will have all stock option markets linked up in such a way that they appear as one.

But as of today, we would like to mention the following exchanges where options are traded and – for the interested investor – provide a massive amount of content on their websites.

It is easy to get overwhelmed by the quantity of information and the differences in details of the various instruments. So never forget the big picture: you decide the underlying first, hopefully with the help of a chart, then you establish your options positions, and most of the details become irrelevant. Moreover, options exchanges are notoriously looking for the next hugely successful product and are therefore continuously launching new options and option-like contracts. But do as we do and stay with the basics: puts and calls on either individual stocks or indices.

Exchange	Location	Website	Instruments
Americas			
AMEX	New York	www.amex.com	Indices, options, stocks
CBOE	Chicago	www.cboe.com	Indices, equity options
CBOT	Chicago	www.cbot.com	Indices, options, stocks
CME	Chicago	www.cme.com	
ISE	New York	www.iseoptions.com	
PSE	San Francisco	www.pacificex.com	
PHLX	Philadelphia	www.phlx.com	
TSE	Toronto		
Europe			
Belfox			
Euronext F			
Eurex			
IDEM			
Euronext NL			
Meff			
Liffe			
AustralAsia			
SNFE			
HKFE			
OSE			

Because you as a trader will most probably use an intermediary for trading options, it is much more important for you to choose a good options broker, e.g., Interactive brokers or OptionsXpress, which is super fast and has excellent execution capabilities, than deciding on what market to trade. For you as the end-user, the exchanges can help you with information and educational material, but it is the broker that is your gateway to the market and therefore should be chosen carefully.

3.4 THE BASIC DIRECTIONAL STRATEGIES

3.4.1 BUY CALLS—NOT STOCK

Most serious investors are looking for great stocks that offer tremendous and immediate upside potential. They are not bottom fishing for down and out securities that are currently trading at a small fraction of yesterday's glorious highs and now bump along at distressed prices making new low after new low. Bottom fishers are trying to buy satisfactory stocks at bargain basement prices, at prices that have little further downside, and may at some far distant time turn around and rise. Study after study has concluded that cheap stocks selling significantly below their earlier highs are cheap because no one wants them, and being out of favor makes it difficult to determine when they may again be highly sought and thus begin to rise. These studies have found that "buying low and selling higher" sounds logical and is theoretically correct, but is normally not as profitable as buying high and selling higher. When purchasing high stocks, you are buying stocks in favor, ones that everyone wants because the company is doing well, and ones that are far more likely to continue to rise than to fall.

Successful traders search for stocks that make new highs, and those securities within a few percentage points of their yearly and/or all time highs. Additionally they seek stocks displaying greater momentum than the market and their industry peer group. Most technical charting packages, data quote providers, and search programs allow the trader to search for securities near their highs and making new highs. Additionally they allow for price comparisons to gauge the relative momentum of a stock against another selected index, industry group, a competitor, or market average.

Having found a great stock, the investor buys shares and never considers the superior alternative, the purchase of a call. This section will demonstrate why buying a call option is normally a better idea than purchasing the stock.

LEVERAGE—THE AMOUNT INVESTED—STOCK VS. CALL:

Compare the leverage of buying stock with buying a call option. When we buy 100 shares in a cash account, we must deposit the full purchase price of the shares with the broker. To purchase 100 shares of a $60 stock requires a cash outlay of $6,000. We are going long the shares today, believing the stock will show healthy price appreciation and the price advance will occur quickly. If a major price increase is not expected, the shares should not be acquired at all, and the money invested in another asset whose value is expected to climb. If a major price advance is anticipated, yet the rise is not imminent, the shares should be purchased later and closer to the expected start date of the rally. This is often the case in the pharmaceuticals industry where a young company has developed a new drug and has submitted it to the FDA for approval, yet the earliest possible release date is a year away. Buying the stock a year prior to the fireworks may not make sense. Too much can happen between now and the approval date which could adversely impact the share price. There are plenty of other stock "plays" to trade in the interim, or the funds could simply be parked in an interest bearing account in the meantime.

Okay, so the investor now owns 100 shares of a great $60 stock with major and immediate upside potential. All the hoped for events happen and the stock shoots to $80 within a month. Can this happen? Absolutely. There are normally hundreds of stocks trading 20 points higher today than one month ago. Just examine charts of a number of tech stocks, internet offerings, or similar high flyers and you will find major moves are commonplace occurrences.

How much has the investor made? The $6,000 investment has increased to $8,000, for a profit of $2,000. Not bad! But the dollar size of a profit is only part of the answer as to the profitability of an investment. The amount of money invested to earn the profit is also important. If the $2,000 is made on an investment of $6,000, that is good. If it was made on an investment of $1 million dollars, that is less than exciting. We quantify the size of the profit in comparison with the size of the investment by calculating the return on the investment (ROI). This is the percentage return we make on each dollar of invested funds. The formula for the (percentage) return on the money invested normally referred to as ROI (Return on Investment) is calculated by dividing the amount of the return by the size of the investment. Having earned $2,000 on a $6,000 investment, we divide the $2,000 return by the $6,000 investment and the ROI is a decimal (.333) or 33.3%. The cash investor of the 100 shares of the $60 stock made 33.3% on his investment. If 100 shares of the stock had been purchased at $150, and the price rose 20 points to $170, the cash investor having invested $15,000, made $2,000, but the ROI was only 13.3% ($2,000 return divided by the $15,000 investment). Why is the ROI in the second example so much lower? Because 2.5 times more money ($15,000 compared with $6,000) had to be invested in the second case to earn the same dollar profit ($2,000).

Another thing that should normally be considered in determining the profitability of an investment is the length of time required to earn the profit. If the $60 stock rose to $80 in one month, the return of $2,000 was realized in just 30 days. The ROI calculated above as 33.3% was a 30 day return. And because there are 12 thirty-day periods in a year, the annual return is 33.3% times 12, or a 400% annualized return. Had it taken 6 months for the stock to appreciate the 20 points, the ROI would be the same 33.3%, but the annualized return would be only 66.6% since there are only 2 six-month periods in the year. The annualized return assumes that the investor can duplicate the periodic return each and every similar time period of the year. Thus if the investor makes 33.3% in a month, the annualized return or 400% is predicated upon the belief the same level of profitability can be made each and every month. If this is true, at the end of the year the $6,000 have grown fourfold to $24,000.

As investors, what we are concerned with can be summarized as follows: the actual dollars of profit we make, the Return of Investment, and the Annualized Return on Investment.

The stock investor who bought 100 shares of a $60 stock in a cash account invested $6,000. If the price moves up to $80 in a month, the profit is $2,000, the ROI is 33.3% and the annualized return is 400%. Had the purchase taken place in a margin account, the investor would only be required to invest 50% of the $6,000 stock purchase cost, or $3,000. The brokerage firm would cover the remaining $3,000 as a debit (loan) and would charge interest on the loan. The interest rate varies from broker to broker and is often scaled, so the more borrowed, the lower the interest rate charged. Generally, the margin interest rate is several points above the prime interest rate. Because the US prime interest rate is so low, the margin interest rates are in the range of 5 – 8% per year.

Ignoring the interest charges and commissions, the margin investor and the cash investor both made the same $2,000 when the stock's price reached $80 within the month. But because the margin investor's investment was only $3,000, the ROI was 66.7% for the month, for an annual return of 800% (figures are rounded), compared with the 33.3% ROI and 400% annualized return for the cash trader.

As these examples have demonstrated, if a great stock is purchased and its price advances, the use of margin has a number of positive benefits. First, if the stock's price appreciation is greater than the interest on the margin loan, the use of margin provides positive leverage and magnifies both the ROI and the annualized return. Thus in this case the use of margin is a very positive thing, for it increases the investment return as a percentage return on the investment. The dollar return is identical (ignoring margin interest charges), yet the percentage return increases.

Second, it allows stock to be purchased with few dollars invested, a help to less well capitalized investors and those investors seeking the maximum portfolio diversification given a limited level of funds. Most of us never seem to have enough cash for all of our "must have" investments. The use of margin spreads the capital out, allowing us to control stock for fewer dollars, or to buy more stock than possible without the margin loan. If the investor only had $6,000 to invest, he could buy 200 shares of a $60 stock in a margin account, but only 100 shares in a cash account. Alternatively, the margin investor could invest only $3,000 to buy 100 shares of the $60 stock, leaving $3,000 available for other attractive investment opportunities.

Third, margin investing permits greater diversification. If the investor has $6,000, 100 shares of two different $60 stocks can be purchased, or 100 shares of a $40 stock and 100 shares of an $80 one, or 100 shares of a $50 security and 100 shares of a $70 one, or any combination of shares to total twice the amount of the deposited money. With $6,000 to invest though a margin account, twice that value of stock or $12,000 could be purchased.

The use of margin provides positive advantages with rising stock prices. It is therefore important for margin investors to buy only great stocks. But margin has a downside: leverage through margin can hurt should the prices drop. The negative aspects of leverage will be covered later.

Investors seldom make a distinction between buying stock in a cash or margin account. But they should. And they should consider opportunities offering even greater leverage than that available in a margin account. The best leverage available to a stock buyer is 50% margin. Yet the call buyer has much greater leverage. The average cost to purchase a one-month call at the money is 6% of the stock value. This translates into an equivalent of 6% margin. Now instead of placing $6,000 with the broker to buy 100 shares of a $60 stock in a cash account, or depositing just $3,000 in a margin account to buy the same 100 shares of the $60 stock, the call buyer has only to deposit the premium, assumed to be 6%, or $360 ($6,000 stock value times 6%). The following table displays the required dollar investment for the cash stock investor, the margin stock investor, and the call buyer to purchase or control 100 shares of stock at $60, and the dollar profit and ROI generated for each financing structure resulting from various price movements of the stock.

Investor Type and Amount Invested to Control 100 Shares of a $60 Stock	Stock Price			
	$70	$80	$90	$100
	Profit Generated in Dollars and as a Return on Investment			
Cash Invested $6,000	$1,000 16.7%	$2,000 33.3%	$3,000 50%	$4,000 66.7%
Margin Investor $3,000	$1,000 33.3%	$2,000 66.7%	$3,000 100%	$4,000 133.3%
Call Buyer $360	$640 177%	$1,640 455.6%	$2,640 733.3%	$3,640 1011.1%

In summary, the call buyer in our example has the following advantages:

FEW DOLLARS INVESTED. The call buyer has only invested $360, compared with $6,000 for the cash stock buyer and $3,000 for the margin stock buyer.

LARGER RETURN ON INVESTMENT. Having invested a smaller amount, the ROI is magnified with the call buyer making over 5 times the return as the margin stock buyer and over 10 times that of the cash stock buyer.

NO INTEREST CHARGE. The margin stock buyer has to pay interest on the margin loan (debit balance), while the call buyer never has a broker loan and thus no interest charge.

DIVERSIFICATION. Since the option buyer is investing such a small amount in the call, most of his capital is available for other investment opportunities.

LOW RISK. How much is the investor risking? Regardless of how much research and analysis we do, and no matter how sure we are the stock we are buying will rise, we are often disappointed. Our great stock turns out to be a real dog. The anticipated merger fails to occur, the new contract does not materialize, the new product is not approved by the FDA, the profit margin decreases, a new competitor appears on the scene, the founder and guiding light resigns suddenly, raw material shortages, slow production, unexpected labor unrest turns into a prolonged strike, insiders dump the shares, an institution bails out, Alan Abelson pans the company, earnings beat the estimates but fall short of the whisper number, a floating decimal glitch is discovered in the new chip, accounting irregularities are discovered, the SEC is investigating the firm, the CEO is indicted for insider trading, or the industry falls from favor... We have heard and seen it all. Our stock heads south from the negative event. The anticipated gain of 20 points (the expectation of rising from 60 to 80) becomes an actual 20 point loss (stock declines from 60 to 40).

How could we have protected ourselves? The immediate answer of most investors is to "use a stop-loss order." When purchasing the stock at $60, we could have entered a stop-loss order at a lower price. If that price was hit, we would have sold the stock. There are no costs or fees to enter a stop-loss order. A commission is only charged if the trade is triggered and the stock is sold. A stop-loss order thus appears to be a simple and effective trading tool that can cut losses short and protect the stock position from suffering a catastrophic decline. Correct? Not quite.

There are problems with stop loss orders. First, at what price should the stop be placed? If the stop is too high, or too close to the stock's current market price, losses are kept to a minimum, but the stop could be triggered with normal price fluctuations without the stock having truly reversed to the downside. Minor daily price fluctuations or price noise could cause the stock to be stopped out (sold), even though the uptrend was still intact. The probability of the stop-loss order being executed increases as the stop is placed closer to the security price. If the stop is placed further from the current market price, the chance of being hit is lessened, but the size of the loss if the stock is sold through the exercise of the stop is increased. The real question becomes: where should the stop order be placed? This represents one of the most difficult of all investment questions. And the problem of stop placement is complicated by a trader's memory of his personal experiences using them. Most investors have experienced numerous instances where they placed the stop-loss at what seemed to be a logical level, only to see the stop hit (stock sold at a loss) followed by the shares then experiencing an immediately major price advance, while the investor is out of the position. The following charts depict just such a situation. The first shows the recent price action and a logical spot to place a stop. The second displays future price action of the shares which declined to the stop point triggering the stop, and then had a huge immediate upward move. The investor missed the big move as he had sold the shares through the exercise of the stop.

FIGURE 20: DNA EXAMPLE

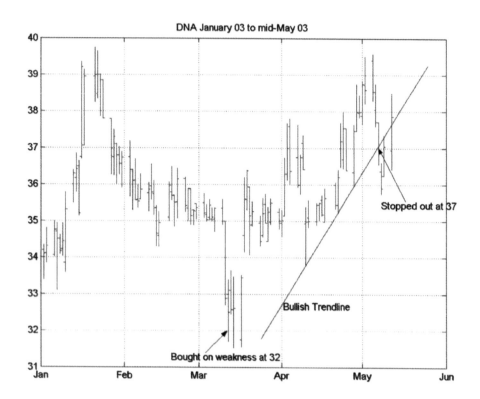

FIGURE 21. DNA EXAMPLE 2

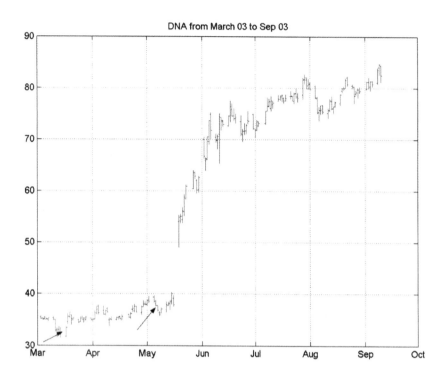

After a few similar occurrences of having winning positions stopped out early and thus missing the major upside move, investors tend to shy away from using formal stops placed with the broker. Instead they migrate to employing mental stops. A mental stop is a price the investor plans to sell the position if its price should decline to the targeted level. There are, however, also several problems with mental stops. Determining the sell price is still a major undertaking. Although the original exit price (mental stop-loss sell price) of 52 may have seemed logical when the stock was first purchased at 60, as its price approaches the mental sell price, a second thought creeps in and all good intensions evaporate in favor of "giving it just a little more room." "I will sell if it drops to 48." As the price approaches 48, the investor decides, "Giving the stock a couple of more points will not hurt." Soon the stock has dropped so low that the resulting loss if sold simply becomes too large to stomach, and the mental stop-loss is abandoned. The short term investment purchased at 60 with the expectation of immediately rising to 80, is now trading at 46, and becomes a long term hold. Human nature being what it is, the investor will now stubbornly hold the position until it has finally risen to a break-even level (60) and can be sold. In this way the investor "never lost any money." The stock may have to be held for years, patiently waiting to break-even. This is faulty reasoning. When stock is purchased and subsequently declines below the purchase price, there is a loss. Until the stock is sold, the loss is not a realized or accounting loss, but it is an equity loss. By making a decision to continue to hold a losing stock, the investor makes the decision equivalent to repurchasing the shares at the lower current price and is therefore foregoing all the opportunities available for the cash in case the shares had been sold. By continuing to hold the losing shares, the investor is actively deciding to keep the money invested in the loser, rather than seeking to employ it in a better trade.

The call buyer need never worry about the appropriate place to enter the stop, whether the stop will be executed, or whether the stop should be lowered. By purchasing a call, the maximum loss (the premium paid) is known and the investor controls the stock for the full life period of the option. The number of times the price drops, and the duration and depth of any price decline, are immaterial because the maximum loss is known. The call buyer's research has revealed the price should advance well beyond the call strike price during the option life, so what happens in the interim is not relevant.

The following example might clarify this point. Assume a one month 60 strike call is purchased for $360, with the stock trading at $60. The stock immediately declines to 52, then rallies to 60, drops to 53, rises to 60, falls to 54, and finally pushes to 67. A stock investor using a 10% stop, meaning that a stop is placed 10% below the stock purchase price, would have been stopped out at 54. If in the subsequent rally the stock was repurchased at 60, it would have been sold again at 54. The investor would probably avoid this stock like the plague on the third up movement, having been twice burned. The stock buyer has lost $1,200 (buying at 60 and being stopped out at 54, repurchasing at 60 and again being stopped out at 54) and missed the rally to 65. The call buyer, on the other hand, could have ignored all declines, comforted in the knowledge that the maximum loss was only $360, representing a loss smaller than the loss suffered by the stock investor being stopped out, and he would still have benefited when the price ultimately hit 65. So which strategy was better? Obviously the call purchase! Since most investment texts recommend the use of stop-loss orders and placing them at least 10% below the entry price, and because a one month call option at-the-money normally trades at about 6% of the stock price, the call is normally a superior vehicle to lessen risk while allowing participation in upward price movement.

The following chart of Genentech, Inc. (DNA) shows the purchase of a one-month call with a 40-strike price maturing on June 13, 2003 purchased on May 2 for $240. The stock declined to 36, then by the expiration date had risen to 75. The call buyer never had to worry about the downside after purchasing the call for $240, for he would participate in any upside movement during the option's life. He made $3,500 (40 strike less the 75 stock price) less the option cost ($240) for a total profit of $3,260 and an ROI of over 1,300%.

FIGURE 22: DNA CALL PROFITABILITY

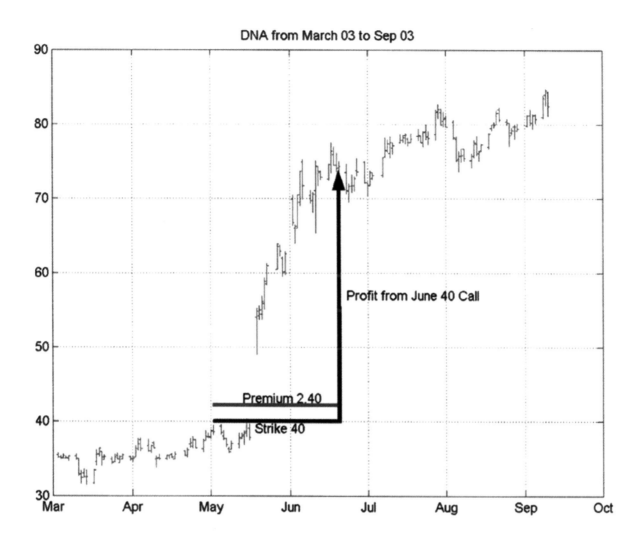

The following table displays the potential loss on a call and on the stock for various price movements. In this example, the stock buyer always loses more dollars than the call buyer when the stock declines more than the call premium amount.

Investor Type and Amount Invested to Control 100 Shares of a $60 Stock	Stock Price			
	$55	$50	$45	$40
	Loss Generated in Dollars			
Cash Invested $6,000	($500)	($1,000)	($1,500)	($2000)
Margin Investor $3,000	($500)	($1,000)	($1,500)	($2,000)
Call Buyer $360	($360)	($360)	($360)	($360)

In this example the call buyer has the following advantages:

MAXIMUM RISK IS KNOWN. The call buyer is only risking $360, no matter how far the stock might decline. The stock buyer has no way to determine the maximum risk unless the stock drops to zero.

MAXIMUM LOSS IS SMALL. The call buyer can only lose the premium, a small amount compared with the much larger loss possible from stock ownership.

NO MARGIN CALLS. The margin stock buyer is subject to margin calls should the share price decline. The call buyer can never get a margin call.

SYNTHETIC STOCK POSITION:

It is a well known fact that most options expire worthless. This is because most options are purchased to provide maximum leverage for the minimum cost, with the buyer investing very little and hoping for a huge return on the investment. The typical option buyer is taking the same approach as a lottery player. Investing almost nothing and expecting to win big or not at all. Options purchased several strike prices out, are way out-of-the-money, and cost very little. For example, a one month call at-the-money on a $60 stock might cost 6% or $360, a call at 65 might cost $100 and a call at 70 could be purchased for $12.50. There is a very low probability of the stock going above 70 in the month, but if it does, the ROI can be huge. Hope springs eternal to these buyers of out-of-the-money options – the company could be acquired at a large premium, it might discover the next miracle drug, its earnings might far exceed even the wildest whisper numbers, or its just released invention will revolutionize computer operating systems. All are unlikely, but who knows? We normally view the purchase of way out-of-the-money options as gambling, but fun entertainment. Unfortunately investing is supposed to be fun, entertaining, and PROFITABLE. In fact, buying far out-of-the-money options may be fun and entertaining, but seldom profitable.

There is a consistently more profitable approach in buying calls: buying a call which represents a synthetic stock position. This means that a call is purchased that acts almost exactly like a stock. A call option deep in-the-money with little time to expiration has very little time value, but a large intrinsic value. If the premium of a one month call at-the-money on a 60 stock is $360, the entire premium represents time value. Similarly, the $100 premium on a 65 call 5 points out-of-the-money is all time value. But the $700 cost of a call with a strike price of $55 is composed of $500 intrinsic and $200 time value. And a 50 call trading at $1,050 only has a time value of $50. This last option acts very much like a stock. As the price of the shares rises, the option will gain in value at nearly dollar for dollar. Conversely, it will lose value dollar for dollar with a price decline of the shares. Thus owning this option provides the same risks and benefits as owning the stock, but with two major differences. The stock buyer is investing $6,000 to control 100 shares of stock, yet the call buyer has an investment of only $1,050. The maximum risk of loss for the call buyer is capped at $1,050, regardless of how low the stock might decline. If the call investor is correct in his prediction of a significant and immediate share price increase, the ROI on the call purchase will be much greater than the ROI on the stock purchase. Why? Because the call buyer is only investing $1,050 compared to the $3,000 of a margin buyer and the $6,000 for a cash stock purchaser. For example, the stock rises from 60 to 80. The margin stock purchaser makes $2,000 on the $3,000 investment for a 66.67% ROI. The cash share buyer makes the same $2,000 profit, but having invested $6,000, his ROI is 33.33%. The option buyer purchasing the 50 strike call for $1,050 earns a gross return of $3,000 (80 market price of the stock less the 50 strike of the call), and a net return after deducting the cost of the call ($1,050) of $1,950 (gross profit of $3,000 less the call premium cost of $1.050). This means the call buyer earns $1,950 on a $1,050 investment yielding an ROI of 185.7%.

Should the shares decline, the maximum dollar loss the call buyer could sustain is known to the penny and is nearly identical to the loss suffered by the share buyer. This is true until the share price declines more than the premium cost of the call option. After the shares have fallen more than the call premium, the stock investor's dollar loss becomes larger than the loss sustained by the call buyer. To illustrate this, had the shares declined from 60 to 55, the share buyer having purchased the stock at 60 would have lost $500 on the 100 shares, and the purchaser of the 50 strike call for $1,050 would also have lost $500, plus part of the time value of $50, for a total loss (assuming no time value remained) of $550. At a share price of 52, the stock holder has lost $800 compared with $850 in loss for the call buyer. At a 50 share price, the stock position has declined $1,000, (60 to 50) and the call buyer is out $1,050. But when the price drops below the call premium level the call buyer has a maximum loss of the call premium paid ($1,050), whereas the share buyer continues to lose dollars. With a share price of 45, the stock position has dropped $1,500, yet the call buyer has already reached his maximum loss of $1,050 and can never lose any more money on this transaction. The stock could actually go to 0 (think of Enron or WorldCom) causing a $6,000 loss on the equity holdings, and still the call purchaser is only out the $1,050 premium investment.

A further benefit to the purchaser of a call deep in-the-money with little time value is that any loss sustained will be nearly identical to that of a stock investor and will seldom be 100% of the premium. When a far out-of-the-money option (a 70 strike call when the underlining stock is trading for 60) is acquired and the stock fails to reach the strike price (70), the entire premium is lost. For the deep in-the-money call (a 50 strike call when the stock is at 60), most of any rise will result in profits. Yet there is little likelihood of a price plunge greater than the premium. Thus in most cases buying a deep in-the-money call, paying little time value premium, results in a profit if the shares rise, or part of the premium is recovered because the shares do not decline more than the premium cost.

The next table clearly demonstrates the similarity of the deep in-the-money call as a synthetic stock position compared with stock ownership for various price moves. As can be observed, the stock investor loses more dollars when a major decline occurs, yet the call buyer makes almost as large a dollar profit with a price rise. In addition, since the call buyer is investing far fewer dollars, the ROI is much larger. Therefore buying a deep in-the-money call with little time value in the premium price has significant advantages over stock ownership and no disadvantages. If we like a stock and have a strong desire to have it in our portfolio because we expect an up move in the very near future, we will always purchase a deep in-the-money call rather than stock, assuming the call premium is primarily intrinsic value with minimal time value. As a rule of thumb, we prefer the time value to be less than 20% of the total premium, and ideally 10% or less.

Investor Type and Amount Invested to Control 100 Shares of a $60 Stock	Profit or Loss Generated in Dollars							
	$45	$50	$55	$60	$65	$70	$75	$80
Cash Investor $6000	($1,500)	($1,000)	($500)	0	$500	$1,000	$1,500	$2,000
Margin Investor $3000	($1,500)	($1,000)	($500)	0	$500	$1,000	$1,500	$2,000
Call Buyer Buying a One-Month 50 Strike Call for $1,050	($1,050)	($1,050)	($550)	($50)	$450	$950	$1,450	$1,950

WORDS OF CAUTION

This section has dealt with a comparison between buying a call and the purchase of 100 shares of stock. In all the examples, calls prove superior to stock ownership. The dollar investment for the purchase of the call is smaller than the required cash outlay to buy the shares resulting in larger Returns on Investment (ROI) for the call buyer if the stock should move up significantly. The call buyer's maximum loss is known to the penny, and the dollar size of the loss is smaller than the loss sustained by the stock investor if stopped out of the position. In each case, a single call and 100 shares of stock are compared. Because a call controls 100 shares of stock, there is logic in substituting one call for 100 shares of the stock. Consider buying one call instead of 100 shares of stock.

The call clearly has benefits over the equity. And there is an additional consideration. If the investor wants to increase profit opportunities, and has the money to purchase 100 shares of stock, (buying 100 shares at 60 involves a cash outlay of $3,000 in a margin account and $6,000 in a cash account) a second call (a one month 60 strike call costing $360) could easily be afforded. This will increase the potential dollar return, but at a price. More dollars are at risk and when an option is a loser, with the option expiring worthless, 100% of the premium is lost. Buying one call for $360 would have resulted in a $360 loss, buying two would double the loss to $720. Because the premium is modest, losing the entire premium on two calls is no worse than being stopped out of the 100 shares of stock. But if most or all of the cash that could have been invested in the stock is diverted into the buying of calls on this stock, and the call buyer is wrong on the future directional move of the share's price, 100% of each and every premium is lost, and the entire capital base is eroded.

If we have done a creditable research job on the stock, like the shares at 60, and can afford to buy 100 shares, only one call should be purchased. If wrong, 100% of the premium is lost. Since the premium for a single one-month at-the-money strike call is small, normally approximately 6% of the stock price, and it is all lost, there is still 94% of the capital base to try again. The loss on a call is usually smaller than the stock loss if stopped out of the shares. If the call buyer uses the entire $6,000 in capital to purchase calls on the stock, and is wrong, the entire capital is lost – defeating the major benefit of buying a call – the limited and small dollar loss. There is flip side. If we are correct in our price forecasts, the added leverage of investing all of the capital in calls can yield tremendous profit. But the price is simply too high.

To state it simply – the rule for the purchase of calls is **"for every 100 shares of stock you would normally purchase, buy one call."** If you are absolutely confident in your judgment of the future move of the shares, buy two calls. But **never** go beyond a ratio of 2 calls for 100 shares of stock. The risks are simply too great and the benefit of limited losses is destroyed.

Summary – Buy Calls, Not Stock

In nearly all situations, and if it is done logically, buying a call is superior to the purchase of 100 shares of stock. The exception is the purchase of "gamble calls," those with a strike price so far out-of-the-money (strike price far over the current stock price, such as buying 80 strike calls on a 60 stock) and with a very short expiration. In gamble calls there is very little likelihood of the security price exceeding the option's strike price prior to maturity.

The numerous advantages of calls as compared to stock ownership are outlined below:
Few Dollars Invested. The call buyer invests only a small percentage of the cost of the stock.

Larger Return on Investment. Having invested a smaller amount of money, the Return on Investment (ROI) is magnified. If the security has a significant move, the call buyer makes a percentage return on invested funds many times greater than that of the stock investor.

No Interest Charge. The margin stock buyer has to pay interest on the margin loan (debit balance), while the call buyer never has a broker loan and thus no interest charge.

Diversification. Since the option buyer is investing such a small amount in the call, most of his capital is available for other investment opportunities.

Direct Substitute for Stock (Synthetic Stock). Deep in-the-money calls with little time value in their premium price, move in value approximately dollar for dollar with the value of the stock. Because the call investment is so much less than required to purchase the stock, the profit on winning calls as a percentage of invested funds is far larger, and the dollar loss on losing calls is similar to the stock loss.

(continue next page)

Maximum Risk is Known. The call buyer is only risking the premium no matter how far the stock might decline. This maximum loss is known to the penny. The stock buyer has no way to determine the maximum risk unless the stock drops to zero.

Maximum Loss is Small. The call buyer can only lose the premium. Because the premium is small, the maximum loss is often less than the loss realized by an equity investor using a stop loss order and getting stopped out.

No Margin Calls. The margin stock buyer is subject to margin calls if the share price declines. The call buyer can never get a margin call.

Continuous Price Protection. A stop loss order provides price protection until the stop is hit. It is therefore a one-shot protection device. Once hit, the position is liquidated, a loss incurred, and there is no further opportunity to profit from future price advances because there is no longer an equity position. Call ownership allows the buyer the opportunity of participating in any price advance, while protecting against a loss greater than the premium. The call provides the protection for the entire life of the option contract regardless of how low the stock may decline or how many times it declines.

With so many advantages, it is easy to conclude, "Never buy stock again." But to maximize the use of calls, there are certain basic rules that, if observed, will keep the buyer out of major trouble.

Do Not Over Buy. If you would buy 100 shares of a stock, buy only one call. Or purchase a maximum of two contracts. To employ most or all of one's stock capital to buy the maximum number of call options on the stock defeats the advantage of small maximum loss.

Do Not Buy Far-Out-of-the-Money Calls. When the strike is several strike prices above the current stock price, the premium is cheap, but the chance of the stock price exceeding the strike price is very remote. Statistics show most calls of this type expire worthless.

Only Buy Calls When a Major Upside Move is Expected Soon. The stock must advance in price for the call to become more valuable. The larger the price rise, the greater the option price gain. And the gain must happen within the life of the contract life. Do your research and purchase calls only on great stocks, i.e., ones most likely to rise dramatically and rise soon.

Use Deep-in-the-Money Calls as a Substitute for Stock. Because deep in-the-money calls fluctuate dollar for dollar with the stock, they are logical substitutes for stock ownership. Their advantage is that they are cheaper in price and as a result offer great leverage.

Compare the Premium with the Size of the Future Move. The premium should be small in relationship to the magnitude of the future move. If we predict a 15-point move, the premium cost should only be a small fraction of the potential move.

3.5 DON'T BE PENNY-WISE AND POUND FOOLISH

Options are great financial instruments. Looking at options literature, though, we see a lot of books treating option pricing in highest detail, books often written by authors who have never run an options-portfolio themselves!

You have to understand that the profits made by using options stem from moves in the markets and not from sophisticated option price calculations. For the average user of options, excluding a dozen of very specialized firms (quantitative traders, software and risk-consulting), there is absolutely no benefit in the modeling of markets and development of new pricing methods for options. Even for options market makers the key to profitability lies in the thorough understanding of the simple models and the intelligence of the dynamic hedge process of the portfolio.

Trying to understand options-pricing at a deep level and ignoring the big picture regarding the market dynamics, which is done by looking at charts, would be penny-wise and pound-foolish!

We include some 50 pages of introduction to options pricing as we believe that it is useful in the sense that it helps you to understand the concepts and the jargon used by the financial intermediaries and the press.

Moreover, we have included the section about options pricing because we think that options pricing has to date not yet been explained in such an easy and straightforward way. Thanks to this chapter the interested reader should get a sufficient understanding of the subject and – if he got confused by other books – he can finally get a clear idea of what it is all about.

But the important point is that technical analysis of the underlying stock and the character of its movements comes first, options pricing second, if at all.

3.6 ALL THAT YOU NEED TO KNOW ABOUT OPTION PRICING

> **Note: If you are not too concerned with the in-depth aspects of an option price and the many aspects of volatility, you can jump directly to Chapter 5, where we explain the trading and money making aspects of the non-directional strategies.**

3.6.1 WHY DO WE EXPLAIN OPTION PRICING?

When trading with options you come across all sorts of expressions that relate to option pricing, such as Theoretical Price, Time value, or Delta. Therefore it is important to acquire some notion about the background of option pricing. We will also show you the background of the famous Black&Scholes formula and we will explain to you Monte Carlo simulation, the methodology which became so important over the last few years.

This chapter is just meant to give you additional background information. The trading strategies that we explain in the later chapters do not require knowledge about Black&Scholes or Monte Carlo.

3.6.2   OPTION PRICING: THE BIG PICTURE

As an interested reader you probably already know quite a bit about pricing options. If you don't, that's fine, too. In our book, we would like to make things as comprehensible as possible and start explaining options and option pricing from scratch.

An option is a bet on the future. Can it be priced? This means, can a method be developed that tells us what an option with a lifetime of several years is worth today? Do we need to know the price of the underlying at the option's expiration date? Obviously not, because it is – unfortunately – not possible to know what a stock will be worth a couple of years from now.

Many methods have been developed in the last 25 years or so. Again, we would like to explain the option pricing in the most straightforward way, using an alternative method that is understandable with a minimum of mathematical knowledge. On the following page you will see we have listed the few basic concepts you will need to help you better understand this book.

> **Option pricing truth: The option price is a present-valued sum, namely the present-value of the sum of all statistically possible outcomes weighted by their probability.**

That means that the option price can be calculated by taking every possible outcome of the stock price, calculate the probability of that outcome and the value of the option for that outcome, multiply the two and sum them all up.

Option pricing is all about knowing the equilibrium price, where an option has exactly the same price as its probability weighted payoff. That means the price where the seller and the buyer of the option would both make the same zero profit in the long run if the markets behaved normally and the exactly the same transaction could be repeated many times, which of course is not possible, but that serves as a theoretical simplification.

But let's go step by step and first talk about options, then volatility, and only afterwards about the applications of non-directional trading strategies for maximum profit.

3.6.3   THE REQUIRED NUMBER-CRUNCHING ABILITIES ARE MINIMAL

The finance literature is notorious for its artificially created mathematical complexity. But trust us, we will present all the required information regarding non-directional trading in terms that are easy to understand. In the following we include the necessary mathematical and statistical notions and define them shortly. We distinguish between the two sciences, mathematics and statistics, because that is done so traditionally. For the sake of understanding calculations in finance, they could be joined and simply be called number crunching.

3.6.3.1   MATHEMATICS

No more than the four basic operations (addition, subtraction, multiplication and division) are needed to understand this book.

3.6.3.2 STATISTICS PRIMER, OR ALL THAT YOU NEED TO NOW ABOUT STATISTICS

Some straightforward statistical concepts have to be understood. They are very natural and common sense, though. We explain them definition by definition.

TIME-SERIES: series of numbers that are presented in a chronological order, e.g., daily closing prices or quarterly earnings.

VARIABILITY: the strength of a time-series move. Time-series are like the sea, "they can show moves or waves of different sizes". A time-series that moves strongly is said to have a high variability.

MEAN: the simple average of data, like the average salary of a certain profession, which is calculated by summing all the salaries of all people interviewed and dividing the sum by the number of people interviewed. Only addition and division are needed as operations.

PROBABILITY: the percentage of occurrence of a certain outcome of an experiment if it were repeated many times. The probability or likelihood to throw heads with a standard coin is 50% as there are two possible outcomes, but only one of those is heads. The probability to throw a 6 with a die is 1/6th as there are in total 6 possible outcomes, but only one of those is a six.

EXPECTED VALUE: the most likely outcome. Let's look at the example of throwing two dice: There are obviously 36 outcomes, namely the 6 outcomes of the first die multiplied with the 6 outcomes of the second die, shown by the square below. The numbers in red indicate the eyes on the individual die; one die is listed as the first horizontal column and the second as the first vertical column.

	1	2	3	4	5	6
1	2	3	4	5	6	7
2	3	4	5	6	7	8
3	4	5	6	7	8	9
4	5	6	7	8	9	10
5	6	7	8	9	10	11
6	7	8	9	10	11	12

There are 36 possible outcomes. There is only one outcome of a 12; therefore its probability is 1/36. There are six possibilities to get a 7; therefore the probability of a 7 is 6 x 1/36. It could also be said that any of each combination occurs with a probability of 1/36, whereby the 7 should be weighted with 6, as 6 of the possible outcomes are a 7.

If for example we thus want to calculate the expected value of the outcome of the throw of the two dice, we would do the following:

We list the possibilities and associate a probability weight to them.

Outcome	Probability Weight
2	1/36
3	2/36
4	3/36
5	4/36
6	5/36
7	6/36
8	5/36
9	4/36
10	3/36
11	2/36
12	1/36

Now we can say that the expected value is 7, as it is the value with the highest probability, and we can also say that with a probability of (5+6+5)/36 = 44% the outcome will be in the range of 6 to 8.

Variance:

Let's look at three series of 6 numbers each.

```
Series 1:  10 10 10 10 10 10

Series 2:  10 12 11 8 9 10

Series 3:  1 19 17 3 18 2
```

They all have the same mean, but other than that they are very different in terms of variability. We quantify the variability by taking for each number the difference from the mean, square it, sum it up and divide it by the number of samples. We have to square the differences so that they all become positive numbers, because a negative number could cancel out a positive number.

The variance of Series 1 is obviously 0.

The variance of series 2 is (10-10)^2 + (10-12)^2 + (10-11)^2 + (10-8)^2 + (10-9)^2 + (10-10)^2 divided by 6 = (0 + 4 + 1 + 4 + 1 + 0) / 6 = 1.67.

The variance of Series 3 is (81 + 81 + 49 + 49 + 64 + 64) / 6 = 65.

STANDARD DEVIATION:

The standard deviation is the square root of the variance. It may be thought of as an average deviation. The standard deviation has also a special meaning in the context of the normal distribution, which is explained below.

The standard deviation is often indicated with the Greek letter sigma.

Sigma of Series 1 = 0

Sigma of Series 2 = 1.29

Sigma of Series 3 = 8.04

NORMAL DISTRIBUTION:

Normal distributions have the bell-curved shape shown below.

FIGURE 23: NORMAL DISTRIBUTION

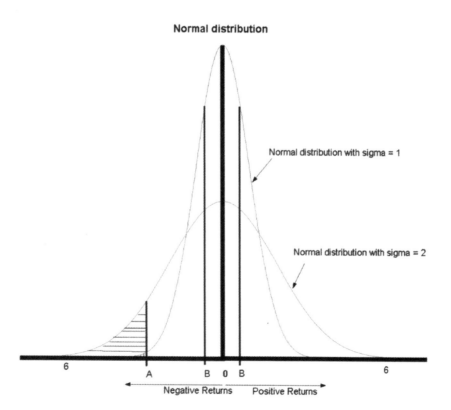

The probability is defined by the surface under the curve, a classic integral. Let us explain this.

The entire surface under the curve equals 1. It encompasses all possible returns, like crashes to the very left and violent upward moves to the very right. We can say that – in terms of the random walk theory of the markets – the next move is either up or down, i.e., fifty-fifty. This is documented by the bell curve as well. You see that half of the surface under the curve is to the left (down moves) and half is to the right (up moves).

If we want to calculate the probability that the next move lies within B left and B right, then we would calculate the surface defined by the two vertical lines and the bell curve on top and the x-axis on the bottom. It is clear that the probability of this happening under the blue curve is greater than under the red curve. This is logical, as the blue curve describes a stock with only half the sigma, or volatility, of the stock described by the red curve.

Now, if we want to know the probability that the stock falls below A, we would look at the surface to the left of A. It is obvious that this surface is much bigger under the red curve than under the blue one. That is logical, too, because the red stock has double the volatility of the blue stock.

Assuming that A is situated at 3 sigma, we can see in a normal distribution table that the probability of moving below A is 50 bigger for red stock than for blue stock.

As a note, the 6 on both sides of the axis indicates 6 sigma, i.e., 6 times the standard deviation of the blue stock, and as the red stock has a standard deviation of 2 sigma, it corresponds to 3 times the volatility or standard deviation of the red stock.

The following small table gives probabilities according to the normal distribution for a stock fall below a value that is expressed in sigma. As sigma=0 is in the center and according to the random walk concept the next stock move is either up or down with the same chance, therefore the probability that the stock falls bellow the center is half or 50%, that the stock falls bellow 1 sigma, that is makes a negative move with a greater magnitude than 1 sigma is obviously smaller, namely 16%. Which also means that 84% of all moves are expected to be between minus 1 sigma and plus infinite.

Below Sigma	Probability
0	50%
1	16%
2	2.30%
3	0.10%

For example, if you look at a stock worth $100 with a daily volatility of 2% (equals an annualized volatility of 32%), the above table tells you get that the probability of the stock being worth less tomorrow is 50% and the stock being worth less than $98 is 16%, representing a 1 sigma move. The stock has a small probability of 2.3% that it will be below 96 (2 sigmas) by tomorrow, but inversely, that the stock has a probability of 97.7% to be above 96.

If these figures sound small to you, just read on, where we explain that stock return distributions have much fatter tails than the normal distribution, which means that the probability of our stock to fall bellow 96 is bigger than what the normal distribution suggests.

FAT TAILS OR HETEROSKEDASTICITY:

Stock returns have fatter tails than the normal distribution, a phenomenon which is also called heteroskedasticity. That means that big moves, such as crashes, happen far more often than normal distribution would foresee.

The problem regarding the fat tails, which we will treat a bit more in detail when we talk about volatility, is substantial. As an illustration we give the following data:

According to the normal distribution a down move of 4% on the Dow Jones index has a probability of 0.000056 and in real history it has had a probability of 0.0066. That means that the probability of such a move is under represented by a factor of about 120. If we look at even bigger moves, the under representation gets even more frightening.

5% down, factor 5,000
6% down, factor 100,000
7% down, factor 30 million!

The tails of the normal distribution, that is the probability for extreme moves, are much too thin in respect to the empirical data. But even so, for many applications the normal distribution makes life for the mathematician much easier and is therefore used as an approximation. When the quantitative analysts or options market makers look at situations where the underestimation of extreme moves matters, they adjust for that by either using a higher volatility for out-of-the-money options, the ones that are most sensitive to extreme moves, or they use alternative models altogether.

CORRELATION:

Correlation is specified by a number between –1 and 1.

1 means that two time series (A and B) are perfectly correlated. That means that each and every time when series A moves up, series B moves up as well. The Dow and the SP100 are nearly perfectly correlated.

-1 means that two time series are perfectly inversely correlated. That means that each and every time when series A moves up, series B moves down. The bond and yields are nearly perfectly inversely correlated.

A correlation of 0 means that one cannot make a prediction of series A based on series B. The birth weights of babies and the stock price of IBM are not correlated, i.e., the correlation is 0.

A major risk in finance is that investments which have been highly correlated suddenly move in total different directions. Such correlation risks for example brought down the famous Long Term Capital hedge fund. Many practitioners and academics consider correlation based trades as dangerous and in general doubt that useful correlations exist at all in the world of finance and view them as short-lived phenomena.

3.6.4 INTRODUCTION TO THE CONCEPT OF OPTION PRICING

It is always much easier to explain concepts by using examples. We therefore propose an example where an investor, let's call him Joe, has a bullish market-view—he thinks prices will move upwards—for the next few days on Intel as of **July 18th, 2003,** and he would like to make some money by buying short-term call options.

At that moment the 12 month line chart of Intel (ticker-symbol: INTC) looks as follows:

FIGURE 24

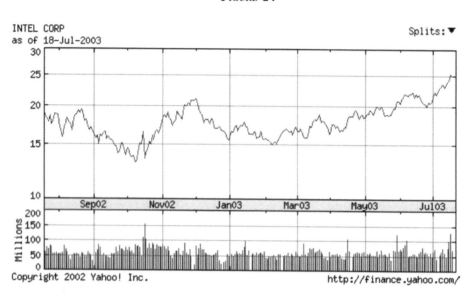

Being bullish for the short term, Joe decides to buy some August <u>Expiration</u> (August 15th) <u>Calls</u> with a <u>Strike</u> of $25. **He gets a quote of $0.80 for the INTC 25 August 2003** from the broker.

The payoff of this call option is the dollar amount above 25 of the closing price of Intel Friday, August 15th, 2003. In the case that Intel closes below $25 the call option expires worthless.

As Joe is ignorant about options-pricing, he cannot assess whether the price of the option or <u>Premium</u> of $0.80 is fair.

However, Joe has access to all sorts of historical data as he uses the Yahoo database, PCQuote and many more online services. Furthermore, he knows that INTC does not pay any dividends nor does any capital structure change until expiration on August 15th. **Intel is closing at $24.50 July 18th, 2003**.

As it is Friday, Joe has the whole weekend to think things over and reflect on the pricing of options.

Joe looks up the different pricing formulas, but they are so complicated, and he just can't understand them in depth. Therefore, in order to solve his question, we suggest to Joe to take a detour and use an example with dice, without, however, losing the context of his initial problem: *What is the fair price of the Intel 25 Aug. 2003 call that expires in 20 days?*

TABLE 1: INTEL OPTIONS QUOTES AS OF 18.7.03:

INTEL CORP(INTC)									24.6600 ▽ -0.2700	
Symbol	Last	Time	Net	Bid	Ask	Open	High	Low	Close	Vol
INTC	24.6600	07/18	-0.2700	24.6100	24.6600	25.1000	25.1500	24.1500	24.9300	65354390
				Calls					Aug 2003	
Ticker	Last	Net	Bid	Ask	Vol	Open Interest			Strike	
.NQ HV	12.00	+2.30	12.10	12.20	12	20			12.5	
.NQ HC	9.70	-0.10	9.60	9.70	14	1116			15	
.NQ HW	7.00	-0.30	7.10	7.20	1138	1538			17.5	
.NQ HD	4.60	-0.20	4.60	4.70	5305	6967			20	
.NQ HX	2.40	-0.35	2.40	2.45	2817	23341			22.5	
.INQHE	0.80	-0.20	0.75	0.80	20598	50116			25	
.INQHY	0.15	-0.10	0.15	0.20	15354	10529			27.5	
.INQHF	0.05	0.00	0.00	0.10	10	1211			30	
.INQHZ	0.00	0.00	0.00	0.05					32.5	

Source: www.pcquote.com

3.6.5   *REDUCING THE COMPLEXITY: A HYPOTHETICAL MARKET PRICED WITH DICE*

Basic options pricing is not complicated, but to our disgrace it is always presented in hyper-complex terms. So, in order to understand the fundamentals of options pricing, the problem has to be simplified. This simplification is achieved by using a much reduced market. This reduced market consists of one stock and call options on this stock. The stock is called "Dot" and it can only have a limited number of prices. Dot can be priced in six different ways, namely $1, $2, … $6. Like a die.

In this imaginary and highly simplified world the Dot is priced with the daily throw of a dice. Therefore each day the price of Dot is between $1 and $6.

A market exists for one-day call options on Dot and can be bought or sold. What would be the fair price of a Dot 4 call, that pays $1 if the die shows 5 and $2 if the die shows 6 and for all other values $0?

As stated above, this call option with a strike of 4 has only three possibilities of a payoff, either $0, $1 or $2. It pays $0 if the throw is 1,2,3 or 4. It pays $1 if it is 5 and pays $2 if it is 6.

SUMMARY: Dot is decided by the throw of a die, taking values from $1 to $6. What is the fair price of a call option with a strike of $4?

Let's start with the following case: Joe buys one Dot Strike 4 One-Day call from the Market Maker for $0.75. The Dot – decided by the die – has a price of 1 the following day, i.e., at expiration of the one-day option. Obviously Joe makes $0 as the option expires worthless with the underlying Dot at 1 and he therefore loses the purchase price of $0.75.

Joe buys another call, again for $0.75.

The die is thrown. A 6 shows up.

Joe's Dot Strike 4 One-Day call pays 2, which is the "in-the-moneyness" of the call given by the strike-price of 4, which equals the Underlying price at fxpiration ($6) minus Strike-price ($4) . The net gain for Joe is therefore $1.25, which is the value of the Dot call of $2 minus the purchase price or premium of $0.75 he paid to the Market Maker.

Joe continues betting and does this for 100 days. The throws or prices of the Dot are listed in the following table:

TABLE 2: THE DOT PRICES OVER 100 DAYS

1	2	6	1	4	3	5	6	2	3	6	1	5	5	2	2	3	5	6	3	3	1	4	3	2	1
6	1	6	5	6	5	1	2	4	2	5	3	6	3	1	5	6	2	3	5	3	1	6	4	1	1
6	5	6	5	5	5	6	1	2	6	5	3	2	3	1	3	4	4	2	6	4	3	5	5	4	1
1	4	6	3	5	1	1	4	6	5	5	2	5	2	5	2	2	3	1	4	2	6				

The outcomes of these 100 days are depicted in the following plot. It is always recommended to look at series of numbers in a graphic representation.

FIGURE 25: DOT PRICES LINE CHART

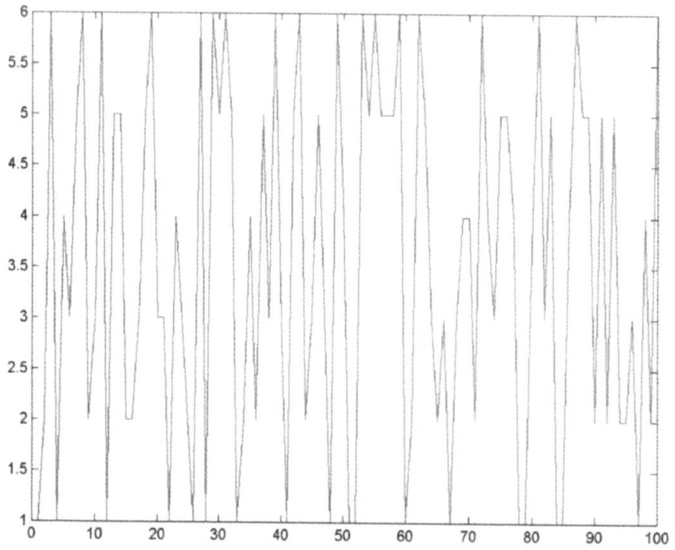

By counting the peaks and valleys one can see on the plot that 17 times a 6 was thrown and 18 times a 1.

3.6.5.1 HISTOGRAMS ARE USEFUL TO VISUALIZE PROBABILITIES

The best way to look at frequencies of outcomes is to create a histogram. For the 'Dot'- case 6 containers or bins are created that represent the 6 possible outcomes of the throw of a die. Then each bin is filled with the number of outcomes that correspond to it, the 'ones' to bin one, the 'twos' to bin two, etc.

The number of occurrences defines the height of each column. One could also imagine that for each occurrence one unit is added to the height of the column.

In practice, one looks at the outcomes above, counts the number of times a 1 was thrown (17) and makes a horizontal line at the height of 17 at bin number 1. Then this is repeated for the remaining 5 possibilities.

Thus what one gets from the histogram is a visual representation of the frequency of the occurrence of the different events, but what one loses is the order of the occurrence, which in the case of a chance-driven or random or stochastic variable is not relevant.

Investor's 100 days of speculation transformed into a histogram looks as follows:

FIGURE 26: HISTOGRAM OF DOT PRICE, LAST 100 DAYS

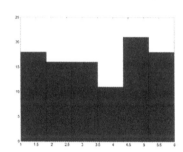

One can see in the histogram that Joe was lucky, for the 5s and 6s had a higher than expected frequency. Of course the expected value for each is $1/6^{th}$, which results in an expected value of 17 being the closest entire number to 16.67.

Interestingly, one learns from this histogram that probabilities can be calculated, but that this does not mean that the reality coincides with them. It is clear that all numbers of the die should appear with a similar frequency, but why the 5s and 6s are more frequent in this run cannot be explained. It is a matter of chance!

WAS IT PROFITABLE?

Now Joe wants to know if his strategy was profitable and he sums the gains from the options bets. The result is the number 57. However, Joe bought the Calls for 0.75 each, therefore he paid 75 in all. He has made a loss of 18. That's no good. We suggest that a further simulation would help to clarify things. Therefore a simulation of another 1000 throws is started by throwing dice and noting down the results and the hypothetical profits, doing the very popular activity of paper trading. We find that we have made a paper profit of 500 in total.

The conclusion is that in order to run this strategy, one should pay a little bit less than 500/1000 in order to make money in the long run.

The approach of simulating many outcomes and then averaging makes a lot of sense and – it has to be said – is the back-bone of modern finance. With the dice example this approach is extremely simple, as one knows the die takes a random value between 1 and 6. Therefore, just a few simulations are needed.

What one could also do (and this is more elegant) is calculate the probability of the outcomes and get the option price directly through one single calculation.

One knows that with a perfect die, each number from 1 to 6 has the same probability of showing up. This means that each number has the probability of $1/6^{th}$ or 16.66…%.

Therefore:
Probability that Call has a Value of **0** = 4/6, namely for the numbers 1,2,3,4.
Probability that Call has a Value of **1** = 1/6, namely for the number 5
Probability that Call has a Value of **2** = 1/6, namely for the number 6

Therefore, Value of Call is **1** * 1/6 plus **2** * 1/6 equals 3/6 = 0.5.

IMPORTANT: these probabilities can be looked up in the histogram by dividing the height of the desired column by the sum of the height of all columns together.

What becomes evident is that the value of an option is the probability weighted potential payoff. It is the equilibrium point where it is most probable—statistically—that the option has a payoff that is identical to the cost of the purchase of the option.

The simulated 1000 throws result in a histogram that is already more regular.

FIGURE 27

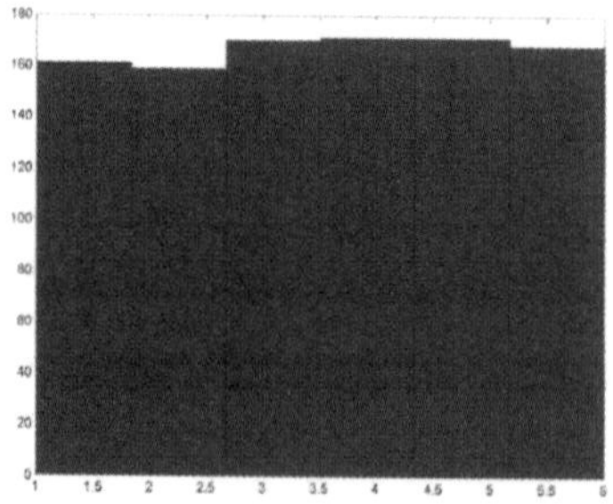

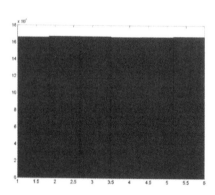

Or for a simulation with 1 million throws we see even more regularity, but it is still not perfectly even! It comes close to the theoretical and expected histogram, though, where all numbers occur with the same frequency.

FIGURE 28

Summary of the insights one gains from the dice example:

*   The option price is the equilibrium value, where the cost of the option equals the most likely statistical payoff or "in-the-moneyness."

*   Histograms are useful to visualize probabilities.

*   Probabilities can be calculated, but that does not mean that reality behaves like the calculated probabilities.

*   Don't pay just any price for an option.

*   It is good to rely on common sense.

3.6.5.2   APPLYING THE INSIGHTS FROM THE DICE MODEL TO THE INTC CALL

Going back to the Intel August 2003 25 call, a sensible beginning is to list the inherent information:

Underlying:	Intel (Ticker symbol "INTC")
Strike:	25
Days till expiration:	20
Price of Intel today:	24.50
Interest rate:	1%

What is clear is that in contrast to the dice example, the Intel stock can take many more distinct prices than the 6 different ones of a die.

The above information is not enough. One has to dig deeper and resort to the Intel price history, which fortunately is easy to retrieve on the internet. With those historical price data or Intel time-series some assumptions can be made regarding the probabilities, the moves and the variability of the stock-price in general.

If one takes the last 250 days – about a year – of Intel the following can be done:

As the option expires in 20 days, all 230 20-day changes in the stock-price—or returns—are calculated, i.e., the difference of the price with the price 20 days ago. This leads to a statistical perspective of the 20-day returns and to a better understanding of the possible difference between the price of Intel today and in 20 days' time when the option expires, hopefully deep-in-the-money!

Now, having calculated the 20-day differences, one can plot a histogram. First the best 20-day return (5.70) and the worst (-5.47) are determined; they are used to set the interval of the histogram. The chosen histogram thus has bins in the range from –6 to 6 with a width of 0.5. That results in 25 bins.

FIGURE 29: INTEL 20 DAY RETURNS AS HISTOGRAM

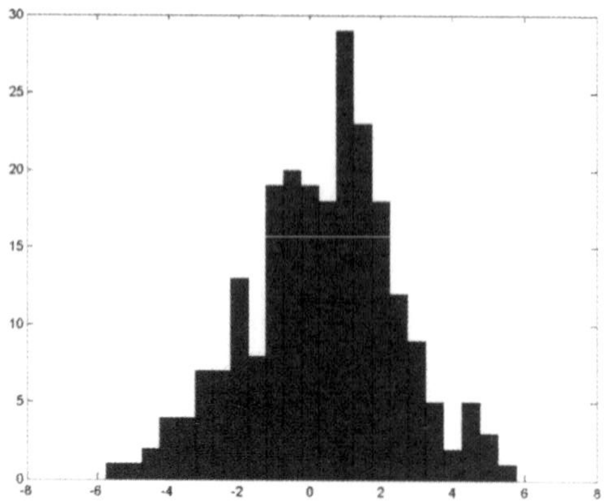

The histogram is not as smooth as one would expect. If, however, a much bigger sample size of 20-day returns is used, the histogram should smooth out, in the sense that coming from the left each column should be higher towards the right side until the peak is reached, and then the columns should decrease, and the histogram would look like a bell-shaped curve, however, with fatter tails than the bell-shaped curve of the Normal distribution.

The 'heights' of the bins are:

```
Columns 1 through 13

   0    1    1    2    4    4    7    7   13    8   19   20   19

Columns 14 through 25

  18   29   23   18   12    9    5    2    5    3    1    0
```

The total amount of 20-day returns in these 250 days is obviously 230, as 20 days are needed to calculate the first 20-day return, namely day 21 minus day 1.

What one wants to know is – exactly like in the dice example – what the probability weighted payoff of the option is. That means, one has to take the total number of returns or price differentials, expressed as 230, and compare it with all the prices which are above 25, the strike price of the option.

In the histogram above, which is centered around 0, one knows that coming from the left, including the bin '0.50', all options expire worthless, as 24.50 (price today) + 0.5 (value of bin) equals the strike. This is because the 20-day returns have to be added to the closing price of the last observation (July 18th, 2003 at 24.50). And the option comes only into-the-money if the price at expiration is above the strike.

Again, the bin values are the observed 20-day differences. To illustrate: the bin centered at $4.00, the forth from the right, has a height of 2. That means that 2 times the 20-day differences had to be put into this $4.00 bin, which has a range from $3.75 two $4.25. Thus, of all the observed 20-day differences two were found between 3.75 and 4.25.

In order to calculate the probability weighted payoff the following Excel table is used:

Calculation of INTC Call via Histogram						
Bin	Return	NumObs	ITMness	Prob	Prob x ITMness	
1	-6.00	0	0.00	0.000	0	
2	-5.50	1	0.00	0.004	0	
3	-5.00	1	0.00	0.004	0	
4	-4.50	2	0.00	0.009	0	
5	-4.00	4	0.00	0.017	0	
6	-3.50	4	0.00	0.017	0	
7	-3.00	7	0.00	0.030	0	
8	-2.50	7	0.00	0.030	0	
9	-2.00	13	0.00	0.057	0	
10	-1.50	8	0.00	0.035	0	
11	-1.00	19	0.00	0.083	0	
12	-0.50	20	0.00	0.087	0	
13	0.00	19	0.00	0.083	0	
14	0.50	18	0.00	0.078	0	
15	1.00	29	0.50	0.126	0.063	
16	1.50	23	1.00	0.100	0.100	
17	2.00	18	1.50	0.078	0.117	
18	2.50	12	2.00	0.052	0.104	
19	3.00	9	2.50	0.039	0.098	
20	3.50	5	3.00	0.022	0.065	
21	4.00	2	3.50	0.009	0.030	
22	4.50	5	4.00	0.022	0.087	
23	5.00	3	4.50	0.013	0.059	
24	5.50	1	5.00	0.004	0.022	
25	6.00	0	5.50	0.000	0.000	
	Sum:	**230**		**Sum:**	**0.746**	

LEGEND:

Bin: the corresponding bin.

Return: the 20-day difference in $, the difference of a price with the price 20 days ago. This is the mid-point of the bin, all 20-day returns equal to that number plus/minus $0.25 get summed up in that bin.

NumObs: the number of occurrences of a return in the range of the bin. The range is the Return plus/minus $0.25.

ITMness: the In-the-moneyness, i.e. the difference of the expiration price with the strike price, all negative numbers are set to 0, as an option is a right and not an obligation, and therefore cannot have a negative value.

Prob: the observed probability over the last 230 20-day returns, taken from the histogram, calculated by dividing the NumObs by the total amount of observations (230)

Prob x ITMness: the probability weighted payoff, which summed up results in 0.746

CONCLUSION FROM THE HISTOGRAM CALCULATION

The fair-price calculated by the summing of the probability weighted payoffs results in $0.75. This value has to be present-valued. In the case of low interest rates of, say, 2% and a short time to expiration of 20 days, the present-value adjustment is irrelevant and thus the value of the option does not change.

The fair-price of $0.75 is at the low-end of the bid-ask of the market of $0.75 - $0.80. That is comforting indeed, proving that the common-sense—though cumbersome—approach of calculating an option price has worked in this example and that the quoted prices are fair.

3.7 FROM MONTE CARLO SIMULATION TO BLACK&SCHOLES

As you have understood the pricing of options via the simple histogram method, we would like to describe – briefly – the famous Black&Scholes option pricing model. We will introduce Monte Carlo simulation as it is a topic that is often referred to in the finance literature and is really the back-bone of modern financial calculations. Moreover, Monte Carlo simulation is a concept that is very easy to grasp.

The major problem of the Black&Scholes model is that it uses volatility as a parameter. Volatility cannot be observed, it can only be guessed. Well, the finance professionals prefer the word 'estimated' in lieu of "guessed," which actually sounds much better.

3.7.1 A FIRST ENCOUNTER WITH VOLATILITY

Because non-directional trading is strongly associated with a number that is called volatility, we have included an entire chapter about it (Chapter 4). But in order to explain the Black&Scholes model we need some notion of volatility already at this stage. The later chapter is mainly dedicated to the problem of calculating and forecasting volatility, and the following paragraphs refer to what volatility actually is.

3.7.1.1 VOLATILITY IS THE VARIABILITY OF THE PRICES, NOT MORE, NOT LESS.

In the following charts, we show simulated price histories of four stocks with different volatilities over a period of 3 years.

Low: 15%
Moderate: 30%
High: 60%
Extreme: 120%

We invite you too look at the charts, so that you really get a sensitivity of how volatility manifests itself in price action charts.

FIGURE 30: LOW VOLATILITY

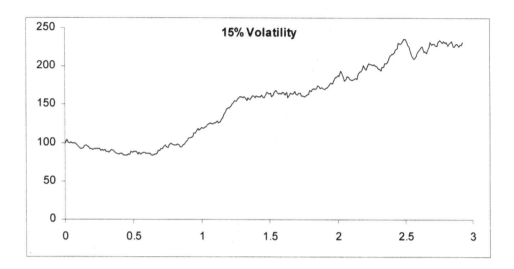

FIGURE 31: MODERATE VOLATILITY

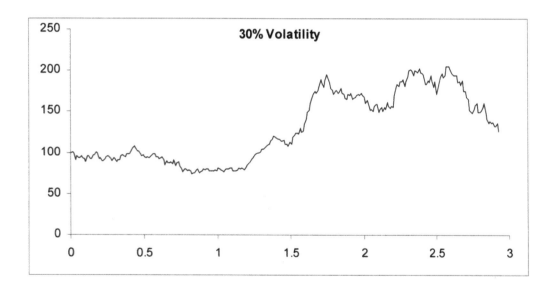

FIGURE 32: HIGH VOLATILITY

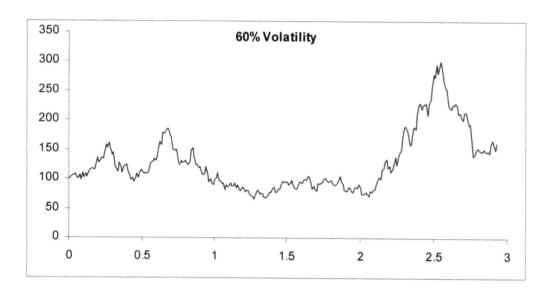

FIGURE 33: EXTREME VOLATILITY

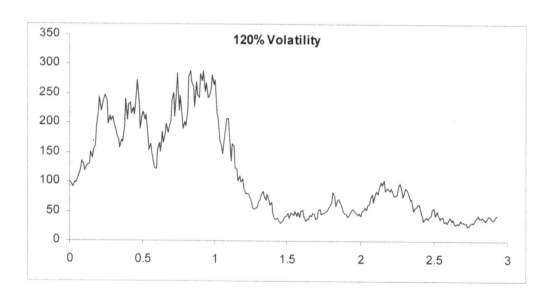

Volatility is the variability of the prices, no more, no less.

Do you like sailing? If so, then you know that there is a scale relating to the state of the wind and water, included here below:

Beaufort Scale of Wind Force and Its Probable Wave Height

Beaufort number	Description term		Wind speeds		Wave height (m)	
	Wind	Wave	knots	m/s	probable	maximum
0	Calm	-	< 1	0 - 0.2	-	-
1	Light air	Ripples	1 - 3	0.3 - 1.5	0.1	0.1
2	Light breeze	Small wavelets	4 - 6	1.6 - 3.3	0.2	0.3
3	Gentle breeze	Large wavelets	7 - 10	3.4 - 5.4	0.6	1.0
4	Moderate breeze	Small waves	11 - 16	5.5 - 7.9	1.0	1.5
5	Fresh breeze	Moderate waves	17 - 21	8.0 - 10.7	2.0	2.5
6	Strong breeze	Large waves	22 - 27	10.8 - 13.8	3.0	4.0
7	Near gale	Large waves	28 - 33	13.9 - 17.1	4.0	5.5
8	Gale	Moderately high waves	34 - 40	17.2 - 20.7	6.0	7.5
9	Strong gale	High waves	41 - 47	20.8 - 24.4	7.0	10.0
10	Storm	Very high waves	48 - 55	24.5 - 28.4	9.0	12.5
11	Violent storm	Exceptionally high waves	56 - 63	28.5 - 32.6	11.5	16.0
12	Hurricane	Exceptionally high waves	64 - 71	32.7 - 36.9	14.0	> 16
13	Hurricane	Exceptionally high waves	72 - 80	37.0 - 41.4	> 14	> 16
14	Hurricane	Exceptionally high waves	81 - 89	41.5 - 46.1	> 14	> 16
15	Hurricane	Exceptionally high waves	90 - 99	46.2 - 50.9	> 14	> 16
16	Hurricane	Exceptionally high waves	100 - 109	51.0 - 56.0	> 14	> 16
17	Hurricane	Exceptionally high waves	109 - 118	56.1 - 61.2	> 14	> 16

Volatility is sort of the same thing if you can imagine the price chart as a representation of the waves in an ocean.

Do you play Golf?

We could also say that the green represents very low volatility, the fairway a bit more, then the sand, the rough, and the heavy rough. On the green it is quite easy to get a good forecast where the ball is going to halt, let's say with an error of 3 meters, if you are a bad golfer as we are. However, the landing spot for a shot from the heavy rough is nearly impossible to predict. Same thing with securities. A government bond with a very low volatility can be predicted much better than a small-cap stock with a high volatility. You can probably assert quite well in which range you expect the government bond within a year; however, about the small-cap, most likely you have no idea, just hopes.

3.7.1.2   DEFINITIONS AND ASPECTS OF VOLATILITY

Volatility can be defined as a measure of the expected degree of the variability of the movement of the stocks. It can also be defined as the annualized standard deviation or the square root of the variance, whereby the variance is the squared sum of the observed value minus the mean value. We write more about this in chapter 4, which is solely dedicated to volatility.

A problematic issue relates to the fact that volatility itself changes over time, which is referred to as heteroskedasticity or volatility of volatility. This fact has led to other non-statistical definitions of volatility, such as the uncertainty of future price levels or future expected trading range. Or it is even called the fear gauge, because of the observed fact that quoted volatility often goes up before big stock market moves.

FIGURE 34: YAHOO PRICE AND VOLATILITY

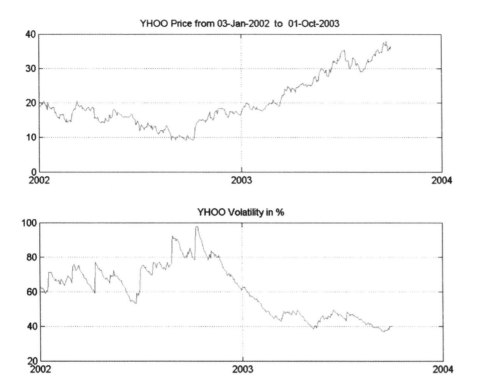

In the above figure it is clear that volatility is not at all constant. It changes in function of the abruptness of the moves in the stock price. Volatility is indicated as annualized volatility in percent.

Standard deviations make a lot of sense in experiments where an average value has a real meaning and the population follows a normal distribution, which is the case in most of the statistical observations made on humans in the social sciences, e.g., size and weight of newborn babies.

The problem in financial markets is that volatility itself is volatile, i.e., volatility changes. Therefore a myriad of problems appear when we want to determine it. A calculation of the variance of birth weight of babies yields nearly the same result if the last 100 or last 500 births in a hospital are considered. In financial markets, however, the volatility calculated on the last 100 samples or 500 samples can show a much bigger difference, because of singular events of huge price moves which are still present in the calculation of the longer series, but are not considered anymore in the shorter one.

The example of birth-weights of babies also serves to illustrate another aspect of volatility calculations. If it were observed that over the last 20 years newborns weighed on average 20 grams more each year, then that information would have to be included in the calculation; it would generate a drift rate. Also, if seasonal patterns were observed, such as the fact that all newborns are heavier in winter, then that information—seasonality—

would have to be considered and filtered out. In stock markets, however, seasonality has never been demonstrated to be significant enough to allow the construction of a filter algorithm. Drift rates, on the other hand, could be parameterized as either dividend return of the stock or its trend. Trends, however, remain problematic to determine, and future dividends are not necessarily possible to extrapolate.

Even considering drift rates and changing volatility, the movements of stocks are best described as a geometric random walk process with returns following closely a Gaussian or normal distribution, though with a changing standard deviation. Therefore the standard volatility calculations make sense viewed in that context.

3.7.2   STOCHASTIC CALCULUS ?!

Already the name of the thing is intimidating. Stochastic calculus is a combination of calculus and statistics. Both are complicated subjects and the combination is close to incomprehensible. We give a short overview and leave it there. As a word of assurance we would like to emphasize that we have not met any successful options traders that understand stochastic calculus. However, some nice hedge-fund disasters were provoked by people that did. Of course, we do not want to state that the understanding of stochastic calculus is a hindrance to becoming successful with options, but we would like to illustrate that it is definitely not a prerequisite.

3.7.2.1   WHAT IS A STOCHASTIC PROCESS?

Let's start with the opposite, namely a deterministic process. If you have a black-box (see bellow, 3.5.4.1) that sums the numbers that you feed it with, you know exactly the outcome. You feed the black-box with the numbers 1, 2 and 3 and you know that the outcome is 6.

In a stochastic process, however, a random variable is involved. A stochastic black-box would for example multiply the fed number with the sum of the dots of the outcome of a dice-throw. Therefore, if you feed this black-box with a 2, you know that the output will be anywhere between 2 and 12. If the input is 10, the output will be 10 with a probability of $1/6^{th}$, 20 with the probability of $1/6^{th}$ etc. Therefore you know the range of the output and the probabilities of a certain output, but you don't know the precise outcome.

3.7.3   BOTANICS AND OPTION PRICING

In this paragraph, we will not talk about the well-known Dutch tulip options, but about the fundamental stochastic process that is used for options pricing, namely Brownian motion. Robert Brown was a botanist and not a highly paid options trader. In 1827 he observed—while looking through a microscope at some plant-cells— that the individual cells were all in frenetic movement, but in an unpredictable way. Later, in 1905, the most illustrious of all scientists– Albert Einstein—also became interested in Brownian motion and he was able to use Brown's earlier findings to develop some important concepts in statistics, as he was intrigued by the wild, irregular movements and thus wanted to develop a method to test irregularity.

Because the Brownian motion is so well researched, financial mathematicians have applied the idea of the Brownian random movement to describe the stock market, where the frenetic moves of the stock prices was modelled in the same way as the frenetic moves of the plant cells.

The result of this application of Brownian motion is the most prominent of all finance formulas, the Black&Scholes formula. The Black&Scholes formula models stock prices as a Brownian motion and uses this input to calculate option prices.

Brownian motion is a random walk, and it should be understood that the Black&Scholes formula is therefore based on the unpredictability of the stock market, which is also called the Efficient Market Hypothesis, and postulates the end of a big part of the financial industry, namely the analysts, stock pickers, and the majority of fund managers. We, however, are not at all convinced of the random movement of stock prices. But what we can be certain of, is that it is definitely difficult to tell whether the next moves are up or down.

However, using such simplifications, like random walk, makes life much easier for the mathematicians and that has to be respected, too. It has to be understood that models can't be created without simplifying reality drastically, otherwise there are just far too many observable quantities in the game.

In the context of random walk one might encounter the expressions Markov and Martingale. Markov refers to the fact that the process has no memory beyond the present. This means that the next move of our plant cell or the model stock price does not depend on prior moves. Like throwing a die, the next number that comes up is not influenced by the prior numbers. The Martingale property refers to the fact that betting based on a random walk is a zero sum game.

By the way, even nowadays with a simple microscope the Brownian movement can easily be observed. If you need a change from looking at a computer screen, go and buy a standard microscope, take the right type of grass-leaf and try it out. You will see that the cell moves are as difficult to predict as the stock market!

3.7.4   BLACK BOX AND BLACK&SCHOLES

The Black&Scholes formula is a true masterpiece. Its development by Fisher Black and Myron Scholes, plus the work of Robert Merton resulted in a Nobel Prize in 1997. Sadly, Fisher Black had passed away just 2 years before and thus could not be awarded his share of the prize.

3.7.4.1   BLACK-BOX

As we will not describe the Black&Scholes formula in detail, but instead describe it as a black-box, we would like to explain what we mean by that.

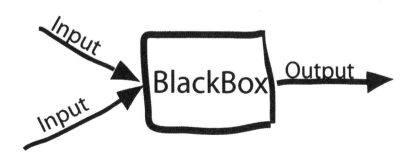

The black-box is normally a computer program. The black-box processes input and generates output. It is called black-box because the way the output is produced is not revealed.

If you are interested in the actual formula, you will find it in the annex.

We like to use that black-box image for many of the advanced finance formulas. Because those formulas get so complicated, we think it is much better to look at them as black-boxes, which liberates us from the feeling that the formulas have to be understood in detail. For practitioners it is therefore comforting to look at many of the new models as such black-boxes, relax, and leave it to the mathematicians to understand and modify them.

3.7.4.2   BLACK&SCHOLES

Like all black boxes, the Black&Scholes formula uses some input to produce the output, namely the option price.

What sort of input is required? The Black&Scholes model assumes a normal distribution of the returns with a mean of 0, therefore the only input parameter regarding the variability of the stock is the standard deviation or volatility. The remaining four parameters are obvious: the current price of the stock, the time until expiration, the strike and the risk free rate.

The output is the Black&Scholes value—often called "fair value"—of the option.

3.7.5   THE GREEKS

The above black-box diagram shows that the Black&Scholes formula depends on 5 Inputs or Parameters. The output is therefore dependent on those inputs. The Greeks are the different sensibilities of the output in respect to the different input parameters, which are Delta, Gamma, Vega, Theta. These are called Greeks, because Delta, Gamma and Theta are Greek letters.

In other words, the Greeks answer the following questions:

Delta: How much does the fair value change if I change the underlying up or down by 1%?

Gamma: How fast does Delta change if the underlying price changes?

Vega: How much does the fair value change if we change the volatility by 1 percentage point?

Theta: How much does the fair value of the option change depending on the lifetime?

Rho: How much does the fair value of the option change depending on the interest rate or dividends?

Often the sensitivities are displayed graphically, because the inherent numbers are of course much too complicated to imagine in a normal brain, and graphics always help. We have included one such graphic, because they look nice and they can help you to get some notion of the non-linearity of the Greeks. However, this is only for the interested reader. If you prefer, you can look at the following graph as a work of art and just enjoy its calming waves.

The graphic depicts the Gamma, the rate of change of the Delta, for a portfolio of straddles and covered calls.

FIGURE 35: PORTFOLIO GAMMA

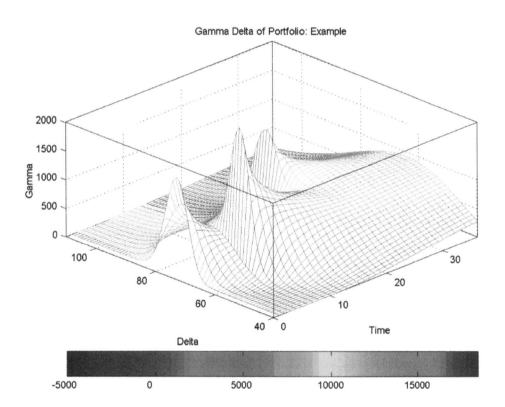

3.7.6   MONTE CARLO SIMULATION: A SUPER SIMPLE CONCEPT

3.7.6.1   AN INTRODUCTION

The Monte Carlo method is based on the idea of games of chance, for example Roulette, which is very popular in the Casino, and therefore on the law of big numbers, which says that if you run the Roulette-wheel many, many times, the chances that a 4 or a 17 occurs is the same. Of course only with fair roulette wheels, but in Monte Carlo they make sure that they are as fair as mechanically possible. Therefore, in the Monte Carlo approach many different outcomes are randomly generated and then statistically quantified.

Monte Carlo simulations are well suited to be used in all domains of finance. Because Monte Carlo simulations need extensive calculation resources, their recent boom is based on the broad availability of fast and relatively cheap computers.

Monte Carlo simulation is best described with the earlier dice example. It is a method to estimate a value by simulating many outcomes randomly. If we want to know what the probability is that we throw a 6, we can just repeat a large number of throws and then count all the 6s and divide this number by the total number of throws.

Monte Carlo simulation is suited for pricing derivatives because in theory their underlying assets such as stocks or bonds follow a random walk. Therefore, the simulation is used to generate a huge amount of such possible random walks or asset paths. The set of generated random walks is used to perform the pricing of the derivatives contract, which, according to the theory, is the present value of the average outcome.

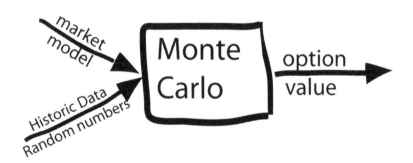

There are many different market models that can be used. These days one often uses a member of the GARCH model family.

The market model tells the black-box how to generate the asset paths, and in order to be precise real historical time series are used as data input. Based on the historical data the computer can calculate all sorts of things, like the magnitude and occurrence of extreme events, the changes in volatility and many more.

3.7.6.2   OPTIONS PRICING WITH MC

In the context of options pricing we simulate a large number of so-called asset-paths. Using random numbers, or special pseudo-random numbers, the computer generates as many different asset paths as we desire. Now for each asset path the option payoff is taken at expiration—by calculating the moneyness exactly as with the histogram option pricing—and all those option prices are simply averaged.

3.7.6.3   OPTIONS PRICING SUMMARY

We think by now you should have a good overall understanding of option pricing. The histogram options pricing explains what it is all about, namely probability times payoff or probability weighted payoff. In certain more rigid cases, options pricing can be done with elegant mathematical, and in most cases with brute force simulation.

OPTION PRICING
* **The price of an option is a sum. It is the sum of all possible payoffs multiplied with the probability that this payoff occurs.**
* **It can be calculated symbolically with elegant math.**
* **In some more restricted cases, it can be calculated with a simulation.**
* **It can also be calculated via the histogram of historic return data.**

3.8   GREEKS, PRICING MODELS AND VOLATILITY

3.8.1   GREEKS

Practitioners—who run large and complex derivatives portfolios—use simulations to generate graphical images of the Greeks—the sensitivities to changes—in order to get a feeling of the risks and to get thus insight how to manage such risks through hedging. Such graphical images have a beauty of their own, and thus we have included one:

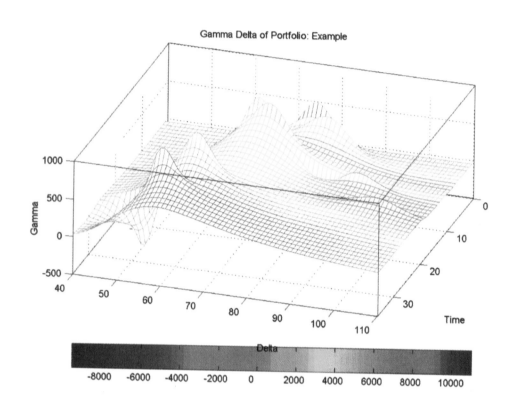

In this 3 dimensional graph you can see how gamma (the height of the surface) and delta (color) behave depending on time (to the right) and depending on the stock price (to the left). Such graphics are useful to get a grasp on complex derivatives portfolios.

For the strategies explained in this book, covered calls and straddles, the Greeks are not relevant, because the positions are set up, all possible outcomes are known, and the positions are not dynamically hedged or substantially altered during their life.

3.8.2   PRICING MODELS

Professionals have to rely on their pricing software. These days it is no longer a mystery how to construct the black-boxes that calculate the fair prices of options, however, the input to those black-boxes will always remain a guess. Most big trading houses use in-house models, whereas the smaller trading operations use one of the many software solutions available on the market. If you are interested in such products, have a look at the following websites for further information:

- www.actant.com
- www.algorithmics.com
- www.riskmetrics.com

The problem associated with the pricing models is well explained with the black-box model and its corollary, which says: trash in, trash out. The professional's task is to feed the models with good input; the rest is taken care of by the black-box.

Moreover, there exists an entire section of risks that are not associated with the data, which basically comes down to problems in the programming of the model as such. Errors provoked at different levels of the computer and software architecture are the most dangerous 'model risks' because they are so difficult to spot and they occur without warning.

Again, the professionals are aware of potential model risks and it is their responsibility to test, test, and test. For this reason, you can be quite secure in the application of the software products we mention.

In this book, we show methods that do not depend on complex calculations. Therefore, in order to apply the strategies presented in the book, you do not need more than a pocket calculator.

3.8.3   VOLATILITY

For the options trader, a good sense for future volatility levels is the key. Many professionals analyze volatility developments with the tools of technical analysis, establishing levels where volatility should be sold and levels where volatility should be bought. Volatility is mean reverting, that is, it will – in the long run – always revert to its long term average value. Based on that premise, volatility behavior should be theoretically a bit easier to predict than the stock price moves.

CHAPTER 4
THE CENTRAL DIFFICULTY:
VOLATILITY ESTIMATION AND VOLATILITY FORECASTING

Working with options pricing and comparing the results with market prices, it becomes clear that volatility is the crucial factor.

Volatility in its most basic definition is the annualized standard deviation of the daily returns.

FIGURE 37: ONE-DAY RETURNS

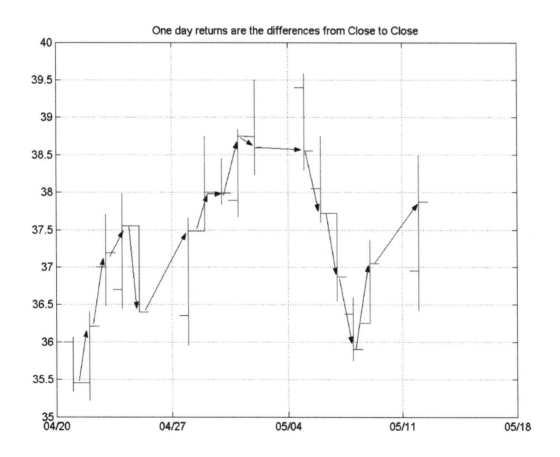

So in order to get the simplest volatility number, one would do the following:

First, all 1 day returns—daily price differences—are calculated.

Second, mean and standard deviation of those returns are calculated.

Third and last, the calculated standard deviation is annualized, by multiplying it with the square root of the number of trading days per year, which is about 16.

4.1 WHAT IS IMPLIED VOLATILITY?

No doubt the most important formula in finance is the Black&Scholes (BS) options pricing formula. The BS-formula calculates the price of an option with the following input parameters: the stock-price of today, the life-span of the option, the exercise price, the risk-free rate, and if applicable, a dividend yield. In addition, one more parameter is needed: volatility.

The BS formula has many flaws, but is still the most widely used formula for pricing options, though with adjustments.

The implied volatility is simply the volatility that has to be plugged into the BS formula that generates the price observed in the market.

It is in a way of the inverse function of the BS formula.

In order to explain the inversion of formulas, let's use a much simpler example. Buying a house, you normally get the price for the house plus its surface in square meters. In order to compare the house prices it is therefore necessary to compare the price per square meter, because the houses are different in size.

The house price is calculated as follows:

House price = price per square meter x square meters.

If one gets a price of 1,000,000 for a house with 200 square meters and one wants to find its price per square meter, then one just has to find the number that has to be plugged into the formula that results in a house price of 1,000,000:

1,000,000 = ??? times 200.

The same is the case with the implied volatility. In the example of the NDX August call that is quoted in the market as 20.30, the value for the volatility has to be found, which when used in the standard BS formula yields 20.30.

Or

OptionPrice = Black&Scholes (Stock, Strike, Time till Expiration, RiskFreeRate, Volatility)

20.30 = Black&Scholes(1280.53, 1300, 14d, 1.04, ???)

Due to the complexity of the BS formula, the implied volatilities are found by iteration, which means that different implied volatility values are tried, until one is found that delivers a result with a small enough error.

Implied volatility—just like price per square meter for houses—is used to normalize options prices.

4.2   CHARACTERISTICS OF VOLATILITY

4.2.1   MEAN REVERTING

This is the most striking feature of volatility, namely that it reverts to its long-term mean.

FIGURE 38: S&P PRICE AND VOLATILITY

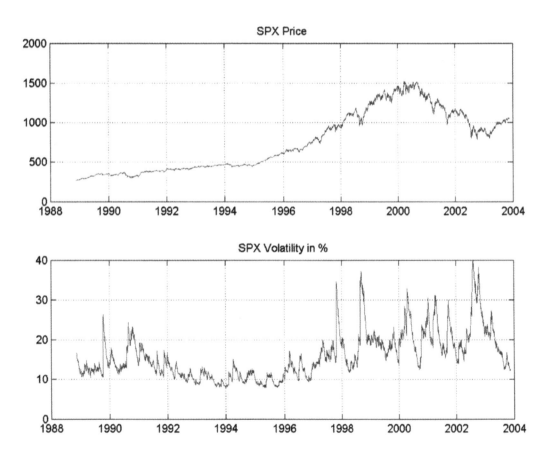

4.2.2 VOLATILITY CLUSTERS

The chart of the daily returns of three selected stocks, Intel, Tyco, and Genesis Micro (Ticker symbols: INTC, TYC, and GNSS) quite clearly show the volatility clusters. Although the charts are completely different, they show an undulating pattern of clusters of big and small values that resembles a radio-signal. Big oscillations are clustered together as well as small oscillations. One can see how big movements normally follow big movements and small movements follow small movements.

The charts input are the compounded returns, which means that the spikes represent big daily differences in the prices. The scale of the daily moves is given on the left side of the chart and in the case of Genesis Microchip it goes from minus 30% to plus 15%.

In the charts below it is important to imagine the graphic without the few exceptional moves, because then the oscillating pattern of low and high volatilities can be appreciated a bit better, since the human eye will not get distracted by those singular events. It is also clearly apparent that every time huge moves occur, further big moves follow during some time, and that periods or clusters of small moves do exist.

The time frame of these charts is January 1st, 1999 until June 15th, 2002.

FIGURE 39: GNSS 1-DAY RETURNS

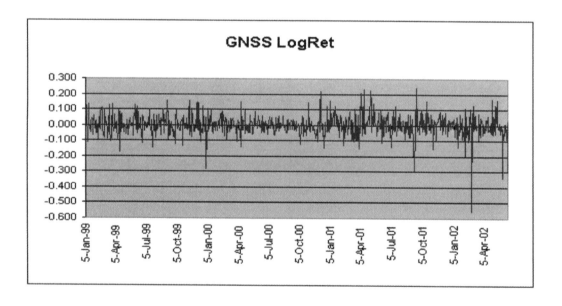

FIGURE 40: INTC 1-DAY RETURNS

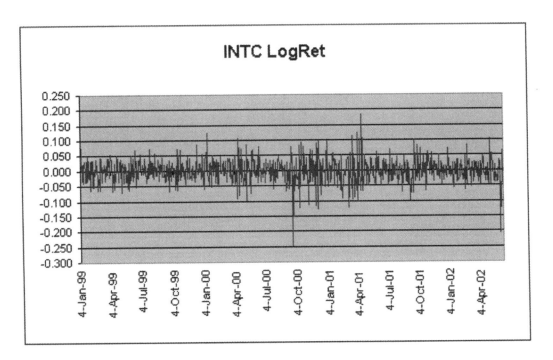

FIGURE 41: TYC ONE-DAY RETURNS

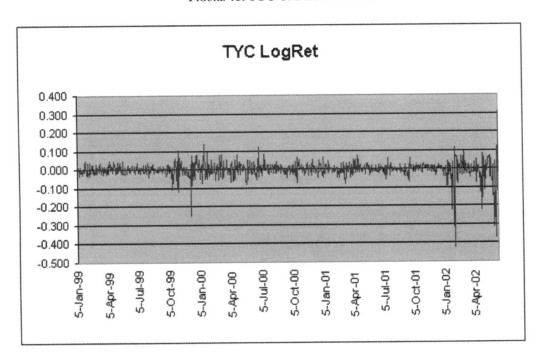

4.2.3   FAT TAILS OR EXCESS KURTOSIS

In order to perform meaningful calculations of the distribution parameters of returns of the stock prices, some assumptions of the distribution have to be made. Based on the charts below, one can see that the returns of the three stocks follow the bell-shaped curve of the Gaussian distribution, though not perfectly. The distributions of Intel and Tyco are quite close, and Genesis is most different to the Gaussian curve.

The following charts furthermore show the excess kurtosis or leptokurtosis. It can be seen that the distribution function has fat tails in comparison to the normal distribution. This means that there are more exceptional market moves than the normal distribution would predict.

FIGURE 42: RETURN DISTRIBUTIONS INTC, TYC, GNSS, NORMAL

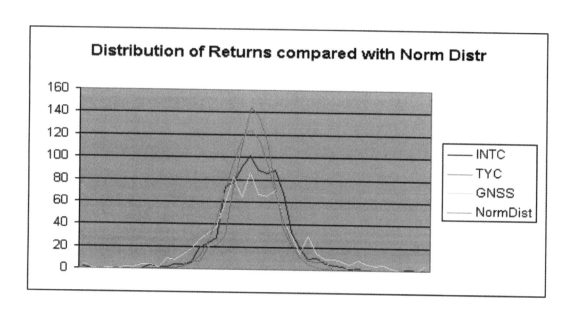

It is also clear from the above graphic that in terms of standard deviation the three stocks have to be rated as follows: GNSS, TYC, and with least standard deviation INTC.

In order to make those fat tails more visual we include three dimensional graphics, first of all three stocks and then the enlargements of the tails to both sides.

FIGURE 43: RETURN DISTRIBUTION INTC, TYC AND GNSS

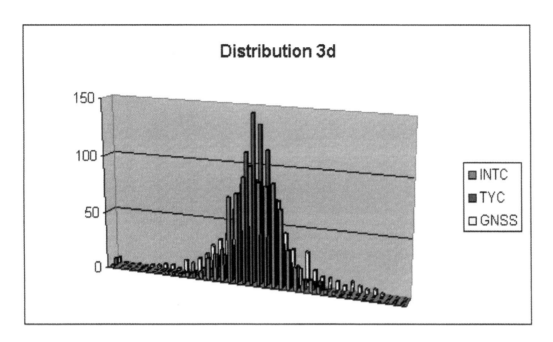

FIGURE 44: FAT TAILS INTC, TYC AND GNSS

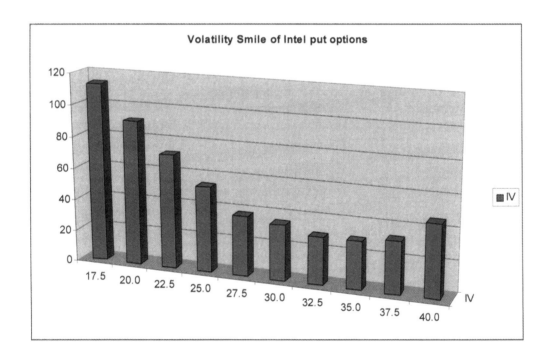

FIGURE 45: INTC, TYC, GNSS FAT TAIL TO THE RIGHT

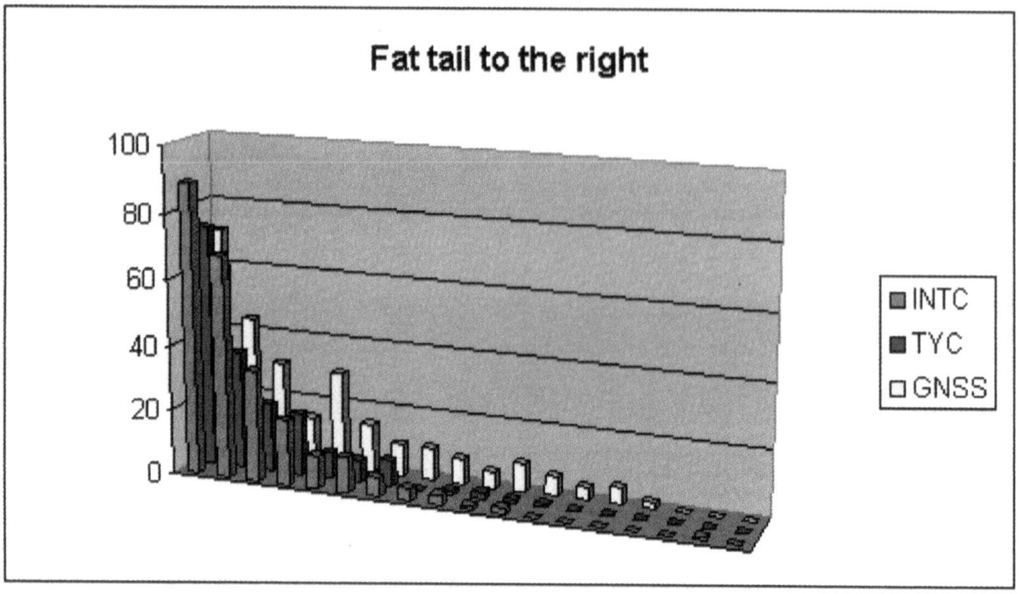

The fat tail to the left graphically displays the frequencies of occurrence of down-moves of the stocks. The irregularities in comparison to the Gaussian distribution curve are evident. For in the Normal distribution the values get smaller the further they are from the centre. In real stock returns it has always been shown that this is not the case and bumps on the distribution curve are present.

4.2.4   VOLATILITY OF VOLATILITY

Volatility changes over time and this phenomenon is illustrated by the two charts below which show the value of calculated historical volatility over time. For example, a peak in volatility of both Intel and Genesis can be detected between December 17th, 2001 and March 17th, 2002.

FIGURE 46

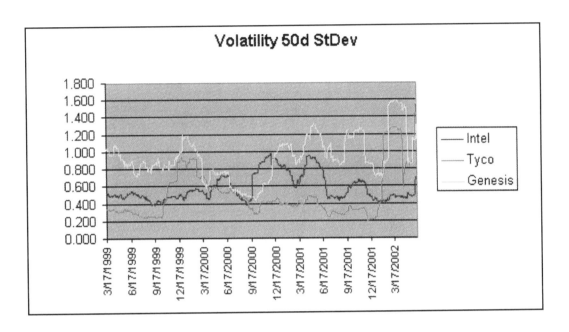

FIGURE 47

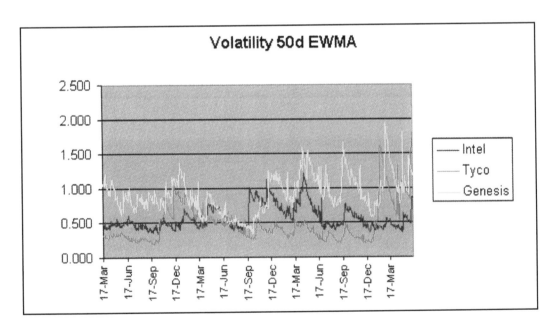

It is important to become aware of the differences of the charts by using the EWMA method described in the next chapter or a simple standard deviation calculation. Both charts clearly show the problem of both methods. In the simple standard deviation calculation which uses the logarithmic return of the last 50 trading days, the effect of one huge move is carried through the full 50 days. That generates the 'steps' in the chart.

The use of an exponential weighted method creates the characteristic exponential decay shape after each huge move.

The two graphs show that the unweighted standard deviation calculation creates jumps in the values which are a function of the length of the time window used, a subjective variable. Therefore we can conclude that it is not a good method for historical volatility calculation. However, it is widely used because of its simplicity.

In practice two methods are widely used, namely EWMA and GARCH.

4.3   VOLATILITY SMILES AND VOLATILITY SURFACES

If we look at options quotes, we observe that each and every option uses a different volatility.

INTEL CORP(INTC)

33.0000 ▲ +0.1100

Symbol	Last	Time	Net	Bid	Ask	Reference price	Div freq	Div amt	Historical Volatility
INTC	33.0000	09:38	+0.1100	33.0000	33.0000	33	4	0.02	18.780%

Calls						Nov 2003	Puts						
Ticker	Last	T-Val	Delta	Gamma	Theta	Implied Volatility	Strike	Ticker	Last	T-Val	Delta	Gamma	Theta	Implied Volatility
.NQ KW	13.60	15.51	1.00	0.000	-0.001	0.00%	17.5	.NQ WW	0.05	0.00	0.00	0.000	-0.000	112.98%
.NQ KD	13.20	13.01	1.00	0.000	-0.001	0.00%	20	.NQ WD	0.05	0.00	0.00	0.000	-0.000	91.22%
.NQ KX	10.50	10.51	1.00	0.000	-0.001	0.00%	22.5	.NQ WX	0.05	0.00	0.00	0.000	-0.000	71.79%
.INQKE	8.10	8.02	1.00	0.000	-0.001	0.00%	25	.INQWE	0.05	0.00	-0.00	0.000	-0.000	54.11%
.INQKY	5.50	5.52	1.00	0.000	-0.001	0.00%	27.5	.INQWY	0.05	0.00	-0.00	0.000	-0.000	37.66%
.INQKF	3.20	3.03	0.98	0.029	-0.002	31.88%	30	.INQWF	0.20	0.01	-0.02	0.029	-0.001	34.74%
.INQKZ	1.20	0.90	0.64	0.245	-0.013	27.78%	32.5	.INQWZ	0.75	0.38	-0.36	0.245	-0.013	30.04%
.INQKG	0.25	0.08	0.11	0.122	-0.007	28.71%	35	.INQWG	2.25	2.05	-0.89	0.122	-0.005	29.65%
.INQKU	0.05	0.00	0.00	0.006	-0.000	27.09%	37.5	.INQWU	4.40	4.48	-1.00	0.006	0.001	33.29%
.INQKH	0.10	0.00	0.00	0.000	-0.000	38.05%	40	.INQWH	7.00	6.97	-1.00	0.000	0.001	46.03%

As we see on the excerpt above—especially looking at the puts on the right—implied volatilities are very different from one exercise price to the next.

If we just take those numbers and enter them into a spreadsheet, we get the following:

Strike	IV
17.5	113
20.0	91
22.5	72
25.0	54
27.5	38
30.0	35
32.5	30
35.0	30
37.5	33
40.0	46

If we plot those numbers we get:

FIGURE 48: VOLATILITY INTEL PUTS

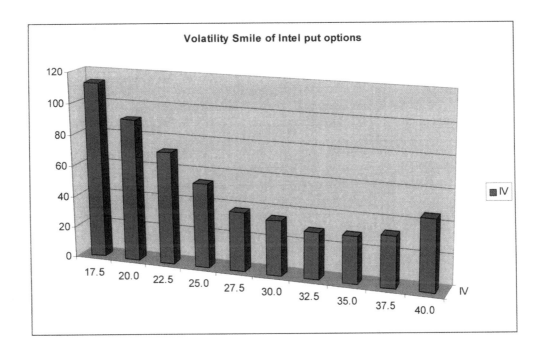

If we join the numbers by a line they look like a smile, nearly as nice a smile as .

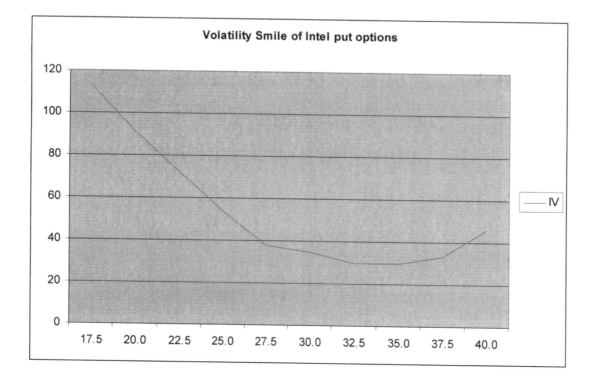

FIGURE 49: VOLATILITY SMILE INTEL PUTS

Simply said, because the Black&Scholes formula is based —as a simplification —on normally distributed stock returns and because stock returns are actually not normally distributed, adjustments have to be made. In practice, those adjustments are made by using different volatilities for the different options of the same stock. The adjustments are made basically to use higher implied volatilities further away from the strike.

> As is said by the practitioners: Using a wrong input (adjusted volatility) in the wrong formula (Black&Scholes) to generate the correct output.

If we vary the expiration dates as well, we can generate a three-dimensional graph: the volatility surface.

What are these implied volatilities and volatility surfaces? They are the expectation of the traders of the future of the market in respect to moves of the underlying and their volatilities in a certain time frame. The volatility surface is a snapshot of the market and it changes continuously in a fashion similar to the price of the underlying.

The volatility surface is a three-dimensional graph. It is created by establishing a square as a base with expiration-dates and strike levels as sides or x and y coordinates. Then for each intersection —strike with expiration—the z-coordinate is established as the implied volatility for the specified strike and the specified expiration. In order to get the surface, we connect all z-coordinates.

If the structure is reduced to two dimensions by eliminating the dimension of the expiration dates, we again get the so-called smile.

4.3.1   AN EXAMPLE: ALCOA'S VOLATILITY SURFACE

The axis on the left (x) displays the strike prices and the axis on the right (y) the remaining option life in trading days. The surface is placed over the implied volatilities for an option with a given strike and a given expiration.

The strike prices are chosen in such a way that the most at-the-money is in the middle.

The surface is plotted with the market data of July, 30th, 2002.

What we can easily see is that the surfaces are concave and that the at-the-money options have the lowest implied volatility. We can also observe that the 'volatility-smile' or curvature is most accentuated in the near month, August 2002, and least in the far month December 2003.

The volatility smile is the two-dimensional plot of the implied volatility done by drawing a line for the implied volatility for just one expiration. The 'smile' for the August expiration can easily be imagined by just looking at the leftmost line.

FIGURE 50: ALCOA VOLATILITY SURFACE

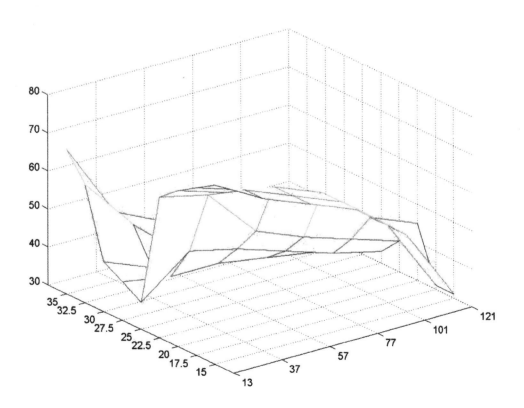

The odious thing about those surfaces and smiles is that they change over time. If you ran a movie of the volatility surface over time, it would look like a manta in the sea, moving gently, sometimes faster, sometimes slower.

We know that the concept of volatility surfaces is very popular amongst derivatives traders and we must ask: what can they be used for? They are used for hedging and pricing of exotic options, giving the trader a feeling of the parameters to be used and giving an idea of what the inherent market expectations are. However, the inherent market expectations unfortunately do not serve as a good forecasting tool of the future volatility action.

ALTERNATIVE TO VOL-SMILES AND SURFACES?

As mentioned before, the fact that volatility smiles and surfaces exist is due to some generalizations in the Black&Scholes formula. But the advantages of the Black&Scholes model, owing to its simplicity, are overwhelming, and therefore in practice no other models are used that would allow for a generalized input like a volatility process instead of the volatility smile, because such models would just be far too complicated to be understood fully and intuitively.

4.3.2 CALCULATING IMPLIED VOLATILITIES

The most primitive way to calculate the implied would be to perform a brute-force approximation by taking two boundary values, say 15% and 200%, divide it by steps of one tenth of a percent and then calculate for the 1850 percentage parameters (15.0% 15.1% ...199.9% 200%) all Black-Scholes option prices each, and then take the value which is closest to the observed market price. Such a method would work; but it would be far too slow.

The standard way, however, to calculate the implied volatilities is to use the Newton-Raphson methodology. This methodology increases the efficiency of the calculations by using the change of the price in relation to volatility. Precise calculation can be obtained with less than 50 iterations because this type of approximation gets to the desired value fast by an optimal choice of the parameters.

The put option implied volatility is calculated indirectly via the relationship known as put/call parity. The put/call Parity connects the call and the put price together and makes it possible to calculate one value given the other if all other parameters are kept the same.

The big problem in respect to the calculation of implied volatility is not the precision of the computational value, but the observation of the market price itself. At the end of a trading day, only limited information is available in respect to the market price. We get:

    Bid Price
    Ask Price
    Last
    Volume
    Open Interest

But we have to decide which price to use as the observed market price. We usually use an average of bid, ask, last.

The reasoning behind this is as follows:

None of the three, bid, ask nor last is significant by itself. This is due to the market mechanics. Option prices are quoted by market makers. They quote bid and ask prices and are obliged to do so for a minimum quantity. The best prices on both the bid side and the ask side of the aggregate of all of the market makers' quotes and open orders are used to establish the market's bid and ask price.

The market makers continuously update their quotes during the trading day in the liquid and delta-sensitive options. The far-out-of-the-money options are quoted much less frequently; therefore they can become targets for manipulation.

The problem associated with the last price in illiquid options contracts is this: it is possible that the last transaction took place at noon and that no other transaction was made during the whole afternoon. However, the underlying has changed. Therefore the last is associated with the underlying at the time of transaction – noon – and not with the closing price of the underlying at 4 o'clock. Such a discrepancy in time means that the published last has actually nothing to do with the last of the underlying.

4.4 VOLATILITY: WHERE TO LOOK IT UP

4.4.1.1 IVOLATILITY SITE

The ivolatility site is very complete. It has a database of different types of volatilities of almost every exchange traded option. We include a couple of screen shots, so that you can get an idea of the site. However, the best way is to visit it yourself.

FIGURE 51

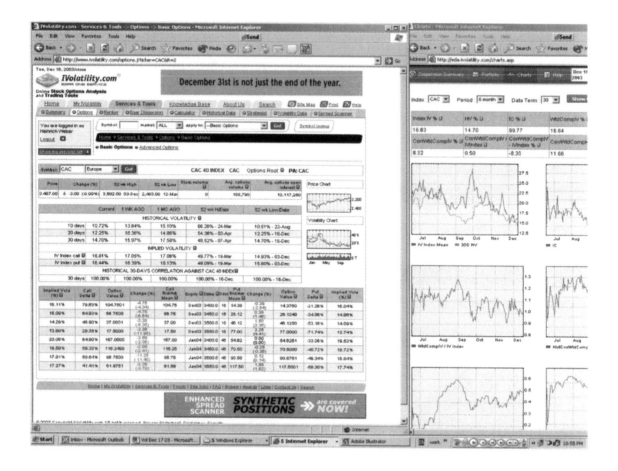

4.4.1.2   PC-QUOTE

FIGURE 52

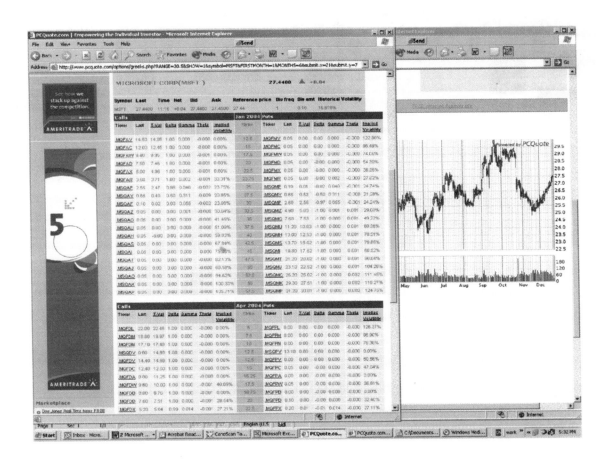

4.4.1.3   YAHOO

Yahoo has an excellent options tool, indicating implied volatility, giving tools sort options, basic strategies, and so forth.

FIGURE 53

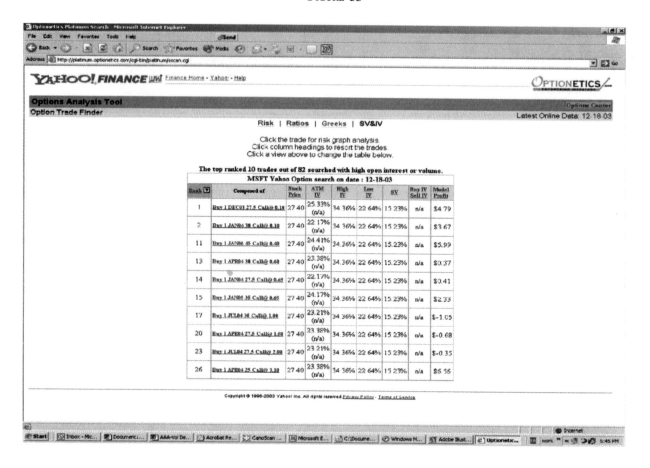

FIGURE 54

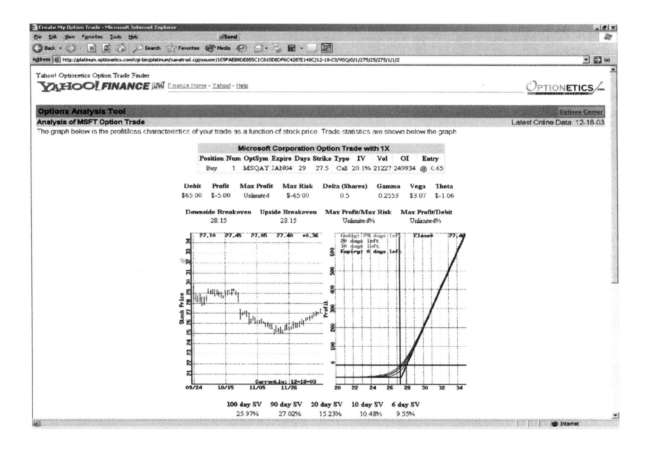

4.5 PREDICTING VOLATILITY WITH P&F CHARTS

We use Point-and-Figure charting for analyzing and predicting volatility. Please review chapter 2 where we give an introduction to P&F stock charting.

For volatility forecasting, we use a logarithmic scale of 5%.

It is a bit confusing that volatility is measured in percent and logarithmic box sizes too. Therefore, just in the following paragraph—we will call the measure for volatility percent V%A logarithmic scale for volatility forecasting is generated as follows:

We start with a minimum volatility of say 10V%; hence the first box has a value of 10V% the second 10.5V%, that is 105% of 10V%.

Adding another 5% gives the third box a value of 11%, and so forth.

117

In practice, such log scales are started at the lowest observed volatility level, which is the reason that a scale for one chart is slightly different than that for another one.

A 5% logarithmic scale that starts at 16.4% (volatility percent) is listed here below. This is the scale we use later on to scale the VIX chart:

Box	Value
1	16.400%
2	17.220%
3	18.081%
4	18.985%
5	19.934%
6	20.931%
7	21.978%
8	23.076%
9	24.230%
10	25.442%
11	26.714%
12	28.050%
13	29.452%
14	30.925%
15	32.471%
16	34.094%
17	35.799%
18	37.589%
19	39.469%
20	41.442%
21	43.514%
22	45.690%
23	47.974%
24	50.373%
25	52.892%
26	55.536%
27	58.313%
28	61.229%
29	64.290%
30	67.505%
31	70.880%
32	74.424%
33	78.145%
34	82.052%
35	86.155%
36	90.463%
37	94.986%
38	99.735%

We primarily analyze the charts according to the channels given by the trendlines and secondarily according to the bullish or bearish quality of the chart, which simply refers to the last signal. If the last signal was buy, then the chart is bullish. If it was sell, then the chart is bearish.

Due to the different characteristics of volatility, the P&F charting, which was developed for stocks, has to be adapted. The main difference is that volatility is mean reverting, which means that volatility tends to oscillate around the long term mean.

The adaptations are as follows:

1. Buy signals on high levels and sell signals on low levels are systematically ignored.
2. On long poles, i.e., long columns of Xs or Os, positions are neutralized on the reversal, which means at three boxes in the opposite direction.

The striking feature of the P&F charts are the crystal-clear trend lines that give clear directions of where volatility is headed. We prefer the P&F volatility charts because they are superior to all other charts in terms of objective chart inherent information and do not need interpretation that renders a chart ambiguous. In order to illustrate this we include the charts of the SP100, NASDAQ 100, and German Dax volatility indices. You will see how much clearer the trend channels are on the P&F chart than on the standard line chart.

4.5.1.1.1   CBOE SPX MARKET VOLATILITY INDEX

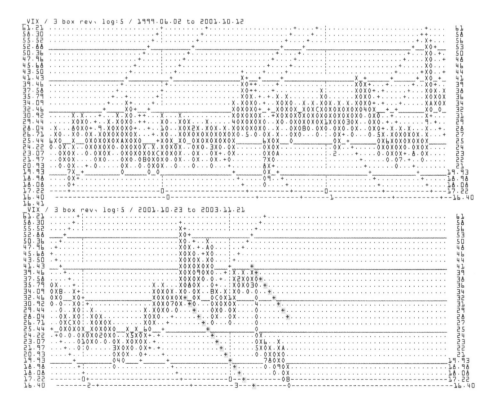

FIGURE 56

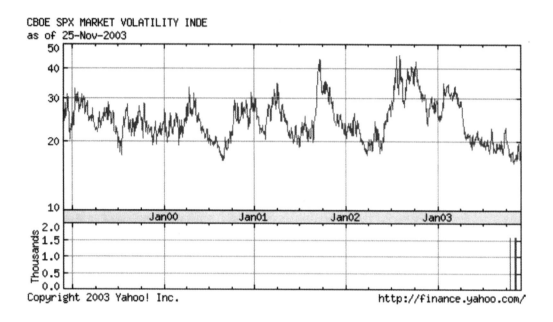

4.5.1.1.2   GERMAN DAX VOLATILITY INDEX

FIGURE 57

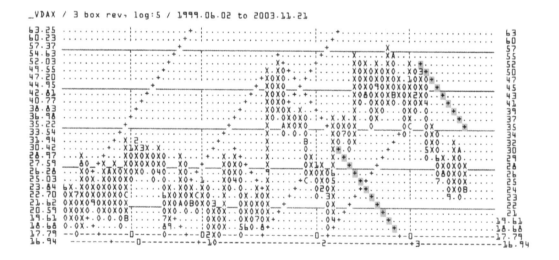

FIGURE 58

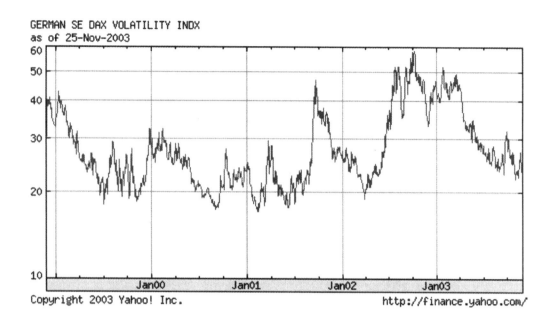

4.5.1.1.3   CBOE NASDAQ VOLATILITY INDEX

FIGURE 59

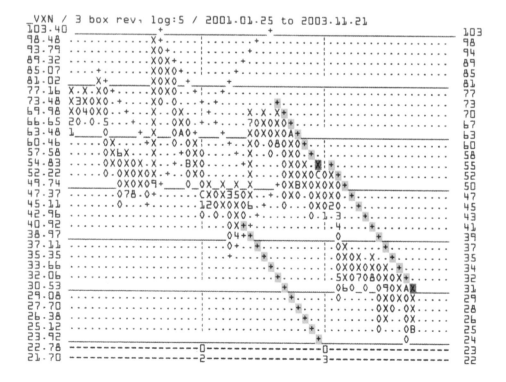

Here we have also indicated two instances where the bearish resistance was touched. The second instance is recent, and we are now watching out if volatility crosses that trendline, and if it does, we become buyers of volatility.

FIGURE 60

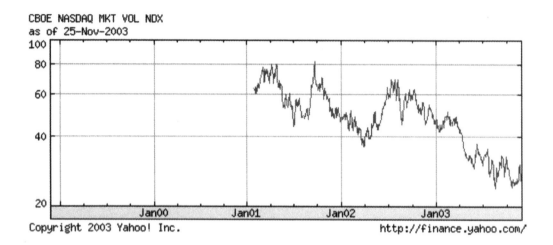

4.6   MAKING PROFITS FROM VOLATILITY

The best way to trade volatility is to buy and sell 'Straddles.' That's our favored way. Straddles are a combination of a call and a put with the same strike and expiration date on the same underlying.

Straddles are so important that we have dedicated them a big part of the book. What we would like to show you at this point are two charts, underlying and volatility, and underlying and relative straddle price. What you see is that both are identical. Therefore, profiting from volatility means trading straddles!

CHAPTER 5
THE SOLUTION: NON-DIRECTIONAL STRATEGIES

5.1 INTRODUCTION

We use the term strategy to describe the process to set up a position that benefits from a certain expected market situation. For example, if you believe that BP stocks will crash by at least 5% over the next week, then your strategy would be to buy BP calls.

In this book we cover the two basic non-directional strategy groups, covered calls and straddles. Non-directional means that the expected market situation that benefits the strategy does not depend on the stock moving in a certain direction.

Most importantly, we are convinced that it is far more profitable to understand and apply the two groups of strategies than to bother with more complex strategies, that imply many more options (such as butterflies) and suffer through their transaction costs.

Believe us and stay with the basic strategies!

5.2 CHECKLISTS

In our trading, we use checklists in order to be sure not to overlook anything. We explain the idea with the checklist used for buying straddles or straddle long.

TABLE 3

Long Straddle	
Increase in news?	
Bias of news?	
Liquidity of options o.k.?	
Spread o.k.?	
Volatility far from year high?	
Graphic analysis	

INCREASE IN NEWS?
We check to see that there is no manifest increase in news coverage of the stock we are interested in. If that where the case we would have to scrutinize that news and analyze it before we decide to set up a strategy. We would have to see when the news coverage started and how it influenced the chart and the volatility.

123

BIAS OF NEWS?

Assuming that there is just the normal amount of news, we take a quick look to see if it does not include a strong bias towards up or down. If it does, then we would again have to see when the bias started and how it influenced the chart and the volatility.

LIQUIDITY OF OPTIONS O.K.?

A look at the screen or a call to the broker gives us insight if there is liquidity in the options we want to use. The bigger the better.

SPREAD O.K.?

We check if the spreads of the option quotes are in line with our expectations. The smaller the better.

VOLATILITY FAR FROM YEAR HIGH (OR LOW)?

Using a service like www.ivolatility.com we check to see if the volatility is not close to the 52-week high if we want to buy options, or that the volatility is not close to the 52-week low if we want to sell options.

GRAPHICAL ANALYSIS

We use a special graphical analysis which we describe later on.

If we have ticked all boxes in our checklist, then we can engage in the strategy, i.e., buy or sell the stocks and/or options.

We recommend that you do the same, especially if you use automatic screening software or services, such as www.optionmonitor.com, to find the best strategies. Often such automatic software detects interesting situations which are related to small companies, where the risks or transaction costs are far too high.

5.3 COVERED-CALL TYPE STRATEGIES

5.3.1 SELL CALLS TO INCREASE INCOME

When most investors think of selling calls, they immediately think of selling covered calls. A covered call is one call sold against 100 shares of the same stock held in the brokerage account. The call could also be written as covered if the account holds a long call position on the same stock.

Selling covered calls against stock is the most common call writing strategy. But there are practices that will improve the writer's income potential that go well beyond the simple technique of selling a call against 100 shares. This section will explore some of the more profitable of these practices.

5.3.2 SELLING COVERED CALLS

In its most basic form, selling a covered call involves the purchase of 100 shares of stock and immediately selling a call against the stock. The premium is credited to the writer's account the following day and is compensation for the writer's obligation to deliver the 100 shares of stock at the strike price at anytime the option purchaser requests the stock, up to the expiration date of the call contract. Typically, the call has a strike price equal to the cost of the stock or one strike higher. Assume the covered call seller purchases 100 shares of the stock at 59, the call would normally be sold having a strike price of 60, and the premium for a one month call with a strike price nearest the current stock market price (at-the-money call) would be approximately 6% of the stock value (the value of 100 shares of the stock at the strike price). Thus the writer would receive a credit of the premium for the one-month call of $360 (less commissions).

Now what can happen? There are three possibilities.

1. The stock rises above the strike price and the option buyer exercises the call buying the 100 shares from the writer for $60 a share.

2. The stock remains below the strike price and the option expires worthless.

3. Or the stock rises above the strike price and the writer eliminates his obligation by the repurchase of the call.

THE STOCK RISES ABOVE THE STRIKE PRICE OF THE CALL AND THE OPTION BUYER EXERCISES THE CALL. When the call is exercised, the writer sells the stock at 60. It was purchased for 59, so there is a $100 profit on the stock sale. Additionally, the writer has made the premium of $360. The total profit to the writer is $460 ($100 equity profit plus the $360 call premium). The writer had invested $5,900 in a cash account or $2,950 in a margin account to hold the stock for 30 days. Calls normally can only be sold in a margin account, but the seller could fully pay for the stock even though it is in a margin account. Margin accounts allow the stock buyer to employ leverage, yet the use of the borrowing feature is a function of the buyer depositing less than the full purchase cost of the shares. If stock is fully paid when held in a margin account, the margin account acts like a cash account. The ROI (Return on Investment) is the profit of $460 divided by the investment of $5,900 or 7.8% (ignoring commissions) in the cash account and 15.6% in the margin account. Annualized, the cash account earns the writer 93.6% (12 30-day periods in a year and the profit is $460 per 30-day period) and the margin account yields an annualized return of 187.2% (ignoring margin interest costs). With such large returns possible from call writing, it is no wonder selling covered calls is so popular.

THE STOCK REMAINS BELOW THE STRIKE PRICE AND THE OPTION EXPIRES WORTHLESS.
If the option expires worthless, the writer made $360 on the $5,900 cash investment for an ROI of 6.1% and the margin investor had an ROI of 12.2% on $2,950 of the funds invested. These equate to 73.2% and 146.4% respectively on an annualized basis. With the option expiring unexercised, the writer's stock position remains intact and available for a repeat covered call write the following option cycle month. Of course the real economic profit on the transaction would be the premium income less any unrealized loss on the stock position. This means that by receiving the premium of $360, or 3.6 points per share, any decline in the value of the underlying equity is offset or cushioned by the premium. So as long as the stock does not decline by more than 3.6 points below its purchase cost ($59) the transaction will be profitable. The purchase cost of the stock minus the premium represents the break-even point of the transaction (59 minus 3.6, or 55.4). Thus as long as the stock remains above 55.4, the writing of the covered call has yielded a profit. If the stock price declines below the break-even price, an economic loss is incurred. Had the stock dropped to 45 from the 59 purchase

price, the economic loss would have been the $1,400 loss in equity (value 59 purchase price less the 45 current market price) reduced by the $360 in premium income earned, for a net economic loss of $1,040. Success in covered call writing is predicated on selecting stocks unlikely to drop in value.

THE STOCK RISES ABOVE THE STRIKE PRICE AND THE WRITER ELIMINATES HIS OBLIGATION BY THE REPURCHASE OF THE CALL. The third possible outcome is where the stock rises, and the writer repurchases the call and in so doing, cancels the obligation. Assume the price rose to 70. The writer buys the call back for an intrinsic value of 10 ($1,000 calculated as the difference between the 60 call strike and the 70 current market price). Since the premium was only $360, it appears as if the writer lost money. But not so. The account was originally credited with the premium of $360, and later charged with the purchase cost to buy back the contract ($1,000), generating a cash flow shortage of $640. But at the same time the stock position rose from 59 a share to 70, a $1,100 gain in equity value. The equity value gain, less the cash flow loss of $640, has resulted in an economic profit of $460. The resulting return of investment is the profit divided by the investment ($460 divided by $5,900) or 7.8%. Had the shares risen to 100 prior to expiration, the profit would still be the same $460. The cost to repurchase the 60 call with the stock at 100 would be the $4,000 intrinsic value (100 minus 60), the premium of $360 would be an offset to the buy back price and the stock would rise from 59 to 100 for $4,100 market appreciation. The net result is the call repurchase cost ($4,000) less the premium ($360) plus the stock appreciation ($4,100), which earned the covered call sell a net gain of $460. So no matter how high the stock might rise, the net gain is similar, as is the ROI.

Selling covered calls appears to be a sure-fired profit maker. But not quite! As we discussed earlier, if the stock had declined and dropped below the break-even point (purchase cost of buying the stock less the premium received from selling the call), there would be an economic loss. This is why a successful covered call-writing program must be built upon a portfolio of great stocks, those with the highest probability of rising in value in the near term. The maximum profit from a covered call-writing program is generated when the stock rises. We therefore want underlying stocks with a strong upward trend.

> ## Coverd call writers and call buyers both want the stock to rise.

Most call buyers assume the call seller is betting against them and wants the stock to decline. The call buyer makes money when the stock rises in price, and believes the writer is hoping the stock will decline in value. This is not the case if the call writer (seller) is selling covered calls. The interest of the call buyer and the covered call writer are in fact identical. The optimal situation for both the call buyer and writer is for a price advance of the shares. The covered call writer is in fact betting the same way as the call buyer—that the stock will rise—for only in this way can the covered call seller earn the maximum ROI.

As a seller of a covered call, the writer has a stock position to secure or cover the call that was sold. Money has been invested in the equity position. A premium is received when the call is written. The maximum return the writer can ever make is fixed and limited to the premium plus any price appreciation of the underlying stock up to the strike price of the call. For example, if 100 shares are purchased at 59 and a one month call with a strike of 60 is sold for a premium of $360, the maximum profit possible is the $100 appreciation of the stock to the 60 strike price plus the premium of $360, for a total of $460. Had the writer sold a call with a 65 strike price for $150, the maximum profit would be the appreciation from the 59 purchase price to the 65 strike price ($600) plus the $150 premium for a total maximum possible profit of $750. Alternatively, if the call's strike price is less than the purchase price of the stock, the maximum profit opportunity is the premium received less the loss of value in the stock price if the call is exercised and the stock is delivered by the writer to the call buyer at the strike price. For clarification, assume stock is purchased at 59, and a one-month call with a strike price of 55 is written for a premium of $650. Should the stock be called away at 55, the writer's profit is the $650 premium less the $400 loss in value on the equity (59 cost less the 55 call strike price), or $250.

Let's examine other possibilities of price movement in the prior examples. In the 60 strike price call situation, should the stock rise to 100 within the month, the writer would still earn the $360 premium and deliver his 59 priced stock at 60 for an additional $100 profit, bringing the total profit to $460. Had the stock risen to 80, the results would still be the same, as they would be for any other price point equal to and above the 60 strike price. In the example where a 65 strike call is written, and the stock rises to 100, the profit is the $150 premium plus the appreciation from 59 to 65 ($600) for a total profit of $750. Again, the results would be the same had it risen to 80 or to any other price above 65. In the third example in which a call is written with a strike price below the current 59 market price of the shares, and the shares rise to 100 the profit is the premium of $650 minus the $400 difference between the stock's cost (59) and the strike price (55), for a total profit of $250. At 80 a share the profit would still be the same $250.

We now know a price rise in the underlying stock positively impacts the call writer. Undoubtedly, the writer will be upset if he has sold a 60 call for $360 and then watched the stock rise to 100, knowing there is an obligation to deliver shares at 60. The further upside appreciation in the stock above the 60 strike price is lost. Yet the profit on the writing process was not impacted regardless of how high the stock ultimately rose. The writer earned the maximum possible profit on the transaction once the stock traded above 60 and the call was exercised.

Let us now examine the impact to the call writer if the price of the stock were to decline. In the example where stock is purchased at 59, and a 60 call is sold for $360, a price decline of the shares to 50 has a major negative result. The premium earned was $360, yet the stock declined from the 59 purchase price to 50, generating a $900 unrealized loss. The loss may not be realized, yet the equity value of the account has been decreased by the $900. The net result for the writer was a gain of $360 in earned premium and a loss of $900 in stock equity value, yielding a net loss of $540. The call expires worthless. Another call can be written the following month for additional premium income, but the initial transaction netted the writer a loss of $540. In the second illustration where a 65 strike call was sold for a premium of $150 followed by the shares dropping to 50, the writer has a $900 loss in equity on the stock offset (59 cost less 50 market price) and only $150 in premium income. The net return on this transaction is a loss of $750.

In the third illustration where a call is written at 55, well below the current 59 market price, for a premium of $750, and then the shares proceed to plummet 9 points to 50, the net return to the writer is an equity loss of $900 on the shares (59 cost less the 50 current market price) plus the larger premium of $750, for a net loss of $150.

In these three cases of writing covered calls followed by a price decline of the share price, there is an erosion of the profit. If the stock price drops far enough, there will be a loss to the call writer. There is a specific reason why this loss occurs. The writer has a maximum potential profit defined as the premium received plus any possible appreciation in the underlying stock from its cost to the strike price. When the stock fails to reach the higher strike price, the profit is cut. And as the shares crumble in price, the writer experiences a loss of equity value. Initially this equity loss is offset by the premium received, but the profit begins to diminish. Should the shares decline by more than the value of the premium received, the call writer sustains a real loss. The loss might be unrealized, but is a loss nevertheless.

These examples have demonstrated the truth of the statements: **call writers earn their maximum profit only if the stock rises to the strike price and the strike price is above the purchase cost of the shares. And if the strike price is below the share buy price, the maximum profit is earned if the shares never drop below the strike price.**

It is true that where the stock shows huge appreciation, the writer would have been better off never to have covered the equity position with a call. The act of writing a call places a cap on the writer's maximum profit potential by capping the ultimate selling price of the shares. Had the stock risen to 100, the covered call writer of a 60 strike call would have made his $460 profit (appreciation between the 59 stock price and the 60 strike plus the premium of $360), while giving up the $4,100 in stock appreciation (100 market price less the 59 purchase price). This would certainly be frustrating to the call writer. But if the writer truly understands his role as an option seller, seeking consistent smaller monthly profits rather than shooting for the sporadic windfall profits, he should be able to remain true to the cause. The covered call writer is in the covered call selling game to make his 6% premium income monthly coupled with some modest stock appreciation. He would gladly forego the benefits of the occasional windfall profits for the consistency of earning monthly income. After all, the 6% monthly return is 72% annually. If there is some modest stock appreciation, the yearly returns become even more enticing.

The writer of covered calls must never lose sight of his goal of consistent monthly premium profits coupled with modest stock appreciation. As has previously been proven, the maximum gains are earned when the stock rises. The writer must always be seeking great stocks—those with little downside risk—as the best, and the only stocks on which to sell covered calls.

5.3.3   WHY COVERED CALL SELLERS GIVE UP

All too often an investor is enticed into the covered call selling strategy believing it to be a win-win situation. Collecting large premiums month after month looks terrific.

The investor buys 100 shares at 59, sells a one month 65 strike call for $150 in premium. The stock fails to rise above 65 in the month, so the call expires. The process is repeated again the following month with a new sale of the 65 call for $150. Again the stock stays below 65 and the call expires. In month 3 the overly confident covered call seller repeats the process once again believing he has finally discovered the perfect investment strategy. A technique proven to be a consistent money printing machine.

But in month three the stock skyrockets to 100. The 65 strike call is exercised and the writer sells the stock at 65. The covered call writer is mad! He was forced to sell 100 shares for only 65. Now he knows covered call selling is a sham. It simply does not work. How could he have been so stupid as to have ever done it? Never again, he promises himself.

Unfortunately, this trader had lost sight of the goal by the loss of profit potential.

The truth is that covered call selling did work for our trader. When the covered call was sold, the stock was trading for 59. He had no idea it would rally so far and so fast. At the time the call was sold, 65 appeared to be a great selling price, a price that would earn the seller $600 in appreciation potential plus the $150 in premium income for a total $750 return on a $2,950 investment in only a month. What a terrific opportunity! And the strategy did work. The 59 stock was sold at 65. The premium and stock appreciation netted the call seller his $750 profit in 30 days for an ROI of 25.4%. (305% annualized).

But is the seller happy? No. He is frustrated that he missed out on the opportunity of making the huge bucks from the run to 100. This in no way means covered call selling did not work. It worked perfectly earning the call seller his $750. A $750 profit he had absolutely no expectation of making when the 65 strike was sold for $150 and the shares were trading at 59.

The moral of this example is that as a covered call seller you should seek and be happy with the consistent monthly premium income and the occasional stock appreciation. The ROI is terrific and the annualized return is outstanding. In those cases where the stock really runs, you ought to be happy, since in such cases you earned the maximum profit on the trade, for the stock was taken from you at the strike price yielding appreciation on top of the premium. Remember it is always better to have the stock rise, thus generating appreciation and maximizing the profit, than for the shares to decline, which results in a loss. Don't be greedy. Don't focus on the opportunity lost in the occasional huge up move. Simply concentrate on finding great stocks that should rise, and on the ROI and annualized returns on the entire portfolio.

5.3.4   PROFIT POTENTIAL FROM WRITING COVERED CALLS

The writing of covered calls can be extremely profitable. The writer receives the premium in one day. Typically a one month at-the-money call premium is in the range of 6 to 7% of the stock value. From the earned premium the writer needs to deduct the commission to purchase the covering stock position, the commission charged to sell the call, and the commission charged should the stock be called from him. If we make some assumptions of commission levels we can quickly arrive at a potential return provided from a program of consistently writing covered calls. 100 shares of stock can normally be purchased through a discount broker for $25 or less with many internet brokers currently offering rates for market orders on up to 5000 shares of only $5. The commission to sell a call is normally higher than the cost to buy the stock and can be estimated at $30 to sell the first call with a rapidly declining charge thereafter. Internet firms are the lowest with commissions as low as $15 for the first call. Some firms like Optionsxpress charge $14.95 to sell between 1 and 10 option contracts and $1.25 for each additional contract sold. The commission charged for the sale of the stock through an exercise runs about the same as for a market sale with $25 being a reasonable average cost factor. Brown and Co, a major deep discount broker owned by Chase Bank, and a leading option firm has one of the lowest stock commission structures, and Optionsxpress has one of the lowest option commission structures. Barron's run a cost and service comparison of online firms at least annually. Broker assisted orders at many firms are more expensive than their own charges for web entered trades.

If we assume the typical covered call written is on a 60 stock, is written at-the-money, is for one month, and the commissions are $25 to buy the 100 shares of stock, $25 to write the call and $30 on the exercise sale of the shares, the writer earns the following:

Gross premium income on sale of one call – 6% of $6,000	$360
Less:	
Commission to write one call	$ 25
Commission to buy 100 shares at $60/share	25
Commission to sell 100 shares on exercise	30
Total dollar return	$280

The investment in the 100 shares purchased at $60 is $6,000 if acquired in a cash account. The total dollar return of $280 divided by the invested sum of $6,000 yields a 4.66% return for one month. Had margin been used, the stock investment would only be $3,000, but there would be a month of interest charges on the $3,000 debit loan balance. At 8% interest on margin loan of $3,000 for a month is $20. The interest charge reduces the dollar return on the transaction from $280 to $260. Because the invested funds are halved in the margin account, the $260 dollar profit is divided by $3,000 for a monthly percentage return of 8.66%. The annualized or 12 month return on the cash account is 4.66% times 12 months or 55.9%, and the yearly return for the margin writer is 8.66 times 12 or 103.9%.

These return calculations are only estimates of profitability of covered call writing. The actual annualized return is impacted by a number of factors that include the percentage the premium represents of the stock price, the commissions charged to buy the stock, sell the option and deliver the stock on a call exercise, the price of the stock, and the distance the strike price is away from the price the shares were purchased at. Another major variable in the return calculations is any appreciation of the stock if the strike price is higher than the purchase price, or a loss in equity value should the shares decline.

To maximize the return from a strategy of writing covered calls, the writer should seek a broker who offers the lowest commissions on stock purchases, option sales and exercises, and the lowest interest rate on the margin loan balance. Furthermore, care must be exercised in the selection of the underlying stock as a means of lessening the possibility of an equity loss on the shares.

Can and do covered call writers make these juicy returns? Absolutely. And so can you. No matter how you crunch the numbers, these returns are very achievable by any covered call writer. But to succeed as a covered call writer, the investor must be psychologically able to forego the possibility of the rare but spectacular run ups in a stock, must carefully select great stocks with little downside risk, and must follow a regimented program of writing calls each and every month with little thought or concern to current market conditions.

There are only two main risk factors in this strategy. The first is the possibility of the underlying stock falling drastically in price, generating an unrealized equity loss greater than the premium earned. This risk is largely overcome by selecting stocks with little downside risk and ones the investor is willing to hold through any minor correction, as it is truly a great stock. The second risk, a cherry picked portfolio, is covered in detail in the next section.

5.3.5   LONG-TERM PORTFOLIO RISK FROM COVERED CALL WRITING

In a covered call writing program, in which calls are written on a diversified portfolio, the quality of the portfolio deteriorates over time. The best performing stocks, those rising the most in price during any option cycle (life of the option), will advance in price above the strike prices and therefore be called from the writer. The poorest performers trade at distressed levels and at prices below the call strike prices. These calls are not exercised, with the shares remaining in the portfolio.

Through the cherry picking process the best appreciating shares are called away (sold), and the weak stocks remain. The natural result of the cherry picking process is that the quality of the portfolio diminishes over time.

The covered call writer must constantly be on guard that the portfolio quality does not deteriorate too much. The best approach is to carefully examine and re-evaluate the under-performing companies (fundamental analysis) and their shares (technical analysis) each and every option cycle to determine if they continue to represent the most effective employment of funds. In other words, the following questions should be asked: Is the stock still a great one, offering far greater upside potential than downside risk? Do these shares currently represent the wisest placement of funds? Can the shares reasonably be expected to outperform the market in the near term? Is the current price weakness only temporary? Is there any weakening of the fundamentals or technicals that might forecast lower future prices? Are there better optionable stocks in which to invest? Probably the most important question to ask is, "If I did not currently own shares of this company, would I buy stock at current price levels with the expectation of a near term price rise?"

If for some reason you would not repurchase the shares at current prices, committing new funds to the stock, the fact that they are now owned in the portfolio is not a justification to continue holding them. If you would not repurchase the shares, they should be sold immediately.

Only through a careful review of every stock position in the portfolio, and a weeding out of all names no longer attractive, can the portfolio remain healthy and avoid quality deterioration over time. Additionally, new funds generated from stock being called out (sold) from the account must be reinvested in the strongest securities currently available. This may mean reacquiring the same shares just sold, or the selection of other names. The emphasis of the investor must always be on liquidating those stocks expected to under-perform, and purchasing stocks anticipated to outperform the market.

5.3.6   SELLING RATIO COVERED CALLS

Simple covered call writing has dealt with the writing of a single covered call for each 100 shares of stock owned. Selling covered calls is one of the most popular writing techniques because there is only a minimal risk if any. The only risk appears in those cases where the share price declines in value more than the premium generated. But since the covered call seller is always diligently searching for the best stocks, those shares expected to rise in price because they are the best, strongest, and safest of the stocks available, the price decline risk is controlled.

In the typical covered call scenario the writer owns the underlying stock and is thus able to deliver on the obligation to sell shares at the strike price regardless of how high the price of the shares might rise. Any loss on the short call position (call that was written or sold) is matched dollar for dollar with a gain on the long stock position.

Most covered writing programs consist of the sale of a single call for each 100 shares of stock held in the account. The call sold is usually the nearest out-of-the-money strike. The profit on the transaction is the premium earned less the commissions to purchase the stock, the commission to write (sell) the option, the commission to deliver stock upon the call exercise plus any appreciation earned from the shares rising in price from their purchase price to the strike price. The returns from a covered call writing program can be, and normally are, substantial as demonstrated in the earlier section.

There is an alternative twist to the traditional covered call writing practice. In the modified approach the call seller writes a ratio of calls to the underlying stock position. In this strategy, more than one call is written for each 100 shares of stock owned. Two, three or even four calls are sold against the round lot of stock (100 shares). Thus the name "ratio writing"—the ratio being the number of calls sold against each round lot (100 shares) of the stock. A ratio of two means two calls are sold against the 100 shares, a ratio of three means three calls are sold covered only by one round lot of stock, etc.

In ratio selling the strike price of the calls that are sold is higher than in the normal covered call scenario. In a traditional covered call write, the strike would usually be the closest out-of-the-money strike. If stock is purchased at 57, a call would be sold at 60. In the ration write, the strike would be the next higher strike or even higher. The strike on a ratio write would be 65, 70, or even 75.

THE OBJECT OF RATIO WRITING IS TO:

Lower the risk of having stock called by selling higher strikes.

Increase the premium income through selling more calls.

Benefit from major appreciation in the underlying stock.

These objectives are accomplished by selling calls at higher strike prices, thereby reducing the probability of an exercise. The premium income is increased by selling a larger number of calls even though the premium on each call is lower because of the higher level of the strike price. Because the strike price is considerably above the current market price of the stock, there is considerable price appreciation potential on the underlying stock position.

A typical ratio call write would involve owning 100 shares of the stock and selling a number of calls several strike prices above the current price level of the shares. Assume the investor owns 100 shares of a stock selling at 93. In a covered writing program, one call would be sold with a strike price of 95. The premium would be approximately 6% or $550 for a one-month call. Alternatively, and using actual premiums from the Investor's Business Daily for this $93 stock, the writer could write a ratio of calls at 100 for a premium of $400 each, or at 105 for $225. Assume the writer sells 3 one-month calls at the 105 strike price. The gross premium income is $675, rather that the $550 if one call had been sold at 95.

Let's now examine the possible outcomes. In the normal covered call scenario, the writer earns $550, and the maximum profit potential is $550 plus appreciation from 93 to 95 ($200) less commissions to buy the stock, sell the option and sell the stock on an exercise. Assuming total commissions are $80, the maximum possible profit is $670 ($550 premium plus stock appreciation of $200 minus commissions of $80). This amount would be earned no matter how high the share price might rise prior to expiration. The maximum loss would be measured as the premium ($550) less the commission to purchase the stock and sell the option ($55) and less any decline in the stock price. Had the shares fallen to 85, the equity loss would have been $800 and the total loss would be $305 (premium of $550 less the $55 in commission costs less the depreciation of the stock from 93 to 85 or $800).

In the ratio write, the maximum income is the total premium (3 calls sold at $225 each for $675), plus maximum appreciation to the strike price (93 to 105, or $1,200), less commissions ($80), for a maximum total profit of $1,795 ($675 total premiums less the commissions of $80, plus the appreciation of $1,200). Should the stock never reach the 105 strike price, the profit would be measured by subtracting the commissions from the total of the premiums received, and then adding any stock appreciation or subtracting any decline in equity value of the underlying shares. If the stock rose from 93 to 103, the dollar profit would be the premium ($675), less commissions ($55 – no selling of stock commission), plus appreciation of $1,000 (93 to 103), or $1,620. Had it risen only to 100, the profit would be $1,320 ($675 premium less $55 in commissions plus appreciation of $700). If the shares declined to 85, the writer would lose money ($675 premium minus commissions of $55, minus equity loss of $800) for a total loss of $180.

Because in the ratio writing of calls the total premium income is greater, there is more cushion to offset a stock decline and lessen or eliminate losses (loss of $180 in the ratio write compared to a loss of $305 in the covered write). Since the strike price is set at a higher level, there is the opportunity to earn additional appreciation which, when added to the high level of total premiums received, magnifies the gains (maximum profit potential of $1,750 for the ratio write compared with only $670 in the covered case).

So far the covered ratio writing of calls looks pretty good! But is there a catch? Possibly. In regular covered call writing, the writer will make the maximum profit once the stock reaches the strike price and this profit will remain constant at the maximum profit level as the stock rises above the strike. Even if the stock goes 10 points above the strike, 20 or even 30 points beyond the strike, the profit on the transaction remains constant.

In the ratio write, the maximum profit is also earned when the stock exactly reaches the strike price. Yet unlike the covered write where the profit remains constant as the stock appreciates above the strike, in the ratio call write, the profit diminishes as the price moves beyond the strike. This is caused by losing money on several calls while only generating appreciation on 100 shares of stock. If in the ratio example where there are three calls written, as the share price advances above the 105 strike price, the writer loses $300 on the calls for each point above 105, but only picks up $100 in stock appreciation, for a net reduction of $200 for each point the share price rises over the strike price. This reduction is a subtraction from the maximum gain ($1,750). If the stock's price increased to 110, the gain would be reduced by $1,000, leaving a profit of $750. Examine the numbers. At 110, the 100 shares of stock is up from 93 to 110 for 17 points in appreciation per share ($1,700 for the 100 shares). The premium was $675 and commissions were $80. Adding the figures yields $2,295. The calls get exercised at 105 (the strike price) with the stock trading at 110 in the market. The writer must purchase 200 shares in the market (110) to be added to the 100 shares currently owned and deliver 300 shares at 105. This represents a reduction of $1,525 (5 points on 300 shares plus a $25 commission to buy

200 shares) from the gross of $2,295. The net is now $770 in profits. Had the stock catapulted further to 115, the profit picture would have deteriorated still further. The 100 shares advanced from 93 to 115 for $2,200 in appreciation. Adding the premium of $675, and subtracting the commissions of $80, leaves a gross figure of $2,795. From this gross we subtract the $3,000 loss on the 300 shares of stock (115 market price minus 105 strike price for 10 points times 300 shares) and subtract the additional commission to purchase the 200 shares ($25), which leaves a net loss of $230.

Should the stock's price move up even further, the loss will magnify in direct relationship between the number of calls and the stock position. In our example, the loss will grow $200 for each point of additional stock price advance.

The truism in doing ratio writing of calls is **the maximum profit on the transaction is earned when the stock price exactly matches the strike price.** As the share price rises toward the out-of-the-money strike price, the profit grows. It reaches its maximum level when the market price of the shares and the strike price are equal. The profit declines as the share price rises above the strike price.

5.3.7   COVERED CALL WRITING VS. RATIO CALL WRITING —WHICH IS BEST?

There is no easy answer as to whether the covered call writing or the ratio writing is best. There is greater profit potential in doing ratio writing through the capture of price appreciation of the underlying stock as it rises toward the higher strike price. Additionally, the total of the premium income generated through the sale of multiple calls at the higher strike price and covered by only 100 shares of stock can exceed the premium revenue from the sale of a single fully covered call at a lower strike price. The greater premium revenues from ratio writing offsets a potential stock price decline, thereby reducing risk. But should the stock have dramatic price acceleration rising well above the strike price, the appreciation on the underlying stock position combined with the premium income can fall short of the losses sustained on the uncovered calls, and a loss is possible.

A call writer must carefully analyze the stock, projecting the maximum price reasonably possible during the option time period, examine the premiums on various strike prices and run a quick analysis of the net results if the stock should actually reach the high projected price. The optimal writing strategy is to sell calls with a strike price closest to the highest stock price anticipated to be reached during the option's life. The ratio call writer maximizes his profit when the stock rises exactly to the strike price. Trying to project the maximum stock movement and then setting the strike price is the challenge. If calls are sold at a strike price considerably above the high stock price, the premium on each call is less because, holding the maturity constant, premiums decline faster the higher the strike price. A 110 call premium would be much lower than the premium on a 105 call. If the calls are sold with too low a strike price, the stock significantly overshoots the call's strike price, which results in losses on the uncovered calls when the price rises above the strike. Initially these losses from the stock's price exceeding the call's strike price will be more than offset by the appreciation of the underlying stock plus the writing premium received. But as the market price of the stock continues to rally there will ultimately come a time based upon the price of the shares where the losses on the naked (uncovered calls) can exceed the sum total of the appreciation of the stock and premium income. At this point a loss on the entire transaction occurs.

The ratio writer faced with a running stock can always protect himself by repurchasing the short call position (all calls sold, both covered and uncovered) before the transaction goes into a total loss situation. Yet it is always better to build a trade that assures a total profit at all reasonable price levels of the underlying stock. This brings us back to the need to make profit and loss calculations prior to entering a ratio call writing trade.

The calculation process consists in simply running several "what if" scenarios of the net profit to be realized at various realistic price points of the stock, given the premium income received from selling calls, and the number of calls written at a particular strike price. For example, with the stock at 93, the writer would logically test the outcome of writing 2, 3 and 4 calls at a 100 strike, at 105 and even at 110, with the stock rising to the strike prices as well as rising 5, 10, and possibly even 115 points above the strikes. The next step would be an estimate of the probability of the price reaching these levels within the time life of the call. The case earning the maximum profit would be the first choice. The first part, the calculation of the profit or loss figures is a simple math problem. The only uncertainty and the part requiring intuition is the guessing of the high price of the shares during the option life.

Experience has taught that greater profits are earned in ratio writing of calls than from traditional covered call writing. The optimal ratio of the number of calls to each 100 shares of stock proving most profitable in the 2 to 4 range. Seldom if ever do we sell more than 4 calls against each 100 shares. Conversely we find that the selling of just one call against 100 share positions to be neither intellectually challenging nor does it generate a large enough bang for the buck.

The premise upon which we build a call writing strategy is this: **the underlying stock must be a great stock offering minimal downside risk but meaningful upside potential.** Wanting to profit handsomely from the stock appreciation, a high strike price call is written. Since the premiums are low at the elevated strike prices, more calls must be written to generate the desired level of positive cash flow from the sale. If more than 4 are sold, the risk of loss if the stock should rise above the strike price is just too great.

5.3.8 ONLINE RESOURCES FOR COVERED CALLS

There are quite some websites dedicated to covered calls and similar strategies. One we like is www.optionmonitor.com, which gives many different ways to find the ideal option to do a covered call. We use this site a lot, because its information is trustworthy and the site in user-friendly.

If you have a stock, say INTC, and you would like to sell some covered calls, you get for example the following screens:

FIGURE 61

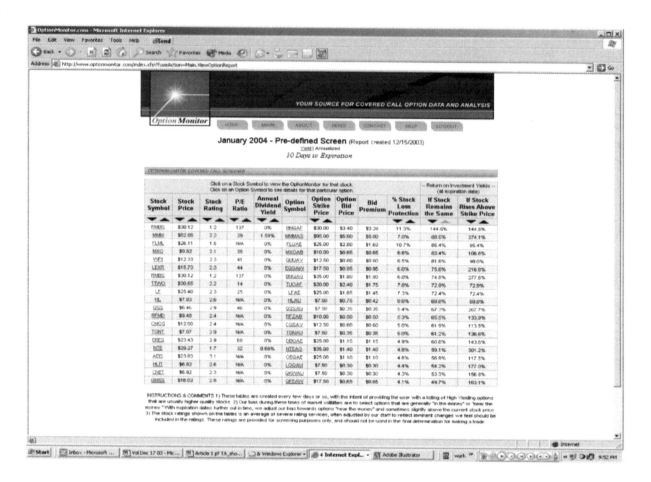

FIGURE 62

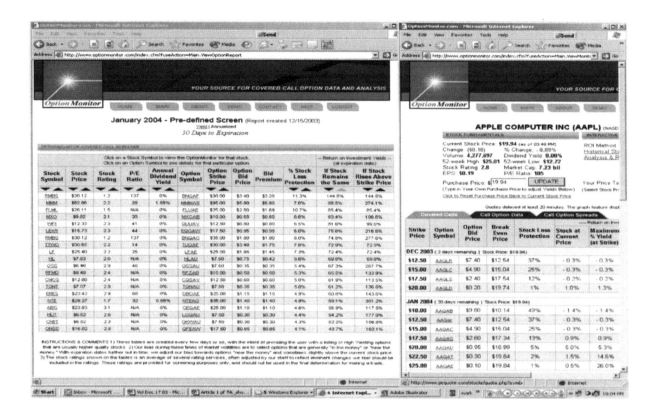

5.3.9   CHECKLIST FOR SELLING COVERED CALLS

Covered Call	
Increase in news?	
Bias of news?	
Liquidity of options o.k.?	
Spread o.k.?	
Volatility far from year high?	
Chart	

This checklist forces us to analyze fundamentals, technicals (the chart), and the level of the stock's volatility. But as you will see the spread and volatility are really the drivers for profitable covered call selling.

5.3.10   SELLING NAKED CALLS

We are not strong supporters of a strategy of selling naked, or totally uncovered, calls. But the strategy of selling naked calls will be discussed if for no other reason than being a widely employed trading technique, naked call selling should be compared with covered call and ratio call writing.

In a naked call selling program the writer owns no stock and backs the obligation to deliver stock with a cash margin equal to 20% (higher at many firms) of the value of the optioned stock, minus points out-of-the-money, plus the premium. The premium initially is a wash since it is generated through the initial sale of the call.

In covered writing, the writer earns the premium. The only possibility of a loss occurring is when the underlying stock drops below its cost by more than the net premium earned. The loss may not be realized, but it does represent an equity loss. If the stock rises, the writer earns the premium and any appreciation up to the strike price. A further price rise in the shares above the strike price has no impact – positively or negatively – on the profitability of the transaction, and the maximum profit potential of the transaction has been achieved. The covered call writer has given up the appreciation potential above the strike price for the premium income received immediately upon selling the call, for the benefit these funds provide in cushioning against price declines in the underlying stock, and for the potential stock appreciation up to the strike price.

The ratio call writer earns more premium dollars, and by writing calls at higher strike prices, benefits more from a large price growth in the shares. The larger premium income allows greater price protection against share prices falling. If the stock's price advances above the strike price, there is an erosion of profits, with the ultimate possibility of a loss.

In both the covered and ratio call writing approaches, the maximum profit is earned when the stock rises to the strike price. The writer by all means wants the stock to go up in price. The covered writer of calls wants any price appreciation. The ratio writer wants appreciation only to the strike price, for further advances lessen the profit. Therefore both covered call writing and ration call writing are techniques requiring the selection of stock with major upside potential and minimal downside risk. The covered writer can write at any strike, while the ratio writer makes an educated guess of the stock's high and attempts to write at a strike close to that peak.

When selling naked calls, the rules are reversed. The writer wants the stock to either do nothing or go down. Only by having the shares remaining below the strike price can the full premium be converted into a profit.

With a stock trading at 72, the naked writer might sell a one-month 75 call for $450. As long as the stock never reaches 75, the $450 becomes profit. Had it declined to 50, the writer would still have made the $450. Owning stock, the covered writer and the ratio writer would have lost some money with the decline, for the value of the shares owned has declined. This is not the case with the naked call writer. Owning no shares of stock, the naked call writer does not suffer value loss with a price decline. On the other hand, had the share price advanced to 77, there would be a loss of $200 on the option. At this level the writer is obligated when the call is exercised to sell stock at 75, which must be purchased in the market at 77. There is still a profit on the transaction of $250 ($450 premium received less the $200 loss on the stock bought in the market at 77 and sold at 75 through the call exercise). Should the rise carry the price to 80, there is a $500 loss on the stock. With a premium receipt of only $450, and a $500 loss on the stock, the net is a $50 loss. At a share market price of 85, the stock has a $1,000 loss. With only $450 in premium income, the net loss is $550 ($1,000 stock loss less the premium received of $450).

The naked call writer wants a stock with no upside potential. The weakest of stocks are ideal candidates for naked call selling. Alternatively, securities that have become overextended in value can be utilized. So while the covered writer is seeking great stocks, the naked writer is searching for dogs.

Why consider selling naked calls? Because of the large profit potential. When selling covered calls, the writer owns 100 shares of stock. This will require tying up 50% of the stock's value to earn a premium of approximately 6% of the stock value from selling one call. The naked seller need only deposit 20% of the stocks value, minus points out-of-the-money, plus the premium (a wash) to earn the same 6%. So if the 75 call is sold for $450 when the stock is trading at 72, the writer deposits 20% of the $7,200 stock value or $1,440, less the 3 points the shares are out-of-the-money ($300), for a total of $1,140. The premium of $450 divided by the investment of $1,140 represents a return of investment of 39.47% for a single month. This annualizes at 473.68%.

Writing naked calls can be extremely profitable. The only hard part is finding terrible, weak, or extremely overpriced stocks lacking upside potential. The terrible and the weak securities, while good naked writing candidates, offer a challenge. Because the market perceives them as weak with little or no appreciation likelihood, their call premiums are often very depressed. The writer might only receive a one-month call premium of 1, 2, or 3% of the strike price value. The annualized returns continue to be superior, but less so. The extremely overpriced stocks offer inflated premiums, but they have a flaw, too. They are extremely overpriced because the market loves them. The market has bid their price sky-high. There is absolutely no assurance the bubble will burst and the price plummet. The shares could just as easily move up another 40 points. In the late 1990's the internet and e-commerce companies were prime examples of vastly overpriced stocks, with no earnings and not even any expectation of earnings for years to come, defying gravity, doubling, redoubling and doubling once again from already dizzying heights. The call premiums on these high flyers with no fundamental substance might seem impressively large, and upside limited, but the risk was enormous. For a long period of time, no matter how overpriced the shares were, they went higher still.

There is also the same danger in selling naked calls as in selling short. Stocks can only decline 100% to zero. But they can rise 200%, 300% 4,000% or to infinity. The risk of loss on short sales of stock and on selling naked calls is therefore theoretically unlimited. This certainly does present a risk. Yet the astute seller of options utilizes techniques to cut losses and by doing so controls the risk at an acceptable level. Also, seldom do stocks move up as quickly as they did in the great bubble of the late 1990's and early 2000's. In truth, stocks have an upward bias. Since 1926 large cap stocks have had a compound annual appreciate of over 10% and small cap securities have experienced yearly returns averaging over 13%. These are long-term average returns, which mask some periods of major deflation of share prices. Yet this upward tendency does stack the deck in favor of covered call selling and against naked call selling.

An offsetting factor in favor of naked call selling is research that has consistently demonstrated the fact that securities do decline faster than they rise. Price declines are usually faster and more magnified than rallies.

> Selling naked calls is certainly a viable strategy. Just be aware of the low premium on the under performing stocks and immense risks of the current market darlings.

5.4   SELL PUTS FOR INCOME AND FOR CHEAP STOCK ACQUISITION

The last section dealt exclusively with the writing of calls. Calls are written to earn premium income on a stock position, profit from further price advances in the underlying stock while generating cash flow to offset against potential price declines in the share holdings, and for speculative profits where no shares are owned and a market decline appears imminent.

> **PUTS ARE WRITTEN FOR ENTIRELY DIFFERENT REASONS. THEY ARE WRITTEN (SOLD):**
>
> As a means of acquiring stock at a future date and at prices lower than currently exist, as a way to earn speculative profits where prices are projected to have only upside potential, and as a method to cover a short position in the stock.

All three reasons to sell puts are covered in detail in this section.

5.4.1.1   SUMMARY

But prior to discussing the benefits of put selling, let's take a moment to review the conceptual basics of what has already been covered. This short review should serve both as a refresher and to reinforce earlier concepts. The seller (writer) of a call has the obligation to deliver 100 shares of stock at the strike price until the expiration date of the contract and is paid a premium as compensation for bearing the risk. The put writer is obligated to buy 100 shares of the stock at the strike price through the expiration date and is also paid a premium for shouldering the risk. Thus the call writer must be willing to *sell* stock and the put writer may be forced to *buy* shares.

5.4.1.2   BUY STOCK CHEAPER LATER

One of the most compelling reasons to write a put is to earn premium income for the willingness to acquire 100 shares of the stock in the future at a purchase price considerably lower than its current market price.

When an option trader writes a 50 strike put on a stock currently trading at 54, he stands ready and willing to pay 50 a share for the 100 shares. He is paid a premium as a consideration for the risk he is bearing. The risk is that he is forced to purchase the shares at the strike price (50) should they fall below the strike price and regardless of how low they might ultimately trade. This risk lasts until one of two events occurs: the put expires at its expiration date, or the put seller closes out his short put position through a closing purchase of a put with an identical strike price and maturity date.

In the typical put selling scenario, the put seller has the capital to buy the shares, either for cash or on margin. The company has been thoroughly analyzed and the seller is willing to own the stock. The shares are currently trading at 54, a fair price given the fundamentals of the firm and the technicals of the stock. Shares could certainly be purchased today at 54 for $5,400 in a cash account or by depositing 50% of the purchase cost ($2,700) in a margin account. But consistent with the theme of this book, "Never Buy Stock Again", the investor knows there is a better approach than buying the shares at their current price. Instead of entering an order today to buy the stock for 54, a put is sold with a 50 strike price and a one-month expiration for a premium of $250. As in all writing situations, the premium is credited to the writer's account the following day. The put writer is now obligated for a month to buy the stock at 50 a share. To back this obligation, and to insure compliance, the put writer must deposit 20% of the stock's value ($5,400 times 20% or $1,080) less the points out-of-the-money (54 market price less 50 strike price or $4 times 100 shares), plus the premium (money just received as premium income of $250). The writer is required to have on deposit $930 ($1,080 as 20% of the stock value minus the $400 for points out-of-the-money, plus the premium of $250). Of this figure,

$250 is immediately being received as premium income, so only $680 of new money is required. This formula always applies with the stipulation that cash required to back the obligation cannot be less than 10% of the current stock value.

Because the writer is quite willing to purchase shares at their current 54 market price, he would be delighted to buy them for $50 in a month. What a deal! The $5,400 in funds available to pay for the shares can be invested elsewhere for the month, or kept on deposit and earning interest for the period. If the shares are acquired through the exercise of the put, their cost is not $5,400 to purchase them today at 54 a share, but the strike price level of 50 for a purchase amount of $5,000. Acquiring the shares through the put exercise at 50, results in a saving of $400 for the 100 shares.

But is the buy price from acquiring the 100 shares through the put exercise at the 50 strike price really $5,000? No! If shares are purchased at the strike price of $50, their real cost is the $50 strike price less the premium per share of $2.50 ($250 total premium for writing the put divided by 100 shares). The stock actually costs only $47.50 a share. And to think the investor was willing to pay $54 a share for the position. What a great outcome from the trade!

But maybe the stock does not decline below the $50 strike price, and the put is therefore not exercised. This is also a very positive outcome for the put writer. The $250 premium is profit on an investment of $680 in new funds required to be deposited (20% of the stock value minus points-out-of-the-money plus the premium). The Return on Investment is 36.76 for a month, or 441.17% annually.

There are two possible results when selling a put. Either the stock declines below the strike price, resulting in shares being purchased at a later date and at a cheaper price than the shares were trading on the date the put was sold, or the shares continue to trade above the put's strike price, meaning the put expires unexercised, no stock is acquired, and the entire premium becomes profit. The cash outlay or margin is relatively small, so the premium profit yields a very large **return on investment**.

The writing of a put on a great stock certainly appears to be a win-win strategy. So what can go wrong? First, the stock could go into a free fall, taking the shares well below the strike price (50) of the put. The price might decline to 40 within the month, with an obligation to purchase 100 shares at $50. A market price decline of the shares to 40 would result in a buy price of $47.50 ($50 strike less the $2.50 premium per share) compared with the market price of only $40. There would be a loss of $750. However, this is not too bad. The writer loved the stock and wanted to own the shares. He got his chance. He was willing to pay $54 for the shares and actually acquired them for only $47.50, a savings of $6.50 a share. It is certainly unfortunate the shares declined so much, but the loss on the shares costing only $47.50 is a lot less than it would have been had they been purchased at $54.

Shares acquired through the exercise of a written put will always have an acquisition cost of less than the market price of the stock on the date the put was sold. This is always true; for the put writer receives a premium, which when subtracted from the strike price lowers the cost basis.

Second, if the stock failed to decline below the strike price, and actually rose in price, the writer of the 50 put made a large **return of investment**, but missed the appreciation from owning the shares had they been purchased at $54.

To further drive this point home, let's compare in contrast buying the stock at $54 with selling the 50 put. If the stock declined below $54, but stayed above the $50 strike price, the stock buyer of shares at $54 lost money, but the put seller has not "put" (sold) the stock and has earned the entire premium of $250. If the shares go below the $50 strike price, the buyer of stock at $54 loses more dollars than the put seller who buys at 50 and was paid a $250 premium, making his actual purchase price $47.50. To illustrate this, had the stock declined to 44; the stock buyer would have lost $1,000 (54 cost less 44 market), with the put writer losing only $350 ($47.50 effective stock cost less the $44 market price). If the stock rises, the stock buyer makes the appreciation of the shares, yet the put writer's maximum profit is the net premium received ($250 less a commission to originally sell the put). So had the market price of the securities rocketed to $60, the share buyer would have earned $600 in profits, compared with the $250 in premium earned by the put writer. The share buyer had to invest at least 50% of the stock's cost, which is $2,700, to earn the $600. The share buyer has made an ROI of 22% ($600 profit divided by $2,700 margin investment), The put writer's out-of-pocket investment was only 20%, not the stock buyer's 50%, and even the 20% is reduced by the $400 in points out-of-the-money on the put ($54 market price of the shares less the $50 strike price). The put writer's profit of $250 is on an investment of only $680 and represents an ROI of 36.76%. Had the stock risen even further, the share buyer would ultimately earn a higher ROI than the put seller. But such major moves are an exception.

From these examples, it is easy to make the following observations:

If the market price of the stock falls below the strike price: The put writer acquires shares at prices well below those existing at the time the put is sold. The stock buyer pays more for the shares than the put writer does. In addition, the put writer purchases the shares at a later time than the stock buyer and thus has the opportunity to earn interest on the uninvested funds for a period of time.

If the market price of the stock falls below the current market price, but not below the strike price: The put buyer earns the entire premium as profit, but does not buy stock. The stock buyer has a loss on the shares.

If the market price of the stock rises: The stock buyer makes a profit on the shares. The put writer makes the entire premium as a profit. The stock buyer invests more dollars, effectively reducing the ROI. The put writer invests fewer dollars, thereby magnifying the ROI.

There is only one instance where the direct purchase of shares proves more profitable than the sale of a put. If the stock rises dramatically, the put writer must be satisfied with the premium as the maximum possible profit from the transaction. The stockowner, on the other hand, profits dollar for dollar with the appreciation in the share price. If the upward thrust of the shares is great enough, the shareowner's ROI can exceed that of the put seller. In all other instances, the put writer gains an advantage in either small dollar losses or larger Return on Investment. Further, the put writer's returns are frequent and consistent. Only with a drastic market price decline does the put writer lose money, and even in such cases, the dollar loss is always smaller than the loss suffered by the stock buyer who purchased shares at the market price that existed when the put was written. Additionally, the put writer wanted to own the shares. The stock appeared to be an outstanding bargain at 54, and was a steal at the strike price. When the premium is subtracted from the strike price, the shares are at an even better acquisition price. Certainly in our example above the market declined to 44, but initially when the price was 54, a 50 buy price through a put exercise looked exceptionally attractive, and the 47.50 cost basis of the potential buy looked even more appealing.

The writing of puts with strike prices below current market prices is an ideal way to acquire stock in the future and at great prices. We never go into the market to buy stock. We purchase stock only through the exercise of puts. Once we are long the shares, we use the securities as the underlying position for covered or ratio call writing.

Words of Caution: First, the writing of puts must begin with a rigorous analysis of companies and the selection of great stocks for inclusion in the portfolio. Because the writer is obligated to purchase the shares, he must like, if not love, the companies on which puts are being sold. He should also have a long-term horizon, for the shares will be put to him in the future, and his security research must have projected bright prospects for many months or years into the future. Second, there is reverse cherry picking in a put writing program. The only stock put to the writer are the weakest shares. The writer must therefore constantly monitor the fundamental quality of the securities on which puts are written, and be willing to buy back and close out those short put positions (puts written) if the quality of the company weakens. The maximum profits are made by put writing where the share price never falls below the strike price. The writer must therefore attempt to locate securities with little or no downside. In addition, the put seller must never overextend. If there are funds adequate to buy 100 shares of stock in a cash account, thus 200 shares in a margin account, only sell 1 or 2 puts. The margin base of the funds available to purchase 100 shares in a cash account will support the selling of up to 5 or more puts, but don't do it. You cannot afford to buy 500 shares if put to you.

5.4.2   *INCREASING THE PROBABILITY OF ACQUIRING THE STOCK*

In the prior examples of writing puts, the put seller liked the stock and was therefore ready and willing to acquire the stock. But buying the shares was not a "must do." In the case where the put seller is willing to buy the stock, but does not feel he has to have it in his portfolio, puts are written with strike prices below the current market price of the shares. If the market price declined below the strike price, the shares would be acquired at an extremely favorable price level. If the market fails to penetrate the lower strike price, no shares are purchased, and the writer has made an extremely attractive return on the investment, having deposited a very small amount of money as compared with the funds required to buy shares directly. Thus in this situation the put writer is ambivalent as to the price action of the shares. It is a win-win situation in either case. Shares are purchased at great prices, or the put expires and the ROI is large.

There are cases where the put writer absolutely wants to purchase shares. The research has been done, the stock appears poised for a significant advance, and the company fits logically into the portfolio. There is a strong desire to buy the stock at current market levels. Here again – **"Never buy stock."** The profit position can be drastically improved through the sale of puts. The probability of purchasing the shares can be raised to nearly 100% and the buy price of the shares lowered below the current market. This is all done through the sale of puts. But the puts have strike prices above the current market price of the stock. The puts are in-the-money.

If the put writer is willing to buy stock, but it is not vital to purchase shares, the put is written with a strike price below the current price of the stock. If shares are ultimately received through the exercise of the put, their price is at the lower strike price, a price further reduced by the premium received. There is a possibility of a share purchase, but no certainty. The stock will only be put (sold) to the writer should its price fall below the strike price and even then there is no absolute certainty the put will be exercised. Options are seldom exercised early. Normally if there is an exercise, it is only at the expiration of the contract, and even then, puts are only

143

exercised if the exercise is advantageous to the option holder. So even if the stock declines below the strike price prior to the expiration date, and rallies back above the strike price by expiration, the shares will not be put (sold) to the writer. The put writer can only expect to buy shares if the stock falls below the strike price and remains below the strike at expiration. Even if it is below the strike, if its price is only a few cents below the strike at the close on the expiration date, the put might not be exercised.

The exercise of options is a much-misunderstood area for new option writers. They assume a put will be exercised when the price falls below the strike price. This seldom occurs for several reasons. When the put is exercised, the put holder that acquired the put to profit from a price decline in the shares has lost an opportunity to profit from any further price drop. The exercise of a put purchased as price protection for a long stock position eliminates the price insurance and converts the long stock position into cash through the sale of the shares at the strike price.

If the put buyer no longer wants the put, it can be exercised. It can also be resold for the currently quoted premium. Since the premium will reflect the intrinsic value of the put and a time value, and since the time value component is lost in any exercise, the put holder will normally resale the put rather than exercise it. Only in this way can the put holder receive the maximum benefit. Assume a one month 50 strike put is purchased for $300 when the stock is selling for 53. The stock rapidly declines to 47, with the put having 2 weeks of life remaining. The put has an intrinsic value of $300 and some time value (estimated at $100). If the put is exercised, the hold will obtain the intrinsic value of $300, but will lose the time value of $100. Thus, the put would not be exercised, but would be resold for the full $400. The new purchaser of this existing put has acquired the put with the intent of speculating on further negative price action of the stock. Again, the put is not exercised until there is no time value remaining in the premium price.

Selling a put with a strike price below the current market price of the shares does not assure that stock will be put to the writer even if the market price declines below the strike price. Even if the price is below the strike price at expiration, shares will not necessarily be put to the writer. Only if the closing price of the stock on expiration is 37 cents or more below the strike, is an exercise almost certain. Exercises can occur even if the stock is only a penny below the strike price. However, if the price is significantly below the strike, we can assume there will certainly be an exercise.

If the put seller's motivation is the acquisition of the stock, selling a put with a low strike price may not accomplish the goal. The goal of selling puts with strike prices below the current market price of the stock is to earn premium income, and possibly buy the stock. If the stock is purchased, its price is always lower than the price existing at the date the put was originally sold. If the put seller simply "must" buy the stock, a different approach is required.

The means of increasing the probability of acquiring the stock, yet still purchase the shares at a price below the current market level, is to write a put with a strike price above the current market price. A put in-the-money will be sold.

Assume the stock is trading at 81. The one month put with an 85 strike price (4 points in-the-money) has a premium of $800 ($400 intrinsic and $400 time value). By selling this put, there is a high probability of being put (buying) the stock. The only reason stock would not be put (sold) to the writer at expiration is when its price has advanced above the put strike price. As long as the stock is trading at least 37 cents below the strike price, the stock will be put, and the writer's goal of buying the shares is accomplished.

But why would the writer want to purchase the stock at $85 in a month? It is currently trading at $81 and could have been purchased at this level. The reason is the actual cost of the shares put (sold) to the writer is not the $85 strike price, but the strike price (85) less the premium received ($800). The cost of the acquired shares would therefore be the $85 strike price of the put less the $8 premium received for an actual cost of $77 a share, four dollars less than the current market of 81.

By writing a put with a strike price above the current market price of the stock, there is a high probability that stock is put (sold) to the writer. But what happens if the stock rises above this higher strike price of the put? If the market price of the stock rallies above the strike price of the put, the stock will not be put (sold) to the writer and the full premium ($800) is profit. The writer's investment as required margin on the sale of the put was 20% of the value of the stock then trading at 81 ($8,100 times 20% equals $1,620), minus points out-of-the-money, which is not applicable with the put being in the money, plus the premium of $800, which was just paid to the writer. The net new money investment is only $1,620. The premium of $800 represents a Return on Investment of 49.38% ($800 divided by the margin investment of $1,620). The put writer has made a 50% return without buying the stock. The only downside to this transaction would be the appreciation potential lost by not owning the stock if its price experienced a huge upside move. Had the shares risen to $95, the stock buyer would have earned $1,400 ($81 buy price to $95 current market price), compared to the $800 premium generated from writing the put. To earn the larger dollar return the stock investor had to invest at least 50% of the stock's $81 purchase price ($4,050 as the minimum investment) compared with the much lower $1,620 investment of the put writer. The stock buyer has made $1,400 on a $4,050 investment (assuming a margin account minimum deposit) or a 34.56% ROI. The put writer has earned $800 on a $1,620 cash outlay for a ROI of 49.38%. If the stock rises far enough, the stock buyer's ROI can match or exceed the ROI of the put seller. This can happen, but is not the norm.

Had the stock not rallied, but declined instead, the put writer would have had a purchase cost of $77 a share ($85 strike price less the $800 premium), compared with the $81 cost of the stock buyer. The put writer therefore will always lose fewer dollars with a share price decline simply because the cost basis of the stock is lower for the put writer.

The probability of being put the stock (accruing the stock through the exercise of the put) can be further increased by writing an even higher strike price put. The higher the strike price of the put being sold, the greater the probability of its exercise and thus the greater the chances of being put (sold) the shares. The $90 put could have been sold for a premium of $1,100. With the stock trading at 81, the $1,100 premium represents $900 of intrinsic value and $200 in time value. If the stock is purchased through being assigned the stock at the $90 strike price, the actual cost is the strike price of $90 less the premium of $11 a share for a cost basis of $79. This continues to represent a nice discount for the writer compared with alternatively having to pay $81 for the shares. Should the stock rise, but remain below the $90 put strike, the share cost basis will always be the same $79. If the price appreciates past the $90 strike price, the put writer will not be sold the shares, and he makes a profit of $1,100 in premium income. With the put seller's investment of only 20% of the stock price (20% of $8,100), the ROI is 67.90% (the premium income of $1,100 divided by the margin investment of $1,620).

What are the risks of selling a put with a high strike price? There is the risk of missing out on any huge price appreciation in the shares if they rally above the put strike price. This risk is only an opportunity loss, not a cash loss risk. The selling of an in-the-money put and having the stock rise beyond the strike creates a profit for the put seller. Sure, a larger profit might have been made had the stock been purchased directly in the market, not no loss occurred for the put sell. This risk, which is not really a risk at all, can effectively be offset by selecting a strike price above any likely price advance.

However, there is a real risk associated with selling high strike price puts: The risk of buying shares that have declined. A real loss will occur if the stock declines below the cost basis purchase price (strike price less the premium received). But because the put writer absolutely wanted to own the stock, and because the cost basis is always going to be less than the current price of the stock at the time the put is written, this strategy is also a win-win for the writer. It allows a lower purchase price of the shares, shares are purchased at a later time, so most of the investment capital can be invested elsewhere at interest for a period of time, and if the stock rises above the strike price, the ROI is dramatic.

Writing puts on stock you absolutely want to own is truly a wonderful investment technique. It has two positive outcome possibilities. It either lowers the cost of the shares acquired or yields a high ROI. The probability of being put the stock is a variable able to be manipulated by the writer. The lower the interest in buying shares, the lower the put strike sold with the strike being below the current market price of the stock. The greater the desire to own the stock, the higher the put strike sold, with the put strike being above the current share trading level.

Selling a put with a strike below the current stock price will yield a lower premium and will lessen the chance of being put (buying) the stock. And should stock be purchased, its cost basis is lower than if a high strike had been sold with a higher premium and higher strike price.

Selling a put with a strike price above the current stock's price earns a higher premium, increases the probability of being put the stock, and raises the cost basis of the acquired shares. They are still purchased at a cost well below the current stock price, but higher than in the case of writing a below-market put.

The following table reflects actual premiums for the Ebay October 2003 puts for September 12, 2003. It also depicts the potential acquisition or cost basis of acquiring stock through the exercise of a short put. Nice that the seller of a 45 put for $65 might earn very few premium dollars, but has a very low probability of being forced to buy the stock, and if the stock is put (sold) to him, his cost basis is only $44.35, compared with the market price of the shares on September 12th of $52.62. There will be a higher probability of being put stock if the 50 put is sold, but with its $170 premium, the buy basis is $48.30. Still far below the current 52.62 price. Selling the 55 strike put significantly increases the likelihood of being put the shares, but the buy price is only $50.90, nearly 2 dollars below the current market price. And should the price rise above 55, the dollar profit (premium) is $410. Selling the 60 put almost certainly guarantees being put the stock at 60. But even in this case the cost basis is $52.00, 62 cents less than buying the shares today at $52.62.

Ebay Close 9/12/2003 $52.62	Money Position	Strike Prices of Oct 2003 Puts	Put Quote	Put Premium in Dollars for Oct. 2003 Puts	Per Share Acquisition Price of Stock
	Out-of-the-Money	40	.25	$25	$39.75
	Out-of-the-Money	42.5	.45	$45	$42.05
	Out-of-the-Money	45	.65	$65	$44.35
	Out-of-the-Money	47.50	1.05	$105	$46.45
	Out-of-the-Money	50	1.70	$170	$48.30
	At-the-Money	52.50	2.65	$265	$49.85
	In-the-Money	55	4.10	$410	$50.90
	In-the-Money	57.50	5.80	$580	$51.70
	In-the-Money	60	8.00	$800	$52.00

SELLING PUTS BELOW, AT, OR ABOVE CURRENT STOCK PRICE

Should the naked puts be sold below, at, or above the current stock price?

There are two reasons to sell naked puts:

* desire to earn premium income without acquiring stock, and
* desire to acquire stock at a price lower than it currently trades.

The strength of the seller's reasons should dictate the strike of the puts being sold. There is also the basic premise that the put seller has done research and believes the stock has significant upside price potential. **Unless there is upside potential in the stock, puts should not be sold.** Furthermore, the put seller must always be ready, willing, and able to purchase the stock if it is put (sold) to him. This means there is adequate capital available to cover the purchase of put stock and psychologically the put seller can live comfortably with owning the stock. Without the capital base or the emotional acceptance of the stock, selling puts is a risky endeavour.

If the put seller is primarily motivated for earning premium income without acquiring the stock, puts should be sold with strikes below the current price of the common, and low enough that there is little likelihood of the stock price falling below the strike within the life of the put. There is not a foolproof, mathematically exact method of determining where the stock might be within a certain time period. But an informed and educated guess can be made from a study of the chart.

One of the easiest practices would be to select a strike below the low of the stock going back in time equal to the option's life. If a 4 week put is being sold, go back 4 weeks on the chart and determine the low during this historical time period and sell the strike immediately below that low price level. Another practice often utilized is to examine the price volatility for an equivalent historical time period up to the period of time covered by the put being sold. If selling a 30-day put, go back 30 days in time. Determine the price range during this historical time period, which means finding the highest and lowest prices the stock traded during this past time period and calculate the difference between the high and low price. Now cut the price range in half and sell the strike price one strike lower than half of the price range. For example, the chart would be examined for the high and low prices for the last 4 weeks (assumed to be 76 as the high and 62 as the low). This price range of 14 points (76 minus 62) is halved equalling 7, and 7 is then subtracted from the current price of the stock (73). The resulting number, the current stock price less half of the historical volatility for the immediate past time period equal in length to the future time life of the put being sold (73 minus 7) or 66 represents the probable lower range for the next time period. The put would be sold at the next lower strike price of 65. This technique assumes that volatility, or price range as measured in points between the high and low prices for a set time period, will remain the same, that it will be spread equally above and below the stock's current price, and there is a low probability the stock will close at the end of the option life period at a price below the strike price which is set at a strike outside and below the lower side of the range. The stock might have increased volatility, the entire movement could be below the current market price, and the stock could close below the strike price, yet years of experience have shown the opposite. These two techniques, while not foolproof, work most of the time. Their ease of calculation, empirical support, and logical application make them perfectly acceptable rules of guidance for the setting of strikes for naked puts where stock acquisition is to be avoided.

When the motivation of the put writer is to acquire stock, the setting of the strike price is different. The stock's price needs to be lower than the strike price at the option expiration date. For stock to be put, or sold, to the put seller, its price needs to trade below the strike price of the put at expiration. Thus in the selection of the appropriate strike price of the put that is sold, the seller needs to anticipate where the stock is likely to be trading at expiration and sell a strike higher than that level. The more anxious the seller is to own the stock, the higher the strike is sold. For example, if the stock is trading at 50 and within the option's life might reasonably be expected to rise to 54, a 55 strike would be sold. But should the strike rise further than anticipated, and top 55, that strike would have been too low and the 60 would have been a better choice. The best way to approach this dilemma is first to decide how important it is to be put the stock (acquire the stock through the exercise of the put). If it is quite important for you to become the owner of the shares, sell a strike price higher than any reasonable price advance would carry the shares, but no higher.

There is a trade-off in selling puts with higher strike prices. The higher the strike price in relationship to the current share price, the greater the premium received by the seller, the larger the intrinsic portion of the premium and the lower the time value component. The time value component of the premium received represents our profit and is also the figure that reduces the cost of the acquired stock. With the stock selling at 50, the one month 55 put might be selling at 8 (5 point intrinsic and 3 point time value), and the put shares would be costing 47 (55 strike less 8 points). The 60 strike would be trading at 11.50 (10 points intrinsic and 1.50 points time value) yielding a share cost of 48.50. The 65 strike would be trading at 15.50 for a stock purchase cost of 49.50. Which is best? The sale of the 65 strike price put gives the highest probability of exercise (being put the stock), for this put will absolutely be exercised unless the stock rises above 65 within the month. There is a lower probability of having stock put on the 60 strike, but the probability is still good. And a still lower probability of acquiring stock through the sale of the 55 strike, but even in this scenario the shares have to rise 5 points to avoid the exercise. Should shares be put, their cost (47) is lowest by selling the 55 strike since it carries the highest time value. The shares cost more under the 60 strike put scenario (48.50), and would have cost more still, (49.50) had the 65 strike put been sold. The trade-off becomes: firstly, increased probability of acquiring the shares with the higher acquisition cost when selling higher strike puts, with, secondly, a lower chance of buying the shares, but with a reduced cost basis if acquired when selling a lower strike put. It becomes obvious the proper approach is to sell the lowest strike put with that strike price above the reasonably anticipated top price the shares are likely to trade prior to option expiration. This will maximize returns from put selling and provide a reasonable probability of being put the shares.

The flip side requires the examination of the profit to be made should the stock really run and in so doing blow through all of the strikes. In this case, with the premium on the 55 put being $800, on the 60 put $1,150, and $1,550 on the 65 put when the stock was trading at 50, the largest dollar profit would have been earned by selling the highest strike, the 65, for its premium was $1,550. Assuming the stock rose and was trading at 69 at expiration, the 55 put earned the seller $800, the 60 put generated $1,150, and the 65 yielded $1,550. The put seller wanted to own the stock and missed the opportunity this time, but earned a premium. Was this a bad alternative? Absolutely not. Had the shares been purchased at 50, the profit on the stock currently trading at 69 would be $1,900. The investment has been $5,000 for a ROI of 38%. The seller of the 55 put made $800 on an out of pocket cash investment of $1,000 (20% of the 50 stock price), for an ROI of 80%. The sell of the 60 put made $1,150 on the $1,000 cash investment for an ROI of 115%, and the sell of the 65 put earned $1,550 on the $1,000 for an ROI of 155%. So even the undesirable outcome, not getting put the shares, has been highly profitable. In fact, more profitable on an ROI basis than a direct market purchase of the shares at 50.

The discussion has been focused on selling out-of-the-money puts for premium income where the seller tries to avoid being put the shares, and selling in-the-money puts in the hope of acquiring the shares in the future at a price less than the current market price quote of the stock. There is a third alternative employed if the option selling is neutral about acquiring the shares. With the stock trading at 50 a trader could logically be interested in both maximizing the return on cash invested (ROI), and be willing to purchase shares at a healthy discount below current share prices. In this case, and to accomplish both goals, puts at-the-money, meaning puts with a strike price closest to the current share price, would be sold. The stock is selling at 51, making the 50 put the nearest strike. Being the nearest strike, the 50 put is the at-the-money put. This 50 put is slightly out-of-the-money (1 point) and with a one month expiration it might trade at $400. By selling this put with its near the market strike, there are two very real potential outcomes. One possibility is the price stays above the strike price, the put expires, and the entire premium is earned. Because the option expired worthless, stock was never acquired. Alternatively, the stock's price declines below the 50 strike and 100 shares are put (acquired) for each put option that had been sold. With the margin requirement of 20% of the stock price, minus the points out of the money, plus the premium, the put seller has invested $920 in the trade (20% of $5,100 or $1,020, minus $100 points out of the money, plus premium of $400. But remember the premium was just paid to the seller for a true out of pocket investment requirement of $920). If the stock is not put to him, his profit is $400 and his ROI for one month is 43% ($400 profit divided by the cash investment of $920). If the stock is acquired because its price declines below the 50 strike, its cost basis is the 50 strike less the premium of $400 yielding a cost basis of 46. So regardless of the ultimate outcome, (either stock is not acquired and the entire premium is a profit, or stock is purchased by being put at the strike price and the premium is a reduction of the buy price), the seller of the put has achieved acceptable results.

> There is a risk associated with selling an at-the-money put when neutral on buying the stock. The risk occurs in the case where the stock price declines below the price level (break-even point) calculated as the strike price less the premium. Below the break-even price, the acquired shares are trading at an economic loss for the put seller.

There are two methods of avoiding, or at least lessening, this risk. The first is to only sell naked puts on shares of great companies, i.e., where you are sure they have very limited downside and significant immediate, intermediate and long-term upside potential. Downward risk is reduced and if the shares are put (acquired by the put seller through the exercise of the put), they can be expected to move higher quickly. The second way to protect yourself from a decline is to roll the put down if the stock price declines below the strike and seems likely to remain below that level until expiration. This practice is explored below.

5.4.3   ROLLING DOWN

Stocks may and often do have volatile price action. This action can easily take the share price below the strike price of the put. Such a decline places the put seller in the position of being forced to acquire the stock. Fortunately there is an easy solution to this problem. It involves rolling the put down and out. And it works because share prices don't go down to zero. A company with optionable stock could go out of business and its share price could decline to zero, but this is so rare that in our many years of trading options, we have only seen such an event occur a few times (Enron and WorldCom). On occasion prices on great stocks do decline dramatically. No matter how severe the share price decline might be, and unless the fundamentals of the firm have changed drastically for the worst, the price drop is usually short lived. When such a price fall happens, the put seller needs to eliminate the immediate risk of acquiring the shares while simultaneously position a put sale for the future. This is accomplished by repurchasing the penetrated put (where the stock price is currently below the strike and is expected to remain below the strike until expiration) and resell a lower strike put with a later expiration date.

Assume a one month (April) 50 strike put is sold for $400 with the stock trading at 51. The share price now drops suddenly and inexpediently to 43. What should the put seller do? Acquiring the stock at 50 less the $400 premium is one choice. The second is to roll the put down and out. The original put at 50 would be repurchased for a cost of intrinsic value ($700) plus time value, (assume $100), for a total buy-back cost of $800. The original $400 premium income has become a $400 loss. The next step is to sell a lower strike put for the next later month. The May 45 put is sold for $500. At this point the total premium income is $900 (the original $400 premium from selling the April 50 put plus the new premium income of $500 from selling the May 45). The net income from all the transactions is $100 ($900 gross premiums received less the $800 cost to buy back the April 50 put). Should the stock rise and stay above the 45 strike during this new option cycle, the seller is back into a realized profit position. If the shares continue to trade lower, the put continues to be rolled down in strike price and out in time until its strike price is ultimately below the share price at expiration. There is a caveat, though. Rolling puts down only effectively works with great stocks that have upside potential far in excess of the downside risk. Stocks in general have an upward bias over time of 10% annual appreciation for large cap issues and 13% for smaller cap and growth shares. This upward bias, coupled with the underlying premise of only selling puts on the shares of the strongest companies, over time will make the rolling process succeed. We have on occasion been forced to roll puts down as many as 7 times prior to establishing a put strike price lower than the share price. This 7 time rolling down effort was ultimately rewarded with a respectable profit. More importantly, throughout the entire process the economic profit/loss position from the put sales has always been superior to the scenario where we would have owned the actual shares of the stock. Why? Because of the premiums captured along the way. These premiums constantly reduced the cost basis of the stock in case it should have been acquired.

When should a roll be done? It is not important to even consider rolling the put down in strike price and out in time until there is the certainty that the price will remain below the strike price at expiration. If the roll is done too early and the shares advance above the strike price, it was a wasted effort. Ideally the roll is done very near the expiration date. Near the expiration date there is negligible time value, and little time remains for the shares to rally above the strike price. As a practical matter, most professional put sellers role on the last trading day of the option's life. This last trading day is the third Friday of the option expiration month.

> As a general rule, the current month's put is rolled out one month and the strike is lowered one or more strike prices. The goal of a roll is to generate the same premium income from selling the new put as was paid to buy back and thus close out the current put with its strike higher than the current market price of the shares.

For example, on option expiration day, with the shares trading at 44, our 50 strike put will have an intrinsic value of $600 and no time value. We buy to close the current 50 strike put and sell the next month's 45 put. For each put we buy to close, we sell one new put one month out and at a lower strike. Hopefully the premium received from the new sale will approximate the premium paid to close the losing put. If the premium on the new 45 strike put is far lower than the premium on the current 50 put, there are two alternative roll strategies. The first is to roll out a month, but keep the strike price the same as the old put. Thus we would buy to close one current 50 put and sell one new 50 put that expires the next month. In this way we will certainly have a positive cash transaction because the premium on a future month put at an identical strike will always, because of time value, trade at a higher price than the current month's put. This approach works best where significant upward price momentum is anticipated in the very near future. Additionally there is positive cash generated from the roll. The second strategy still involves going out one month and down at least one strike price, but "doubling up." More later expiration, lower strike puts are sold than the number being closed out. Overall, risk is increases because the number of new puts being originated (sold) exceeds the number being closed out. Yet this risk is partly offset because the new puts have lower strike prices. Because the original put was sold on a great company and one whose shares were an appropriate purchase, and assuming the company's fundamentals have not changed, risking buying more shares of this great firm at the lower price should be viewed as an opportunity, not a risk. There is risk only if the put seller lacks the financial capability of buying the increased number of shares. Thus if buying power is not a constraint, "doubling up" is a very useful tool, especially so since doubling up can continue until such time as the stock actually rises above the new and lower strike price. Stocks of great companies do not go to zero and have major price bounces even if the market is currently in a major downturn. Having the financial ability to double up when necessary to keep positive roll cash, enough rolls, or a stock bounce, will eventually bail the put seller out by having a strike price lower than the stock price at expiration.

5.4.4 SUMMARY

Selling puts is an ideal investment strategy. Premium income is earned from the put sale. The capital requirement is low allowing for a large ROI. If stock is acquired through the exercise of the put, its net cost is always lower than the price existing in the market when the put was originally sold. And the stock purchase will be at a later date allowing the funds to be employed elsewhere at interest until needed.

Selling puts is a can't lose technique when compared with the immediate purchase of shares. The purchased stock always has a lower cost basis.

The risks result from buying shares that have dropped precipitously. But even in such cases, the buy price as adjusted for the receipt of the premium is always less than the market price at the time the put was sold.

Some simple but "must follow" rules for selling puts:

* Only sell puts on great stocks expected to rise.

* Never sell more puts than you have funds available to purchase the stock if put (sold) to you.

* Constantly monitor your portfolio, weeding out the weakest stocks acquired throught put exercise.

5.5   STRADDLE-TYPE STRATEGIES

5.5.1   BUY STRADDLES—NEVER HAVING TO PREDICT THE DIRECTION OF THE MARKET

In over four decades of trading stocks and options, there is one thing we have learned and relearned numerous times: *It is very difficult to predict the direction of the market as a whole or for a single stock.*

Predicting that a great stock like Cisco, Microsoft, AOL-Time Warner, Qualcomm, Yahoo and the like will be trading higher in price several years into the future than it is today is not too difficult. Had you made that statement in 2000 looking out to 2003, in most cases it would have been incorrect.

FIGURE 63

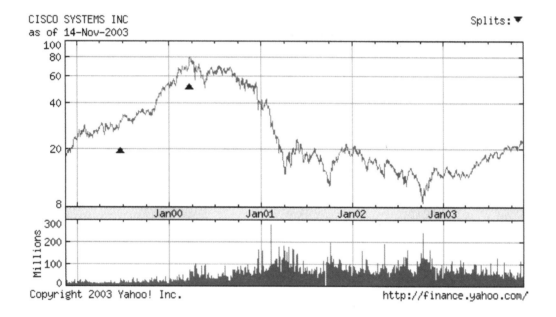

153

FIGURE 64

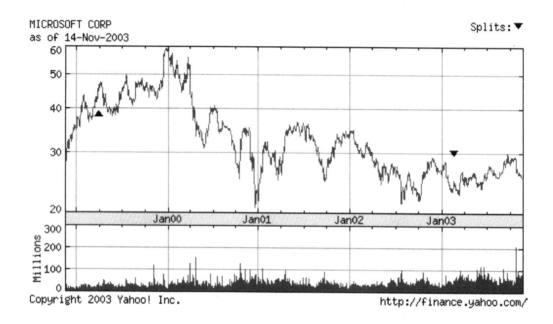

FIGURE 65

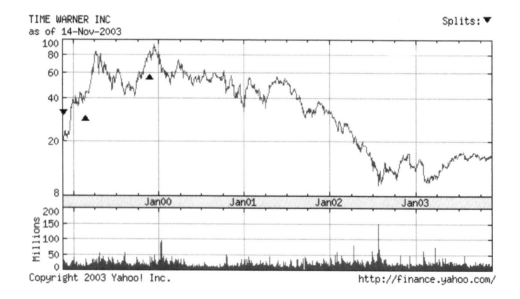

FIGURE 66

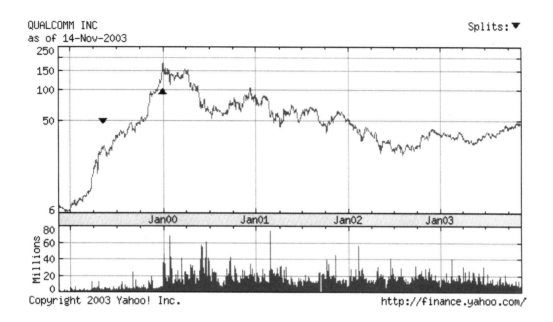

FIGURE 67

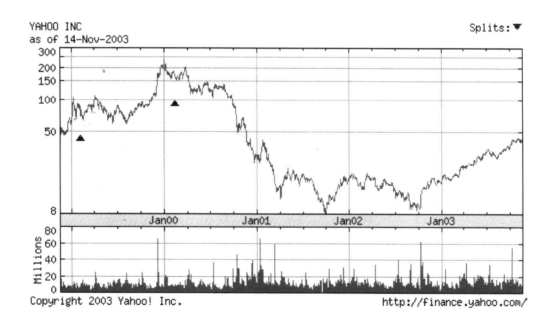

But very long term general price trend predictions for horizons of 10 to 20 years is not hard. Numerous academic studies have all arrived at the same conclusion: Over many years stocks have had an upward bias with large cap stocks gaining approximately 10% per year, with small and medium cap shares rising an annual 13%. Knowing the general trend over the next 10 or 20 years does not help the trader at all. Unfortunately forecasting where the entire stock market or a certain stock will be trading 30, 60 or 90 days in the future is difficult at best and frequently impossible.

We are not talking about accurately forecasting an exact price at a future point in time, or even an approximate price. We are speaking of correctly guessing a very basic fact: Will the shares be trading higher or lower than today's price? Even accurately predicting the short-term price direction – up or down – is defeating. We are certainly not subscribers to the pure Random Walk Theories of market behavior, but we concede that accurate short-term price projections or even predicting the direction of movement is normally rather art than science.

Having concluded near-term price forecasting needs some luck, what is an unlucky trader to do? He can choose from two different solutions, either he engages in a reactive-type trading strategy (like point-and-figure) or he follows our advice and starts to use straddles, which is the subject of this chapter, which moreover gives a clear explanation of our favorite strategy.

THE REASON FOR TRADING STRADDLES

The reason for trading straddles is as follows: Although we may have no idea whether a certain stock will be trading higher or lower at a future point in time, it is relatively easy to predict volatility or price-swings.

A stock, that in the last month had a price swing of 20 points from its high to low price and the month before 18 points and the month before that 21 points, can be projected to continue to have wide price swings in the range of 20 points. It is impossible to know exactly where the price may be a month from now, or even if it will be higher or lower. Yet we can draw one conclusion. The probabilities are that the shares will trade somewhere between 20 points higher than the current price to 20 points lower. It is highly unlikely for the shares to trade at both extremes, because to do so would double their recent volatility. Their outside price range can be expected not to exceed either of these extreme levels.

> When a straddle is purchased, the buyer is not betting on the direction of the price movement, but only on the expectation that the price is likely to have significant movement.

5.5.1.1 STRADDLE DEFINED

A straddle is a combination of a put and a call on the same stock, both with the same strike price and the same maturity. A buy straddle would be a straddle purchased for the premium of the put and the premium of the call.

> Straddle: Same number of contracts of calls and puts with identical underlying, strike price and maturity.

For example, in June 2003 a one month straddle is purchased on Genentech (DNA) with a strike price of 70. That means that a one month call is purchased on DNA with a strike price of 70, and a one month put with a 70 strike price is also purchased. If the call costs 4 points ($400) and the put costs 3 points ($300), the straddle costs a total of 7 points ($700).

FIGURE 68: DNA LONG STRADDLE

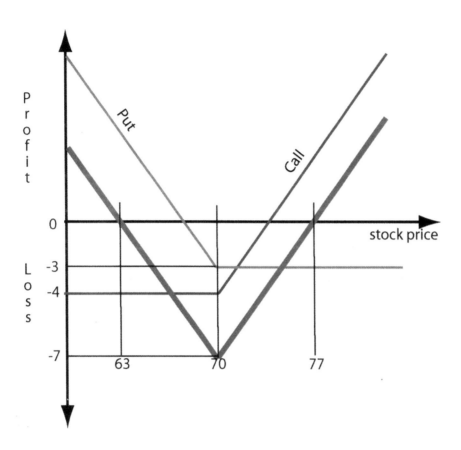

On the above payoff diagram the call, the put and the straddle - thick line – are drawn. The break-even points for this straddle are 63 and 77, which is the strike plus/minus the cost for the two options that totals 7. Therefore, if the stock price does not move outside the break-even points, that is above 77 or below 63 until expiration, the position is a loss, which can clearly be seen by the thick line being situated below the horizontal break-even line. If the stock, hopefully, moves outside the 63-77 range the position generates a profit.

To be a straddle, the put (green line in the above figure) and call (blue line in the above figure) need not be purchased at the same time. A straddle exists even if not acquired as a straddle. The only requirement is that the trader owns both a put and a call on the same stock and both the put and the call have identical expiration dates and strike prices.

How and when the two sides were purchased is not important. Until both are owned, no straddle exists. Even when both a put and a call with the same strike price and expiration date are owned, and a straddle exists, the brokerage account statement will simply show a put and a separate call, for both the put and the call are separate option contracts and not linked in any way.

> Owning a straddle is a difinitional thing, not a separate option instrument.

As said before, you own a straddle if you own both a put and a call on the same stock and identical strike prices and expiration dates. Each can be purchased at different times and each can be sold, closed out, or exercised independently of the other. The straddle could be purchased as a straddle, by the simultaneous purchase of a put and a call, or the sides could have been bought at different dates. Once owned, the two sides can be treated and traded differently.

In our example of the DNA straddle with a one month put and call at 70 strike prices, if DNA declined to 60, the put could be exercised or sold. After closing out the put, the straddle no longer exists. Only a call remains. The call could also be sold or exercised at a later date if the shares rise above their 70 strike.

> By owning a straddle, the buyer is hoping there will be a major move above the call strike or below the put strike prior to expiration.

The DNA straddle at 70 cost 7 points ($700). The buyer is thus hoping that the stock price will rise above 77 (70 call strike plus the straddle premium of 7 points) or below 63 (70 put strike price less the entire straddle premium of 7 points).

At 77, the straddle buyer can recover the entire straddle premium cost of 7 points by exercising or selling the call.

And at 63, the entire 7 point straddle premium can be recaptured through the exercise or resale of the put.

At 77 or 63, the intrinsic value of one side of the straddle is equal to the entire premium paid for the two sides of the straddle. If one side were sold to close it out, the other side may still have some value and could also be closed out simultaneously for an additional profit, or the straddle buyer could speculate that the stock would reverse in price and the other side would gain in value.

Assume that DNA declined to 63 and the put is resold for at least intrinsic value. The put will always be worth at least intrinsic value, and if time remains, there may also be additional time value over and above intrinsic value. At the point in time when the put is exercised or resold in the market, the call at 70 may have some time value and could also be liquidated.

> The point is that each side of the straddle lives independently and either can be traded, exercised, resold, or held for future price changes independently.

But if the stock fails to reach the break-even price of 63 or 77, a loss would be incurred. Our straddle example cost 7 points ($700). This premium cost is the absolute maximized amount in dollars the straddle buyer can lose even if the stock never moves off the 70 strike price. As the price rises above the strike price of 70 or falls below the 70 strike price, the maximum loss on the straddle transaction is reduced.

If the stock stays exactly at 70, the straddle buyer loses $700.

If it declines only to 66 at maturity of the contracts, the put is worth $300 in intrinsic value and the call is worthless. The straddle buyer sells the put for the intrinsic value of $300, and in so doing recaptures $300 of the $700 straddle cost, which yields a transaction loss of $400.

If the stock has declined to 64, the put is worth $600, the call is worthless, and there is a $600 recapture of the $700 cost for a loss of only $100.

At a share price of 63, break-even has been achieved, the put is resold for $700, fully returning the straddle's entire cost (ignoring the commissions to buy the straddle and resell the put), and no money is made or lost on the straddle purchase.

Similarly, if the shares have risen to 73, the call is worth an intrinsic $33, so the net straddle loss is $400 (straddle cost of $700, less the recapture of $300 through the sale of the call). At a price of 76 for the shares, there is a $600 recapture resulting in a $100 loss. And at 77 for the shares, there is a break-even.

Once the price reaches either the upper or lower break-even price (the straddle premium cost of 7 points added to the strike price (70) of the call giving an upper break-even of 77, and subtracted from the 70 strike prices of the put giving a lower break even of 63), the entire straddle premium can be recovered through the resale of the side of the straddle reaching the break-even price.

If the price reaches the break-even level quickly with a long time remaining until expiration, there will likely be time value remaining on the call and on the put. Had a 2 month straddle been purchased for a premium of 7 and a strike price of 70, and had the stock within 2 days of the straddle purchase risen to 77, the call would be worth the intrinsic value of $700 plus a time value of $200 (time values are estimates in this example) and the put would have no intrinsic value but a time value of $100.

In such a case, the straddle would be valued at $1,000, even though the shares are only at the break-even level. Thus when the shares reach the break-even price on the upside or downside, the straddle value will always be worth at least the cost of the straddle, and in many cases worth more if significant time remains until expiration to provide some time value.

Therefore the break-even price levels as calculated by adding the straddle premium cost to the strike price of the call and subtracting that same straddle premium from the strike price of the put, represent the maximum amount the share price has to reach to break-even. Break-even likely occurs at a share price even closer to the strike price than the full straddle premium added to the call and subtracted from the put strikes.

As the price moves beyond the break-even level, profits are earned.

If the price rose to 80, the 70 strike call would be sold for at least the 10 point intrinsic value, yielding a 3 point profit.

At 85, the call has an intrinsic value of 15 points and the profit on the straddle is 8 points.

At 90, the call is worth at least 20 points and the profit is 13 points ($1,300).

If the shares declined to 60, there would be a 10-point intrinsic value on the put for a 3-point profit on the straddle.

At 55, the value of the 70 put is at least 15 points, providing an 8-point profit.

5.5.1.2 WHAT DRIVES THE PRICE OF A STRADDLE

The price of the straddle depends on the same parameters as any call or put, that is: stock price, volatility, risk free rate and expiration. The two most intriguing parameters, though, are stock price and volatility, as they do not influence the straddle in a linear way. The following figures should give you a feeling of the influence of stock price and volatility on the price of the straddle. On the first, you see the stock price and the price of the theoretical 1 month straddle. The price oscillates between 1.70 and 3.70. On the second figure, you see the stock price and the volatility. The reason the straddle did not become more expensive during the up move of Yahoo is that the volatility decreased substantially.

FIGURE 69: YAHOO STOCK AND STRADDLE VALUE

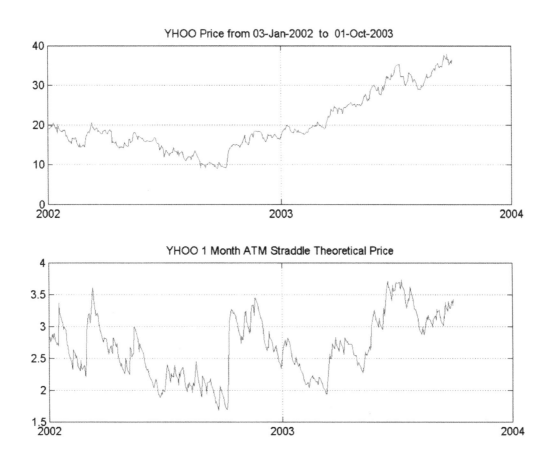

In the above graphic we see the price of a 22 day straddle over time below the actual chart of the price movement of the underlying. It is obvious that there is no linear relationship between the two. The explanation is volatility which is depicted in the next figure.

FIGURE 70: YAHOO STOCK PRICE AND VOLATILITY

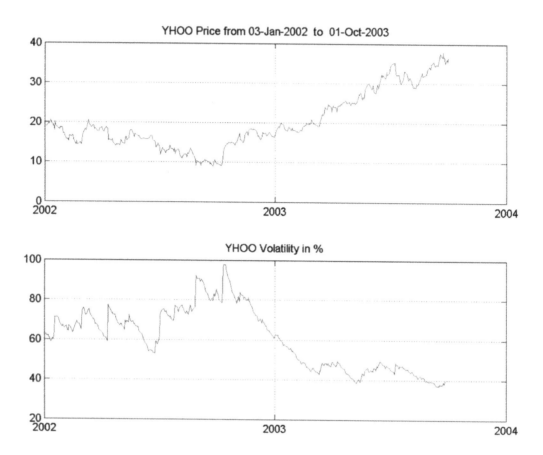

The massive drop in volatility is the reason why the Yahoo straddles were not more expensive at a stock price level of 20 than at a level of 40.

5.5.1.3 PAY-OFF DIAGRAM OF A STRADDLES, BOTH LONG AND SHORT

> Short positions are mirror images of long positions.

The long straddle looks like a V and the short straddle like an A. The peak is situated at the strike. It is obvious from the graphic that the worst outcome is when the option expires at the level of that strike. We have also indicated two scenarios, a sharp drop (A) and a moderate rise (B) in stock price. You can see on the Long Straddle payoff diagram that A is outside the break-even point – that is where the blue line crosses the red line – and therefore a profit is generated.

FIGURE 71

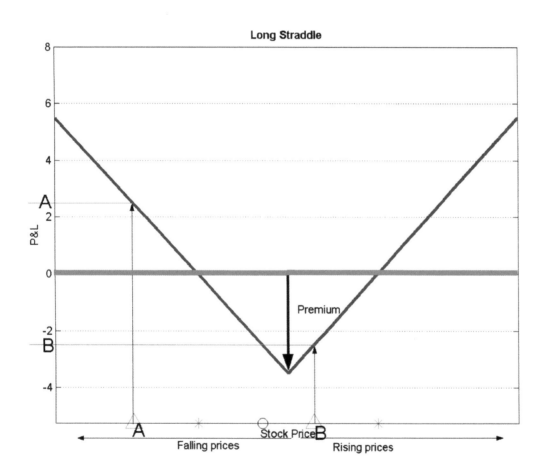

On this typical payoff diagram – that we have explained in detail earlier – you find some additional symbols. The circle (last stock price), the asterisk (break-even points) and triangle (recent stock price range). These symbols are included, because we have taken the graphic directly from our straddle screening program and we did not bother to eliminate them, trusting that they would not confuse the reader if explained properly.

On the following Short Straddle payoff diagram, you see that the sharp drop creates the loss and the moderate rise the profit. This is what you can expect of opposite positions.

FIGURE 72

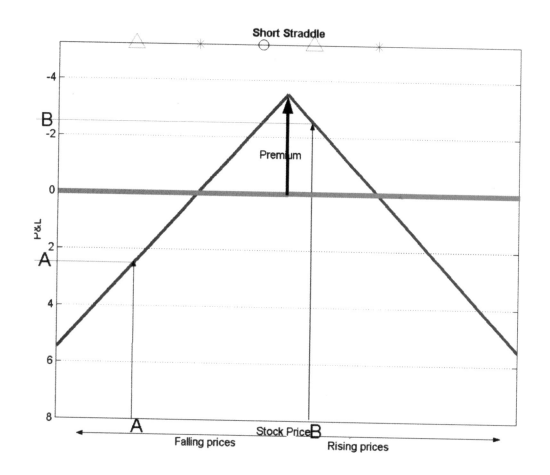

The idea of buying the straddle is to pay premium and hope for big moves. Selling straddle is the opposite, cashing in premium and hoping for small moves, in order to keep most of the premium.

This becomes really evident with the payoff diagrams. As the share price moves away from the strike price, the potential profit from the writing of a straddle is reduced. When the share price is exactly at the strike price, the maximum profit is possible. When the share price is at either the upper or lower break-even level, the writer has neither a profit nor a loss. When the share price crosses above the upper break-even point or below the lower break-even point, the writing of the straddle moves into a loss position.

5.5.1.4   MOTIVATION FOR BUYING STRADDLES

There are two prime motivations for buying a straddle. First, the straddle buyer need not predict the direction of future price movement.

The second justification is that market timing can be eliminated. A straddle buyer need never worry about when the big move will occur. The move must simply happen at some point during the broad time span as defined by the life of the straddle.

In the rank order scheme of investment predictions, correctly judging volatility is easy as compared with the difficulty of guessing direction.

If an investor has the absolute conviction the stock is going to have a major move, and he has a broad estimate of the timing of the move, yet is unsure of the direction of this move, straddle buying might be an ideal investment strategy.

But before investing the money to buy a straddle, gauge the straddle premium cost in comparison with the anticipated move in the underlying stock. The purchase of a straddle can only be justified if its cost is a small percentage of the projected movement. In a later section we will provide specific guidelines as to the appropriate amounts to pay for a straddle.

5.5.1.5   PRACTICAL LESSONS IN BUYING STRADDLES

Success in straddle buying depends on following a few simple rules.

1. BUY DOUBLE THE TIME. Be conservative. Always analyze the recent historical price action of the stock and pay only a small percentage of the spread between the high and low price of the stock for a time period equal to half of the time being purchased.

If you plan to buy a 3-month straddle, carefully examine the spread for the underlying stock for a six-week period and then only pay a small percentage of the spread. We analyze a short time period for price movement and then buy twice that time amount in order to assure ourselves that even if volatility diminishes, we have doubled the time for the price to move by the desired amount.

Had we observed a high of 160 and a low of 120 for the 6 weeks and thus a 40 point spread, by buying a 3 month straddle we have allowed twice the observed time for the stock to again move 40 points.

Thus even if the price fluctuations are halved, the purchase of double the time period will permit enough movement in the shares to bring profit.

2. PAY VERY LITTLE. Once we know the probable price movement for our option time period through observing the spread for a historical period half as long as the time being purchased, we must be careful not to over-pay. Ideally we would pay no more than one-third of the historical spread.

Assume that the 6-week spread was 40 points (high of 160 and a low of 120). By buying twice the time, we can reasonably expect to have at least the same gross spread. In the worst-case scenario half of the future movement would be above and half below our straddle strike price.

If the straddle has a 150 strike, it is logical to expect the high for the range will be 150 plus half the 40 point spread for a high or 170 and the low to be 150 minus half of the 40 point spread or 130.

It would be wonderful if all of the 40-point price action was above or all was below the strike price, yet a conservative posture should prevail and we must expect the worst – that half is above and half is below the strike.

If we pay only one-third of the 40 point spread, or $1,334 ($4000 divided by 3), we can earn a profit on the call side of the straddle when the stock hits the worst case scenario high of only 170 and can also profit on the put side when its price declines to its worst case scenario low of 130.

Even if we fail to hit the exact high or the exact low, there is enough cushion that we can still profit. If the full spread is on one side of the strike price, timing the exit of the winning side is simplified and a healthy profit is earned.

3. HIGH CONSISTENT VOLATILITY IS A KEY. Some story stocks become extremely volatile for a short time period pending an announcement, in anticipation of being acquired, with the expectation of a split, or for some other one-time occurrence. In such cases the shares quickly transition from having low volatility to having high volatility and just as quickly revert back to their traditional pattern of volatility.

Buying a straddle on the story stock during the peak of its price action will require paying up for the straddle based upon recent and unsustainable price movements. When its action settles down and reverts to the norm, the straddle buyer is holding an over-priced straddle in relationship to the traditional level of price movement. The ideal straddle purchase candidate is on a stock that consistently has large price fluctuations, and where there is no reason to expect that volatility will be smaller in the future than has been the norm.

Alternatively, it is an intelligent play to buy a straddle on a low volatile stock as long as the premium cost of the straddle is a very low percentage of the traditional low spread, and volatility expansion is a reasonable projection.

4. STAY SHORT TERM. Volatility is normally non-directional and usually non-cumulative. A stock may have a 40 point range every 6 weeks, yet for an entire year may only have had a 60 point spread. Stocks also have an upward price bias over time, with small cap growth stocks averaging 13% per year and large cap stocks averaging 10% annually. For these reasons, it is usually prudent to purchase shorter term straddles in the one to three month range. They have sufficient time to capture normal volatility without costing extra premium for unneeded time.

REDUCING STRADDLE COSTS

Having purchased a straddle for a price that is low in relationship to historical volatility for a period half the time period of the option life, the premium cost of the straddle can be reduced further and in this way magnify the profit potential of the trade.

The premium on the straddle is reduced if a covered call is sold against the call side of the straddle and a covered put is sold against the put side of the straddle. The premiums received by selling the covered call and covered put effectively reduce the straddle buyer's premium investment.

Assume that a 3 month 150 strike straddle was purchased for $1,600. The break-even point for the straddle buyer is calculated by adding the total premium paid to the strike price and subtracting the total premium cost from the strike price. The break-even price is 150 plus 16 (166) and 150 minus 16 (134). We also know historical volatility (price range) is 40 points per month and this range is expected to fall half above and half below the strike price.

Adding and subtracting half of the spread from the strike price yields the minimum price levels likely to be reached by the stock. Knowing the break-even price and the minimum anticipated move on either side of the current strike price of the straddle, we could sell a covered call well above the upper price band and sell a put well below the lower band.

If we sold a one month 180 call for 1 point and a one month 120 put for 1 point, we would generate 2 points, which reduces the premium paid by $200. The straddle therefore costs a net of $1,400 ($1,600 straddle cost less the $200 premiums received for selling the covered put and covered call).

Since both the call and the put being sold are covered, there is no additional market money required on the transaction. The premium earned for the sales of the covered options lowers the premium cost of the straddle.

Because we own a 3 month straddle and have sold the one month covered call and put, the sale could be repeated two additional times, generating further premium income and thereby reducing the out-of-pocket cost of the straddle purchase even more.

If the strike price of either the covered call or the covered put is reached, the side being hit could be repurchased and in this way totally eliminate the exposure on the covered side. Or the covered contract could be allowed to be exercised. Regardless of which strategy is employed, the straddle buyer has a healthy profit on the straddle, for both the covered put and the covered call have been sold with strike prices well away from the break-even level of the straddle.

The covered call was sold with a strike of 180 and the covered put with a 120 strike. The break-even levels for the straddle were 150 strike plus the 16 premium cost or 166, and the 150 strike less the straddle premium of 16 or 134. Because the covered put and covered call sales have generated a premium income of $200 (1 point for each), the break-even level is reduced from the 166 and 134 levels to 164 and 136 ($1,600 straddle cost less the premiums earned from the sale of the covered call and covered put).

Had the stock risen to the 180 strike price of the covered call, the call side of the straddle would be worth the intrinsic value of 30 and the covered call would have a zero intrinsic value. Thus the straddle buyer has a profit of $1,600 ($3,000 intrinsic value less the straddle cost of $1,600 less the $200 of premiums earned from the sale of the covered put and covered call).

As the stock continues to rise in price above the strike of the covered call or fall below the strike of the covered put, the profit position remains at its maximum level.

If the stock goes up to 220, the straddle call is worth 70 (220 market price less the 150 strike price of the call portion of the straddle), the covered call with its 180 strike price is worth 40 (220 market price less the 180 strike price of the covered call) and the total profit is still the 30 points less the straddle cost of $1,400 (straddle cost of $1,600 less the $200 in premiums earned from the sale of the covered call and covered put) for a net profit of $1,600.

No matter how high the shares rise in price or fall in value, the profit remains the same on the straddle once the strike of the covered put or covered call is hit. Additionally, this profit is the maximum possible profit on the long straddle, covered put and covered call combination.

By selling the covered put and covered call, the straddle's break-even level is adjusted to prices closer to the strike prices of the straddle's put and call, and the profit potential of the straddle purchase is capped. If the covered options had not been sold, the straddle buyer would have a greater profit potential, yet would require a larger price rise or decline in the share price to reach break-even.

As a practical trading strategy we often sell a covered put and a covered call against the straddle to lower the break-even level of the straddle. But the strikes of the covered contracts are at such distant strike prices from the straddle as to yield a large straddle profit should one or the other be hit. The covered put and covered call are sold with strikes not only assuring a straddle profit if hit, but also at levels extremely unlikely to be reached. The ideal price level of the covered contracts is slightly higher in the case of the covered call and slightly lower for the covered put than the likely magnitude of the maximum move, but close to the level of the maximum move.

If covered options are sold with strikes too close to the straddle strikes, one of them will be hit. The selling premium for the covered put and call are larger, but the cap on the straddle profit is minimized. If the covered contracts are sold with more distance strike prices, the premiums earned are lower, yet the straddle profit potential is larger. If the strikes are too far away, the premium received is minimal, which provides little benefit to the straddle buyer. So why bother to cap the straddle potential in any manner for only minuscule premium receipts?

5.5.2 SELLING STRADDLES—PROFITING FROM LOW VOLATILITY AND EARNING TWO PREMIUMS

The preceding chapter dealt with the purchase of straddles whose aim is to avoid having to make directional predictions as to whether the stock will move up or down from its current price level. One of the most difficult things for an investor is to predict the direction of price movements. Gauging the volatility of a security is far easier to judge accurately.

There are often opportunities where a security has historically demonstrated a high degree of volatility (the difference between the stock's high and low price for a time period), and where a straddle can be purchased for a small percentage of the volatility. In such cases it would be logical to purchase the straddle. The straddle being bought should have an at-the-money strike, meaning the strike price of both the put and the call are identical and the strike is that strike price closest to the current price of the underlying share price.

Having purchased the straddle with its premium cost low in relationship to past price movement of the shares, the investor need only patiently wait. Ultimately, and within the option life, the price of the stock should rise significantly above the break-even point of the call or fall dramatically below the break-even point of the put. The break-even points are calculated by adding the entire premium cost of the straddle to the strike price of the call (upper break-even point) and subtracting the full premium cost of the straddle from the strike price of the put (lower break-even point).

We only want to purchase straddles that are cheap, straddles whose premium costs are low in comparison to their historical volatility. For a straddle to be inexpensive, its premium cost should only be a small percentage of the recent price range of the stock.

As an example of a cheap straddle, let's consider a stock currently trading at 50. Over the last 30 days, this stock has had a high price of 60 and a low price of 40. Its shares therefore have a 30-day volatility of 20 (high price of 60 minus the low price of 40).

If a 60 day straddle with a 50 strike price can be purchased for six points, it should be bought. The life of the straddle is twice the time period producing the 20 point volatility, and the straddle costs only 30% of the volatility (price range). The purchase of this straddle should prove a highly profitable trade.

The straddle is cheap in relationship to past historical volatility (price range of the shares). The straddle has a break-even price of 56 on the upside (adding the straddle cost of 6 to the 50 strike price of the call). The break-even on the downside is 44 (subtracting the 6 point straddle cost from the 50 strike of the put). Additionally the straddle has 60 days of life, while the volatility was calculated for only 30 days. It is reasonable to expect that in the next 60 days the shares will move at least as much as they did in the last 30. We can logically anticipate that the shares will have a price range of at least 20 points because they have consistently had 20 point monthly swings in price in the past.

Assuming the worst case scenario, the future price range (20 points) is exactly centered on 50. This means half of the range is above 50 and half is below. The shares would therefore have a peak of 60 and a low of 40. With the break-even points of the straddle being 56 and 44, both the peak and low prices yield profits on the straddle if the buyer is agile enough to exercise both sides (the put and the call).

More likely, the price range over the next 60 days will be more to one side or the other of the 50 straddle strike price. That is, most likely more of the future price action will be above the 50 strike or below it as opposed to being equally centered on both sides of the strike.

From the straddle buyer's standpoint, the most profitable case is for the entire future 20 point move to be either above or below the strike. If all of the range is above 50, the price will have a peak of 70. If all of the range is below the 50 strike, the low price will be 30. In either case a large profit will accrue through the sale or exercise of one side of the straddle.

5.5.2.1 SELLING OVER-PRICED STRADDLES FOR INCOME

Unfortunately, straddles are not always cheap. Thus they are not always good purchases. Straddles can, and often do, have premium costs representing a high percentage of volatility. Such over-priced straddles should not be purchased. They should be sold.

Let us refer back to the 60 day straddle in our prior example. The shares were trading at 50 and they had a 20 point average monthly historical price range. If the straddle cost $600, it was cheap and should have been bought. But what if it had cost $1,800? At $1,800 the straddle is expensive.

Overly expensive straddles should not be purchased. The future price action of the shares will trade in too narrow a range for the straddle buyer to profit. It is unlikely the share price for the overpriced straddle will reach or exceed the upper or lower break-even levels. Why? Because the high premium cost to buy the straddle places the break-even levels beyond the reasonable reach of the price swings.

With a total straddle premium cost of $1,800, the break-even levels are not the 56 and 44 as was the case for the straddle costing $600. Instead they are 68 and 32 (the $1,800 premium added to the call strike price or 50 and subtracted from the put strike price of 50). The 20 point probable move, as estimated from average historical price ranges of the shares, will place the maximum level of the rise at 70 and the low of 30. One of these extreme prices will be achieved if and only if all of the 20 point range is on one side of the strike price.

Let's consider the more normal event. The 20 point future price range is equally distributed on both sides of the current market price (50) of the shares. This means the maximum share price is 60 and the minimum is 40. The stock still has the 20 point price range, yet 50% is above and 50% below the current price of 50 for the shares. If the stock never moves beyond one of the break-even levels of the straddle, the straddle buyer cannot make a profit. But the writer of the straddle did profit.

If the straddle is expensive, meaning the straddle premium is a high percentage of the historical range, it should not be bought. A trader should reject the purchase of over-priced straddles. Yet this same over-priced straddle would be an appropriate candidate for a short sale (writing).

Selling an over-priced straddle would earn the writer two premiums, a premium from writing (selling) the put and the premium from writing the call. Because for over-priced straddles the premiums are high when compared with historical volatility (price ranges), it is unlikely that during the option life of the share the price will rise above the upper break-even level (strike price of the call plus the premium received from selling the straddle) or below the lower break-even (strike price of the put less the premium received from selling the straddle).

The maximum profit the straddle writer can make is limited to the total straddle premium received. The premiums from the writing (sale) of both the put and the call are immediately credited to the writer's account. If the stock trades at exactly the strike price of the straddle, the full premium becomes profit. As the share price rises above the call strike or falls below the put strike, the straddle seller incurs a reduction of the potential profit. When the share price reaches the break-even level, the entire premium received has been surrendered and if the share price crosses above the upper break-even point or below the lower break-even point, the writing of the straddle moves into a loss position.

Again consider our example of the 50 strike straddle with a premium of $1,800. If at the end of the option life the stock closes at exactly 50, the full $1,800 received is profit because both the put and the call expire unexercised.

Had the stock risen to 60, and remained at 60 at expiration, the call would need to be repurchased to eliminate the seller's obligation. To buy back the in-the-money call would cost the straddle writer the intrinsic value (10) of the call (60 market price of the stock less the 50 strike price of the call). The put would expire unexercised. Having received $1,800 from the straddle sale, and having had to buy back the call at the intrinsic value of 10 ($1,000), the writer has made a net profit on the entire transaction of $800 (total premiums received less the amount paid to repurchase the in-the-money side of the straddle).

If the stock was 63 at expiration, the 50 strike call would have an intrinsic value of 13. The net profit on the selling of the straddle would thus be $500 (total premiums received of $1,800 less the $1,300 repurchase cost of the in-the-money call).

Rather than rising, assume the shares declined. If they were trading at 42 at expiration, the put would be bought back for its intrinsic value of 8 or $800 (put strike price of 50 less the market price of 42 for the shares). The call would expire. Having received $1,800 from the straddle sale and having to give back $800 to repurchase the in-the-money put would result in the straddle writer making $1,000 on the transaction.

If the shares had declined to 37, the put would have been closed out (repurchased) for 13 points ($1,300) and the seller would have made $500.

The reason to sell a straddle is to earn two premiums, one for selling the put and the other for selling the call. The ideal straddle to write (sell) is one whose premiums are high in comparison to the price volatility of the stock. In the case of selling over-priced straddles, a significant amount of premium cash is received and there is a low probability the share price will move enough to require giving all of the total premium back through the repurchase of the side of the straddle which is in-the-money on the option expiration date. A straddle seller always attempts to collect more premium cash than required to give back. The net positive cash at expiration is the profit on the transaction.

This net profit is always the total of premiums received for selling the straddle, less any money paid to repurchase the in-the-money side.

5.5.2.2 SELLING STRADDLES FOR MARGIN LEVERAGE

There is an additional justification for selling a straddle (combination of a put and a call) compared with selling only one side, writing either the put or the call. A writer of an uncovered (naked) option, whether a put or a call, must deposit margin with the broker to assure the broker the obligation will be met. The minimum margin to sell a naked option is normally set at the greater of A) 10% of the current stock value (100 shares of stock times its current market price) or B) 20% of the current stock value, minus the points out-of-the-money, plus the premium received. Therefore, the minimum amount required to be deposited is never less than the 10% of the stock value for 100 shares.

For example, consider the writing of a call for a $200 premium, with a strike of 50, and with the stock currently trading at 45. In this example the call writer must deposit 20% of $4,500 (the current market value of 100 shares of stock), which is $900, less the 5 points ($500) the call is out-of-the-money, plus the premium received ($200). The net to be deposited is thus $600 ($900 less $500 plus $200). The writer need only come up with out-of-pocket $400 because $200 of the required $600 in margin was just paid to the writer as premium.

While the writer of a naked put or call must post a margin on each option sold, the seller of a straddle has an advantage. Even though the straddle writer is selling two contracts, a put and a call, he needs only to post margin on one side of the straddle plus the premium for the option on the other side. The side of the straddle currently in-the-money is the option that must be margined. To this required margin is added the premium value of the option on the other side. The writer of a straddle with strike prices of 50 and with a stock price of 52 would be required to margin the call, plus the premium value of the put.

The net impact of having only to margin one side of the straddle means an option seller can generate twice the premium income on one margin. By posting the required margin on the call (the call is in-the-money) plus the premium on the put, the seller gets a "free margin ride" on the put (the side of the straddle currently out-of-the-money). No margin is required for selling the put side of the straddle other than the premium. And the put premium required to be posted is simply money just received from the sale of the put. No 20% on the put is necessary as margin. In essence, the straddle seller earns two premiums by posting just one margin.

The selling of straddles is a prime example of margin leverage, earning the maximum in premium cash income for the smallest possible margin.

5.5.2.3 NEUTRAL ON THE STOCK – BUY LOW, SELL HIGH

Another interesting straddle writing strategy is to combine the selling of straddles with a neutral opinion on the stock.

A stock is trading at 60. We have no strong convictions on the future price action of the shares. We are therefore neutral on the stock at 60. Should the price rise to 70, we would be bearish on the stock believing it to be over-priced. At 70 we would be a seller of the stock. At 70 we would want to sell any long position we hold and might even go short. At 50 we consider the shares undervalued and representing a terrific purchase level.

The sale of a straddle for $1,000 with a strike price of 60 on the put and call accomplishes the following. It allows us to sell shares at over-priced levels and buy at bargain basement prices. Having received $1,000 in straddle writing premium, and if the stock rises in price, we are in effect selling shares at 70 if the call is exercised, forcing us to deliver 100 shares of stock at the 60 strike price. We would be selling and delivering the stock at the 60 strike of the call. Because we have received a premium of $1,000 for the sale of the straddle, the actual selling price of the stock is the strike price of the call (60) plus the premium of 10, or 70. We have accomplished a major goal, to sell shares at an over inflated price.

Alternatively, assume the stock has declined during the option's life. At expiration the shares are trading below the 60 strike price of the put. As a seller of the straddle, we are obligated to take deliver (purchase) 100 shares of stock at the strike price of the put (60). Having been paid $1,000 (10 points) as a writing premium for the selling of the straddle, the actual cost of the purchased shares is the put strike price (60) less the straddle premium received (10 points). Our stock only cost 50 a share, a price point considered to be a real steal.

When we sell a naked straddle, we are neutral on the current price of the stock. We do not expect a dramatic price move in the shares, either up or down. We are willing to sell shares at higher prices if the call is exercised against us. If the call is exercised because the stock is above the call strike at expiration, we are going short the stock at the call strike price plus the straddle premium received. Additionally, we are committed to buying shares at much lower prices. Should the price decline below the put strike price, we would be put (buy) shares at the put strike price less the premium received from the sale of the straddle. Should the put be exercised, we would buy shares and go long the stock.

The net result is that we earn premiums on the sale of a put and a call (straddle). We end up either selling shares and going short at high prices, or purchasing and going long shares at low prices.

If the straddle is sold naked, the option writer has no position either long or short in the stock. The exercise of the call will involve the straddle writer selling 100 shares of stock at the strike price of the call and in so doing he will create a short position of 100 shares of stock. The exercise of the put will require the straddle writer to buy 100 shares of stock at the strike price of the put. Buying the shares results in the creation of a long position in the shares.

Not always will the investor be flat (neither long nor short) the shares. Often a position is held. Usually a long position.

Assume 100 shares of Qualcomm (QCOM) are held long. The investor is neutral on the stock at its current price of 55. While neutral at 55, he would be delighted to liquidate the 100 shares at 59 within the next 30 days, believing at 59 the shares have over-reached their full price potential. Likewise, in the next month he would love to acquire 100 more shares at a lower price, say 51. An ideal technique when you are neutral on the stock at current price levels, but willing to sell an existing position at higher levels and to buy more shares at a depressed prices scenario, would be to write a straddle.

In the QCOM example, a one month straddle would be written with a strike price of 55. The premium on the straddle is $400. Should the shares rise above 55 in the month, the long position of 100 shares would be sold at an effective price of 59 (55 strike price of the call plus the straddle premium of 4). If the stock declines below the 55 strike price of the put, 100 shares are acquired through the exercise of the put. These new shares are purchased at the 55 strike price less the straddle premium received (4). The cost of the shares bought is 51.

FIGURE 73: QCOM

The key to success in selling straddles when neutral on the stock is the willingness to sell shares at prices higher than they currently trade and both the capability and the desire to buy stock at price levels lower than current quotes. The effective selling price or acquisition price of the shares is measured by the premium received through selling the straddle. The higher the premium paid to the writer of the straddle, the higher the net sale price of shares if the call is exercised, and the lower the buy price of the shares if the put is exercised.

5.5.3 BUY OR SELL THE STRADDLE?

Straddle trading is an exciting option strategy. The use of straddles eliminates the most difficult of all investment predictions, the price direction of future market moves. To succeed in buying and writing straddles, the investor need only to make an informed judgment on the amount or range the price is likely to move (volatility) and compare this anticipated range with the cost of the straddle.

We have already explained the properties of volatility. A stock which has consistently shown extreme volatility in the past is likely to remain volatile in the future and continue to show big moves. A security with limited price movement is probably going to remain in a tight price range.

Beta is one measure of volatility for a security. Beta measures the price volatility of a security against the market as a whole.

A Beta of 1.0 means the shares move at the same speed and in the same direction as the market. If the market advances 5%, the shares should rise the same 5%. If the market declines 3%, the shares should also drop 3%.

A Beta of 2.0 means the stock can be expected to move in the same direction as the market, but move twice as fast as the market.

A Beta of 0.5 reflects a security which will move in the direction of the entire market, but only half as much. If the market advances 8%, the shares of the 0.5 Beta stock will advance only 4%.

The beta for a security tends to remain similar in its values over time. This being so, we can anticipate the future price action of a stock will be like its past price fluctuation actions.

THE FIRST STEP in developing a straddle trade is to determine the likely volatility of the future price movement of the shares. Here we rely heavily on the examination of the degree of price fluctuations of the shares in the recent past. After determining historical volatility or price ranges, we then generally assume the future price action of the shares will be close in characteristics and magnitude to their past. Such analysis provides a reasonably reliable yardstick against which to evaluate a straddle price structure.

THE SECOND STEP, after making the estimate of future price action of the shares, is to decide whether the straddle should be purchased or written (sold). This is done by checking the current option quotes to determine the premium costs of both the put and the call component of the straddle. The premium cost of the straddle (the sum of the put and the call premiums) is then compared with the projected future price action (volatility or price range) of the shares. This comparison will answer the basic question, 'Should the straddle be purchased or sold (written)?' If the premium cost of the straddle is extremely low in comparison with the calculated future volatility (price range) of the stock, the straddle is cheap and should be purchased. If the premium is close in value to the full future price range, the straddle is expensive and should be written (sold).

The deciding factor in determining whether the straddle is cheap and should be purchased, or is expensive and should be written (sold), is the comparative value of the straddle premium in relationship to the future volatility or price range. This sounds simple enough. Cheap straddles are bought. Expensive straddles are sold.

But in real life how do we determine whether the straddle is expensive or cheap? What guidelines should we use to define cheap and expensive? What are the simple tools to be employed in deciding whether the straddle is cheap or expensive?

There are two techniques for evaluating the cheapness or expensiveness of a straddle. Both are straightforward in their approach. Both are simple to use. And both provide highly reliable results.

The first is a Graphical Chart Approach. The second involves a simple mathematical calculation. They can be used together or independently. Both will be explained in detail following the discussion of the half-life concept.

5.5.3.1   HALF LIFE—BUILDING A CONSERVATIVE BIAS INTO THE VOLATILITY PROJECTION

Volatility tends to remain consistent over certain periods of time. A stock that has shown a pattern of being extremely volatile with large daily, weekly and monthly price swings over an extended time period is most likely to continue to show wild price swings. A historically volatile stock is unlikely quickly to become a small mover. If a stock has had normal daily swings of 4 points over the last 3 months, what is the probability of its near term future daily moves being measured in pennies? Pretty low. Likewise, shares that are up a nickel one day and down 7 cents the next, with a 20-cent daily price range being the rarity, are not likely to start swinging 3 or 4 dollars a trading session.

On occasion volatility does change rapidly. Sleepy shares become a hot acquisition candidate. A new drug with huge market potential is discovered. Speculative fervour for the shares abates. But external events and unexpected news that dramatically alter normal volatility are the rarity. In most cases volatility only increases or decreases slowly over time.

Option strategies are all about reducing risk and increasing returns. Because straddle buy and writing decisions and their ultimate profitability are so dependent on the future price range (volatility) of the shares, we want to build a conservative bias into the model.

We add conservatism into the evaluation process by an approach we call half-life. It is assumed the volatility of the stock will be similar in the near term future as it has been in the recent past. But when considering the purchase of a straddle, we want to play it safe. We want to make money even if volatility slows down. If traditional price ranges for the shares are 20 points per month, we want to have a winning position even if the monthly range is halved. Alternatively, we assume it might take twice as much time in the future for the shares to realize the 20 point move. This is the half-life concept.

If we are buying a straddle which is cheap based upon the average historical 20 point monthly price range, as straddle maturity time we want to buy twice the time required in the past for the price to achieve the 20 point range. The straddle purchased would thus have a 2 month life. For we want to give the security twice the future time span to develop the same price range.

To implement this concept, we calculate the average historical price range for a certain increment of time. We then buy twice the time into the future as the unit of measure used historically. Or working in reverse, if we are viewing the purchase of a straddle for a certain period of time, we closely examine the historical price range for half that time unit. If we were examining the buy of a 6 month straddle, we would calculate the stock price range for the past 3 months. If the 3 month price range was sufficient to produce a profit on the straddle given its current premium cost, having a life length of twice the time span magnifies the probability of having the movement necessary to earn a profit.

The half-life rule is simple. Only purchase straddles that are cheap when their premium cost is compared with the price range of the stock over half the historical time period as the life unit of the straddle. If you are buying a one month straddle, examine the range over the last 2 weeks. A premium cost of a 60 day straddle would be measured against the 30 day volatility. A 6 month straddle would be evaluated with the three month price action of the shares. The purchase price of a 2 year leap straddle would only be cheap if its premium cost was a low percentage of the last 12 month price range of the shares.

5.5.3.2   GRAPHIC CHART APPROACH

The best method of determining whether a straddle should be bought or sold is the use of a stock chart. On this chart are drawn two horizontal lines representing the straddle premium cost added to the strike price of the call and subtracted from the strike price of the put. We call these lines break-even lines. These lines are drawn back in time (drawn to the left) equal to approximately half of the life length (half-life concept) of the straddle that is being evaluated.

FIGURE 74: BASIC STRADDLE CHART

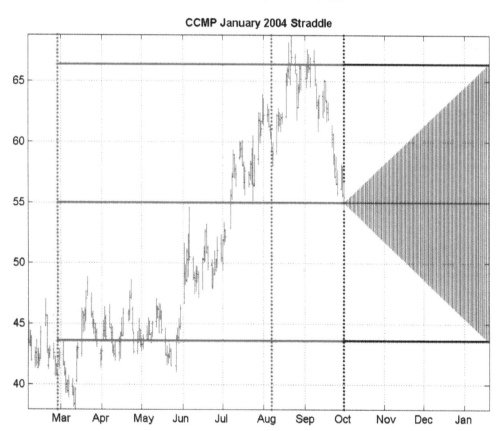

This is the basic chart that we have developed and use with great confidence. The horizontal line in the middle (at 55) is the level of the strike price. The lines above and below are called the break-even lines and are drawn by adding/subtracting the total cost of the straddle. The triangle to the right indicates horizontally the time until expiration and vertically the type of price action required to touch the break-even lines. The red vertical line indicates the half time and the green vertical line the double time.

FIGURE 75: STRADDLE CHART WITH EXPLANATION

This is the type of chart that we use normally to quickly screen potential straddle trades. The chart indicates the half time ('horizontal arrow, '50 %') and the double time (horizontal arrow, '200%'). Moreover it shows the strike level 'StriKe' and by adding the straddle premium ('Spremium') the break-even levels are also drawn. Additionally, two circles on the break-even lines mark the time span in the past that corresponds to the remaining life of the straddle (indicated as 'Exp or 100 %'), useful if you want to engage in positions with a bit more risk. Moreover, to the left this chart indicates the levels calculated by the price range approach - explained in the next chapter.

FIGURE 76: SAME CHART WITHOUT EXPLANATIONS

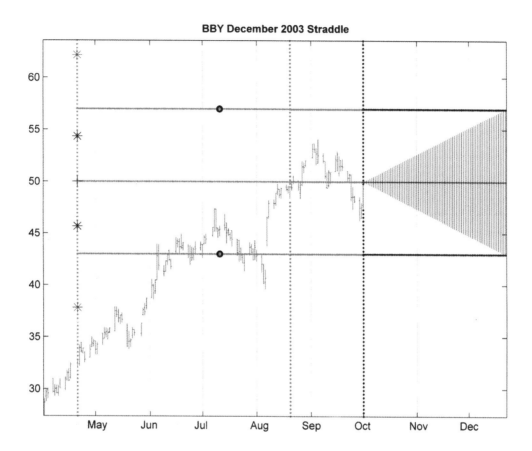

Same chart as above, but without the explanations, which eat up a lot of space and might make the chart look a bit dense. The straddle charts are really straight forward and easy to interpret.

For example, assume a 60 day straddle with its at-the-money strikes of 50 cost $800. The shares currently trade at 52. After securing a price chart (bar chart works best), horizontal lines would be drawn at 58 and at 42. These levels represent the $800 (8 point) straddle premium added to the 50 strike price of the call and subtracted for the 50 strike price of the put. The lines are drawn back in time equal to half of the remaining life duration of the straddle. Because the straddle has 60 days of remaining life, the lines are drawn back, or to the left, 30 days. Going back in time approximately 50% is fine. Accuracy to the exact 50% day is nice, but certainly not required.

First the break-even lines are plotted back for half the straddle life. Then they are drawn forward in time (to the right) to depict the life length of the straddle. In our example, because the straddle matures in 60 days, the lines are taken forward (drawn to the right) 60 days.

The analysis process involves observing two things. First we determine the frequency of (the number of times) the share's historical half-life (time covered by the lines) price action penetrating either or both of the break-even lines. Second we examine the amount of the penetration of the break-even lines (distance beyond a line the price moves).

In regard to the frequency of the price action reaching the break-even lines, repeated crossing of the drawn lines means the share volatility was sufficient to reach break-even levels numerous times. The more often the price reached the break-even lines, the more opportunity the straddle buyer had of at least getting out of the trade without any loss. For the straddle buyer, numerous penetrations of a break-even line or of both break-even lines are good. A failure to reach either break-even line is bad.

FIGURE 77

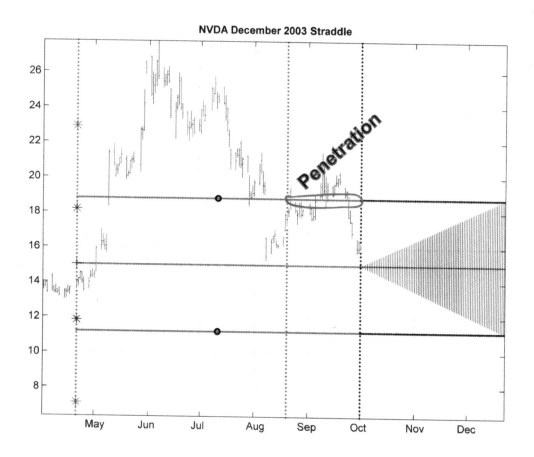

In the above chart of NVIDIA you can see the half-time penetration very clearly. The penetration goes far above the break-even line, to about 21.50. This straddle will therefore be considered a buy. The stock reaches a price of 21 at expiration – December 19th. Therefore the return on that trade has been in the range of 70%.

The second observation, the magnitude of the price move beyond a break-even line, is extremely important. Reaching a break-even line means the straddle buyer can get out even (no gain or loss). But breaking even is not the object of trading options. Making a profit is. Profits are realized when the price rises above the upper break-even line or falls below the lower break-even line. The further the price rises above the upper line or declines below the lower line, the greater is the profit. We therefore want significant moves beyond and outside of a break-even line. The greater the move above or below one of the break-even lines, the more profitable the straddle purchase becomes. The smaller the move beyond the line, the smaller the profit opportunity.

We logically anticipate that future range moves of the stock will be similar to historical moves. Therefore the more times the historical price action took the share price to a break-even line, the more likely the same thing will occur in the future. And the further the price broke through and beyond a break-even line, the more we can expect it do so in the future. Additionally, by examining the price action over a half-life historical time period, and purchasing twice that time span of future time, what worked well in the small increment of past time, has twice the future amount of time to "do its thing."

The decision to purchase a straddle using the Graphical Chart Method is somewhat subjective. Of course we want numerous crossings of the break-even line and major penetrations when a cross does occur. If we have few crossings and minimal moves beyond the line, the straddle should be rejected, for little profit is to be expected. Many break-even line hits but no penetrations would still be a reject decision for the straddle because there was never the chance of making a profit. But what is the right number of line crosses? And how much should the penetration be? The cheaper the straddle premium cost is in relationship to the historical half-life price movement of the stock, the greater the penetration move, and thus the better the straddle is as a purchase. The higher the premium cost of the straddle, the lower the penetration move, and the worse the straddle is as a buy.

It is important to know the facts. The more times the break-even lines are crossed, the better, and the greater the penetration of a line, the better. But unfortunately there are no exact rules as to the optimal number of crossings or the ideal magnitude of the penetration for a straddle to be a perfect buy. Therefore the actual decision is subjective and often intuitive. A straddle buyer must study the chart, observe the number of break-even line crosses, and the distance the price moves after crossing a break-even line, and then decide. It is really not hard to decide. Cases of no penetration are automatically rejected as straddle purchases. Few penetrations with insignificant moves beyond the break-even lines are easy rejects. Lots of penetrations and huge moves beyond the lines yield positive buy recommendations. Even a limited number of penetrations, but penetrations always accompanied by major moves beyond the break-even line, are always buy straddle decisions.

Reasonable numbers of penetrations with reasonable moves beyond the line are cases falling into the ambiguous arena. "Reasonable number" and "reasonable move" require subjective decisions and intuition. Here we have two pieces of advice. First, in these unclear cases "go with your gut reaction." Secondly, if you are a risk taker and have an abundance of capital, buy the straddle. If you avoid risks, or have limited funds, reject these borderline straddles, keeping your powder dry for better and more clearly defined straddle buying opportunities.

Always remember that when utilizing the half-life concept, you will be buying twice the future time period as the length of time being observed. This normally means the better the chart looks as measured by numbers of penetrations and their magnitude of move beyond the break-even lines, the better the actual results will be in trading. Why? Because what worked well in a short time past period has twice the future time to function. This is why we have drawn the break-even lines on the chart to the right and into the future: In order to provide a focal relevance for time perspective. The length of the line to the right is the future time span equal to the straddle life. During this future time period, the stock price can reasonably be expected to have price movement characteristics similar to those realized in the past half-life period (the distance the lines go back in time, to the left) on the chart. Since we have twice the time on our side, even greater movement is a distinct possibility. Once this perspective concept of half-life historical time and full life future time is fully understood, there is no longer the need to draw the lines to the right and into the future. The half-life historical lines as analytical measurement tools are all that will be required to evaluate the straddle effectively and to make a buy or reject decision.

To be successful in buying straddles, it is important that there are numerous half-life break-even line penetrations with some level of movement beyond the line, or alternatively, if few cross, there should be major movement after a penetration of the break-even line.

The straddle seller is looking for exactly the opposite chart pattern. A straddle writer makes money when the share price remains between the upper and lower break even lines. Upon touching a break-even line, the short straddle position is neither a profit nor a loss. As the price moves beyond a line, above the upper break-even line or below the lower break-even line, the position is in a loss posture and further movement beyond the line magnifies the loss. Therefore the straddle writer wants few if any penetrations of the break-even lines. When penetrations do occur, the movement beyond the line should be extremely limited. As the premium cost of the straddle increases, the break-even lines move further from the strike price. The result is a decrease in the number of penetrations and the lessening of the distance of moves beyond the lines. The more the straddle premium has cost, the better the straddle is as a write and the worse it is as a purchase.

A great straddle write is a lousy straddle purchase and a terrible straddle write is a super straddle buy. If a straddle is a great write, why would anyone want to buy it? Or if a straddle is a wonderful buy, why would anyone want to write it? The answer to both questions is they would not. Does this interfere with the sale or purchase of straddles? Absolutely not. Remember a straddle is simply a combination of a put and a call. If a straddle is sold, most likely there are separate buyers of each side of the straddle. Each has different motivations, dreams, fears, goals and uses for the contracts. Likewise, when a straddle is purchased, the put and the call were probably written by different individuals and for different reasons. Seldom are straddles bought and sold as straddles. The norm is for the parts (the put and the call) to be assembled when a straddle is bought and to be sold separately when a straddle is sold.

The traditional half-life concept as explained above works against the straddle writer. In writing a straddle, the trader is selling twice the time as examined for volatility. There is twice the time period for the share price to do hurtful things, having the price cross a break-even line and to keep going. A cross with major penetration might not have occurred in the half-life period, but we are now living with twice as much time.

For straddle selling our recommendation is therefore to modify the half-life concept and thus the Graphical Charting method chart. Basically we reverse the half-life concept to one in which the straddle being sold has the half-life and the chart depicts lines equal in length to the full life. We thus write a straddle for half-life. We are in effect selling a straddle whose life is only half of the historical time analyzed. If you consider the writing of a one month straddle, draw the historical break-even line back in time twice the life of the straddle, or two months. When contemplating a 6 month straddle sale, go back historically a year. Having historical break-even lines twice the buy straddles future life, examine the number and magnitude of the penetrations. If no break-even lines were crossed or if there were only a small number of penetrations, and the penetrations were small, the straddle would be a logical write. Especially since you would be selling only half as much time as you have reviewed in the analysis.

> When looking at the historical chart, if numerous penetrations were depicted and these penetrations were large, reject the straddle sale. Selling straddles have unlimited loss potential, and there is no point in taking a risk that would not have produced a profit in the past.

FIGURE 78: STRADDLE TO SELL

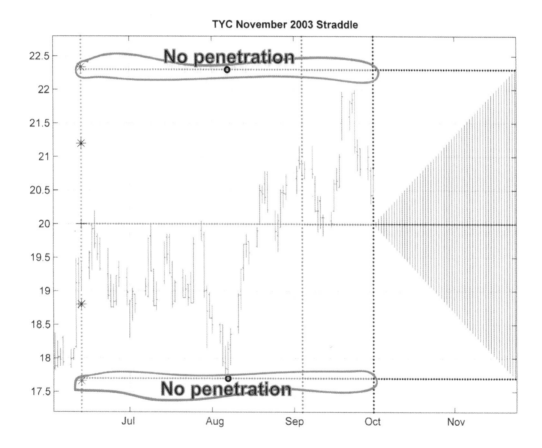

In the above Tyco straddle chart we see that the price has not penetrated the double-life zone. Therefore, we would consider this straddle as a candidate for shorting. The stock closed at 21.57 at expiration, thus the sold straddle resulted in a good profit of about 0.65.

FIGURE 79

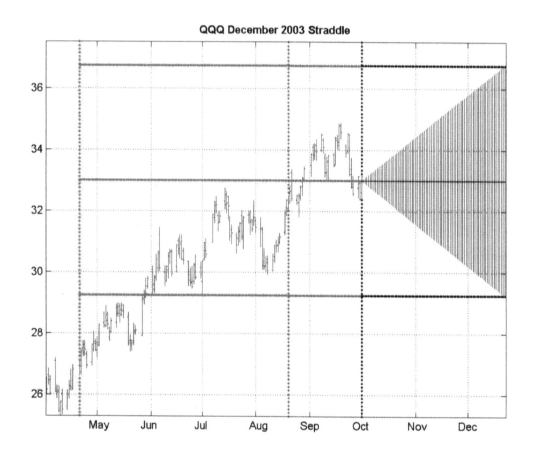

Looking at the QQQ (NASDAQ index) chart we see that the break-even lines are far away from the price movements during the half-time period. We also see that a strong penetration of the double-time has however occurred at the very beginning of that period, namely in May. This might therefore be an aggressive sell, considering that the double-time was only penetrated at the very beginning and that since June the prices have never again touched the break-even lines.

FIGURE 80

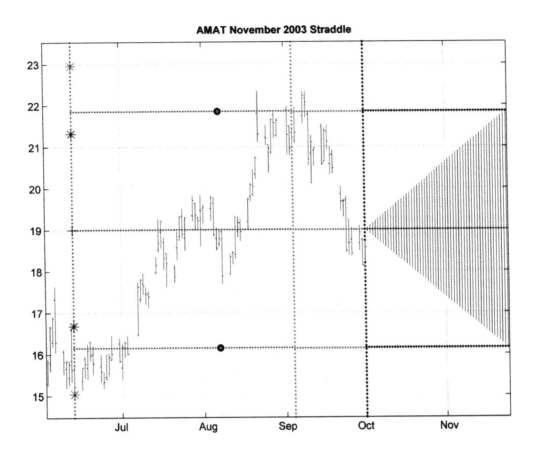

AMAT shows a penetration in the half-time: a buy signal. This position would have made a profit in the range of 40%.

The Graphical charting approach has the advantages of being easy to perform, visually appealing, and logical. By incorporating the half-life concept into the chart, and in so doing giving the straddle buyer the advantage of having twice the time to perform profitably and the straddle seller half the time to fail and lose money, an element of conservatism is built into the analysis. And as the age-old expression goes, "a picture is worth a thousand words." Or taking liberty with the quote, "a chart picture is worth a thousand mathematical equations."

FIGURE 81

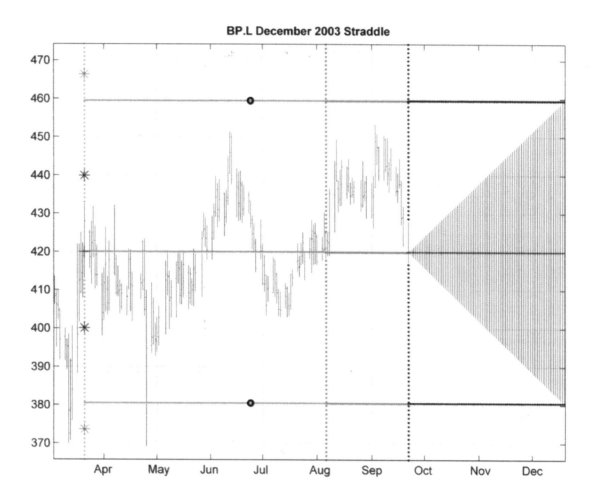

This is BP straddle that we have sold. It shows no penetration of the double-life lines and is therefore an ideal candidate to sell. As the straddle expired with the stock trading around 445, the trade was profitable.

5.5.3.2.1   SOFTENING OF THE DECISION RULES

The following two examples show instances where we have softened the decision rules regarding the sale of a straddle. We do this if the penetrations are to the very left of the chart, or if strong trends are present or if we discard a penetration as a singular move.

However, in both cases, we carefully followed our straddle sell checklist to be assured in our position-taking. As a general rule, we prefer not to take a position than to take one where we are doubtful.

FIGURE 82

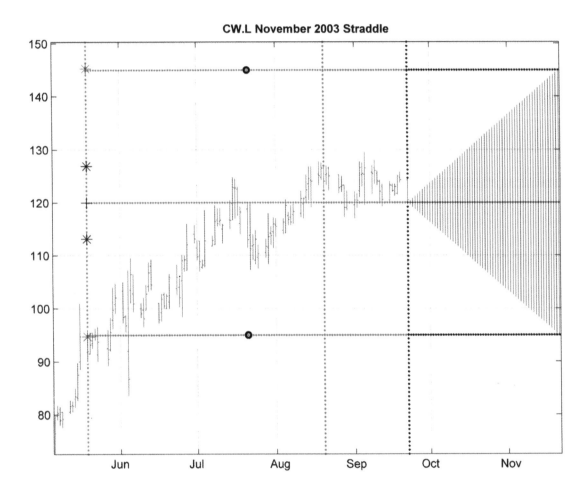

We sold the Cable and Wireless straddle based on the fact that the penetration of the double-life lines was well to the right and that during that penetration a strong upwards trend was present. The expiration happened at 128, generating a nice profit.

FIGURE 83

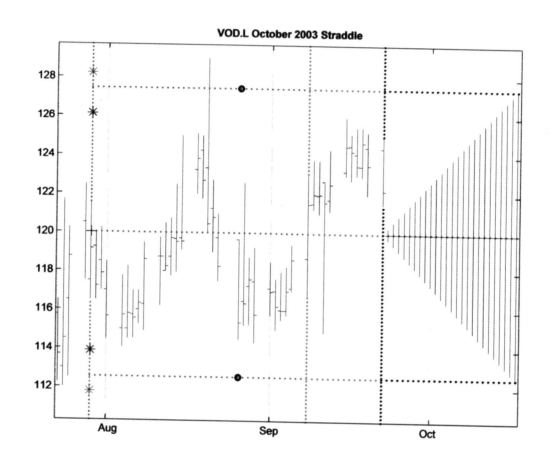

We sold this straddle even though there was a penetration of the double-life levels. However, the penetration looks like a singular movement and it happened before the full-life period, marked by the black dots.

5.5.3.2.2   DOING THE STRADDLE GRAPHIC WITH METASTOCK

MetaStock is a well-known technical analysis package. It is very well suited for creating the type of straddle charts we propose. It works well because it is extremely easy to draw vertical and horizontal lines. So, the first thing you do is draw the chart, then you look up the quotes for the at-the-money call and put, sum both the call ask and put ask price. Then you add to this number the amount of commission you would pay. This number is your straddle break-even.

Then you draw a first horizontal line on the level of the strike; in our example of a Dell January 2004 Straddle, it is set at 32.5. Then we draw horizontal lines above and below with the distance of the straddle break-even. Then we draw the vertical lines, the first at half time, full time and double time. In our example – 20 days from the Jan expiration – we have drawn the lines at 10, 20 and 40.

The following is the screen shot of the result.

FIGURE 84: STRADDLE CHART WITH METASTOCK

We analyze the Dell January 2004 32.50 straddle, using the well-known charting package MetaStock, using the data-downloader Hquote with data from Yahoo and volatility information from Ivolatility. We have used MetaStock's tools to draw the horizontal straddle break-even lines (thick) and the level of the strike (thin) The vertical lines from left to right are: the double time line (thick), time (thin, this line is not strictly necessary), half-time (thick), a thin line that represents today. We see that the stock does not make an important penetration in the half-time, but many in the double time. Doing our homework, according to the check-list, we study whether there is an increase in fundamental information, which is not the case. We check that the volatility is not trading near a 52-week high using the chart below, which is also not the case. Moreover we know that Dell options are very liquid, and concluding from all of this, we would rather buy that straddle. However, as said before, due to the lack of important penetrations, we look for straddles which are more attractive.

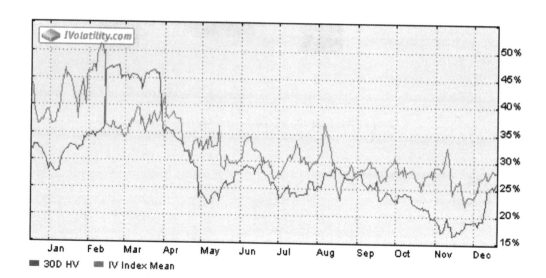

5.5.3.3   PRICE RANGE APPROACH

The alternative to the graphical chart approach is the price range approach. The price range approach is ideally suited for the trader who likes to run optimizations and back-tests and has a purely numerical approach to trading.

The price range approach might lack the visual appeal of the graphical chart methodology, but it has the advantage of excluding all interpretation in setting required "go, no go" decision filters.

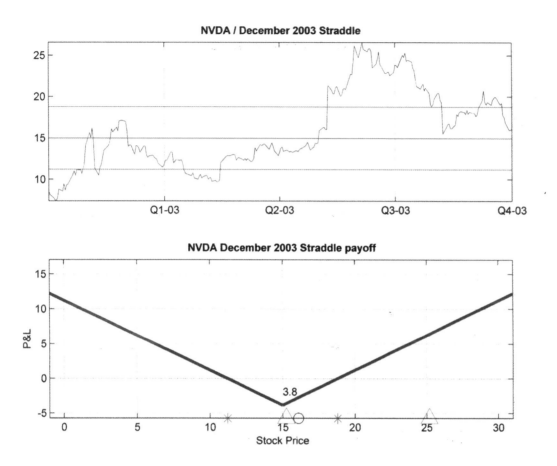

The upper graphic shows a line chart of the stock—NVIDIA—and the break-even levels of the straddle as well as its mid-point or strike.

The lower graphic is an enhanced pay-off diagram with the blue lines showing the payoff at expiration. The figure (3.8) in the middle is the cost of the straddle. The horizontal axis—as in all payoff diagrams —is the stock price. The two red asterisks are the break-even points, thus we know that the stock should move above or below that point in order for the straddle to become profitable. The green triangles indicate the price range of the stock over the same period back as until expiration. The small black circle indicates the last price of the stock.

FIGURE 87:

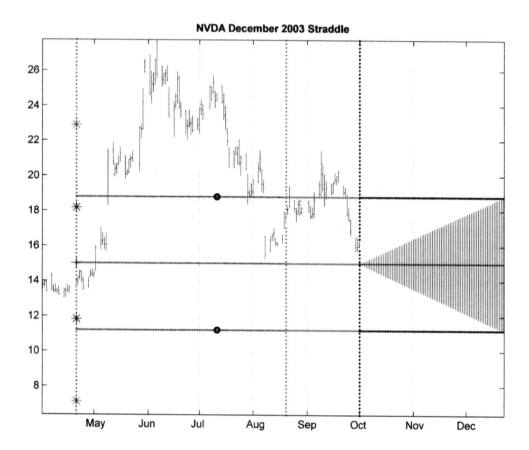

Looking at this graphic we focus on the asterisks on the leftmost vertical line, indicating in black the price-range buy levels and in blue the price-range sell levels. We see in the graphic that the calculated price-range buy levels are inside the horizontal lines drawn at the distance of the straddle-cost from the strike. Being inside those lines, the price range approach gives us a buy-signal for that straddle.

The disadvantage of the Price Range technique is its inability to easily draw attention to the number of times historical price moves took the price to and through the break-even lines and the distance of the penetrations beyond a line.

The risk in using this approach is that errors in the historical data may stay undetected. Therefore, we suggest that in any case you draw a chart of the security based on the data that you are going to use for calculating the price-range. That way you can be sure that you do not fall victim to a erroneous price spark or a non-correction of a split.

In the Price Range Approach using our historical price data base, or our chart or figures supplied by a quote provider, we simply calculate the high and low price points for our half-life when we consider the purchase of a straddle, or the full life when we sell a straddle (with the sale straddle life being half the full life). This price range is then compared to the premium cost of the straddle to determine whether the straddle is cheap (buy) or expensive (write). Additionally, we would normally set specific percentage guidelines as definitive cut-off levels.

For the evaluation of buy straddles, we determine the half-life price range. If considering the purchase of a 2 month straddle, we determine the price range for 30 days. For a 4 month straddle purchase, we will use the 2 month price range. No matter how long the life of the buy straddle is under review, always make the historical price range calculation on half of its future life length. If the straddle premium cost is extremely low in comparison with the half-life price range, the straddle should be purchased. If the straddle premium is quite high as a percentage of the half-life price range, reject its purchase.

But what should the percentage of the half-life price range be for the straddle premium cost to be low enough to make its purchase profitable? The answer to this question requires some explanations.

Think of the stock's price range and its orientation to the strikes price of the straddle. Assume the stock is trading at 60 and has a half-life 30 day price range of 20 points. Over the last 30 days the stock has had a high price 20 points above its low price. The straddle being examined for purchase is composed of two 60 day contracts (a put and a call each expiring in 60 days), thus the half-life is 30 days. To be conservative, we are considering the purchase of a 60 day straddle to allow the shares twice as much time in the future to move the same 20 points. But where will this 20 point move be in relationship to the current 60 share price? We have no way of knowing what the future price action will look like. But we do know the possibilities. The 20 points could all be above the current 60 price, meaning the 60 day range would be 80 as a high and 60 as a low. Or it might all be below today's 60 market level, resulting in a 60 high and a 40 low. Most commonly, it will be somewhere in between, meaning part of the range will be above and part of the range will be below today's share market price. Maybe the future 60 day high will be 75 and the low 55, or the high might be 68 and the low 48. Or the future price range might be spread exactly equally above and below the current 60 price, making the high 70 and the low 50.

If we are buying a straddle with a 60 strike price, we want the maximum price movement to occur either above the call strike or below the put strike. This will maximize our profit. Ideally the high is 80 or the low 40 (price range added to and subtracted from the strike prices).

It is unusual for all of the future price range to be either above or below the strike price. It is more common for the price to be partly above and partly below the strike. The least profitable occurrence is having exactly half of it above and half of it below the strike. Should this worst case event happen with the range spread equally on both sides of the strike prices, the straddle buyer could only profit if the straddle premium cost was less than half of the total anticipated range (assumed to be a range similar in points to the historical half-life range).

In this worst case event with 50% of the 20 point range (10 points) above the 60 strike of the call and 50% of the 20 points or 10 points below the strike of the put, the high is 70 and the low is 50. We will further assume the straddle buyer has purchased the straddle to avoid the need to predict market direction in the future and will therefore only exercise one side of the straddle (would actually sell to close one side) and will do the closing transaction only at expiration. To exercise or sell to close one side of the straddle earlier than at expiration means the straddle buyer is making a judgment call of the future price action of the price action. The straddle was purchased to avoid the need to make market directional calls. If in fact the future stock price range rests equally on each side of the strike, the only way the straddle buyer can profit is to have paid less than 50% of the anticipated future price range, and to have exercised or resold to close one side of the straddle (either the put or the call) at a price level exceeding the total premium cost of the entire straddle. Therefore the straddle must have cost less than 50% of the range and must have been exercised or resold near one extreme of the price range. The lower the premium cost is as a percentage of the historical share price range, the more opportunity the buyer has to profit. The higher the premium cost is as a percentage, the less the chances of a meaningful profit.

To the extent that the range is skewed to one side of the strike, the probability of profit increases. But to be conservative, we always need to make sure we have a profit potential even under the worst case scenario. Thus as straddle buyers we should pay only a small percentage of the half-life historical price range of the shares, and this percentage should always be less than 50% of the half-life range.

Through research and experience we have discovered that 40% of the half-life range usually proves profitable. This 40% figure allows for profits if the future range is equally spread above and below the strike price, the future price range matches the half-life point range, and if we exercise or sell to close only one side of the straddle and do so near the extreme of the range. Our actual real life experience has demonstrated profitable trading success when paying 40% or less of the half-life range to buy the straddle. We have also found future price ranges to be similar to the half-life, yet frequently higher since the full straddle life is twice the half-life. The longer straddle life gives more time for the shares to fluctuate and for the trade to work into a profitable posture.

Additionally our market experience is that the price range is dramatically skewed to one side of the strike. Normally one side is far enough away for the strike to be exercised or sold to close for a net profit on the entire straddle cost at or near the expiration date. Furthermore, because we make it a practice to sell covered strike puts and calls against the straddle with their strikes being a far distance from those of the straddle, we are generating premium income to lower the net cost of the straddle, and paying 40% of the half-life proves highly profitable.

The lower the percentage cost of the straddle of the half-life price range, the more profitable the straddle proves to be. Above 40% the frequency of profitable straddles and the ROI of profit decline rapidly. We will never purchase straddles costing more than 70% of the half-life price range. So why ever pay above 40%? In certain market environments it is hard to locate straddles trading at premiums below or even at 40% of the half-life range. By selling near month distance strike covered options, we can pay up slightly for the straddle and still maintain a high profit profile. We also know the full life range regularly exceeds the half-life range, thus giving us a cushion. Last, in many trades we are fortunate enough to be able to resell the in–the-money one side for intrinsic value plus some time value, thereby increasing total profitability, and we are able to liquidate the out-of-the money side for some minimal time value figure that further swells the profit.

But our advice remains firm: Pay only 40% of the half-life range for a straddle. Then just relax and let the price do its fluctuating. Finally sell the in-the-money side at or near the expiration date. The purchase of these low priced straddles is one of the easiest, safest and most profitable of all the option strategies. It is easy because it eliminates the need to predict the future price direction of the stock. It is easy, for there is a formula to follow

– pay 40% of the half-life price range. It is safe because the maximum possible loss on a straddle purchase is the premium paid for the purchase of the put and call, the necessary elements of the straddle. And it is profitable because the future price swings regularly match or exceed the half-life price range and are skewed to one side of the strike, therefore providing significant movement above or below the strike to resell the in-the-money side at a large profit on the net straddle cost.

Using the Price Range Approach in order to evaluate the potential profitability of straddle writing requires a modification. When considering the sale of a straddle, a specific life length is being analyzed. This straddle life length becomes the half-life factor. We then double the future life of the straddle that is considered for sale. We call this double time period the whole life or double life length (if that is easier to contemplate). The historical price range for the whole life (double life length) is determined. The straddle makes sense as a sale if its premium (the funds we will receive from selling both the put and the call) is more the 70% of the historical whole life price range.

Now for an example. Consider a 30 day straddle with a strike price of 50. Its life is considered the half-life. We double the half-life to obtain the whole life (double life), which is 60 days. We calculate the average whole life historical price range (for the 60 days) and find it to be 18 points. We assume the future price will move the same or less in the future half-life as it did in the historical whole life.

For a straddle seller, the worst outcome is for all of the future range to be on one side of the strike. The best outcome is for it to be equally spread on both sides of the strike. Being skewed to one side or the other is the normal market pattern. A 2/3 to 1/3 skew is common. This skew means two-thirds of the range is on one side of the strike and the remaining one-third is on the other side. It is also quite unusual for prices to be at the extreme top or bottom of a range at expiration. More likely the share price at expiration will be at some level between the two distant price extremes of the range. Last, options are usually exercised at expiration and not before. Given all these probabilities, the extreme price point will be 66.67% above or below the strike, and the price will not be at the price range extreme at expiration. The straddle seller could thus risk selling the straddle for 70% of the whole life range with a reasonable chance of profiting.

The problem with selling straddles is the risk factor. For the straddle purchaser the maximum risk is the premium paid. All movement away from the strike prices lowers losses and a large move generates profits. Price fluctuation is the friend of straddle buyers. Random world events of major market importance, (think of 9-11,) unexpected stock specific events, (consider Enron,) are windfalls for straddle buyers. Market or stock volatility skyrockets. But for the straddle seller, the profit potential is capped at the level of the premium received. The straddle writer can never make a profit greater than the premiums credited to his account from the sale of the put and the call. Any price movement away from the strike lowers the profit potential. A large enough move wipes out the premium receipts and places the entire straddle write in a loss position. A huge move causes a disastrous loss. The straddle seller has two enemies, movement and trend. Unexpected and unforeseen events are the causes of instant and dramatic price movements. They are random and by their very nature cannot be anticipated. They are not usually factored into the straddle premium because they are unexpected. When they occur, and occur they do, they push the share prices far beyond the straddle seller's break-even levels.

There are very few things that bring a stock's volatility to a minimal level that helps the straddle seller. But the unexpected and random events greatly magnify the volatility and the price range of the shares, and these hurt the straddle writer.

Our advice is to sell straddles only under the following conditions:

* Their premium is above 70% of the historical double life price range.

* When willing to buy shares at low levels in the future, if the put should be exercised. (The buy price of the stock purchase is the strike of the put less the entire straddle premium.)

* When willing either to sell existing shares or to go short shares in the future at high prices. (Selling price of the stock is the call strike price plus the entire straddle premium.)

5.5.3.3.1   HOW TO OPTIMIZE THE PRICE RANGE APPROACH

The price range approach is best when optimized. That means that you find the optimal percentage levels for buying or selling straddles that correspond to your appetite for risk. We have included conservative figures, 40% and 70%.

You can also try more aggressive numbers, like 50% for both. To sell straddles for less than 50% of double time should be avoided, as such positions carry substantial risks. Buying straddles can be done above the 50% mark of half-time, as in this case the money which is at stake is clearly defined and limited to your premium outlay.

But please, when using the price range approach, run some paper trades or best optimizations before utilizing it for big positions.

5.5.3.4   CHECKLISTS FOR STRADDLES

The checklists that we use for straddles are the following:

Long Straddle	
Increase in news?	
Bias of news?	
Liquidity of options o.k.?	
Spread o.k.?	
Volatility far from year high?	
Graphic analysis	

And

Short Straddle	
Increase in news?	
Bias of news?	
Liquidity of options o.k.?	
Spread o.k.?	
Volatility far from year high?	
Graphic analysis	

Because the long straddle appreciates when volatility increases we check that the volatility is not close to the year high. For selling a straddle the opposite applies, we would be reluctant to sell a straddle if it were trading close to its 52-week low.

Of course high volatility can go even higher and low volatility can even go lower, however, due to the mean reverting property of volatility – volatility levels tend to approach their historic long-term average level – we know that it is more advantageous to take positions that benefit from a volatility move in the direction of the level of the long-term mean.

Again, we refer to www.ivolatiliy.com to do your quick check regarding the volatility.

The other items in the checklists can be grouped into fundamentals (increase in news and bias of news), market (liquidity and spread), technicals (volatility and chart) and therefore the checklists make sure that we look into the three aspects – each from two different angles - before we set up a position.

5.5.4   ABOUT DIVERSIFICATION

Diversification is the process of running different positions or bets at the same time. But portfolio diversification is a dilemma in itself. We know that we should not 'put all the eggs in one basket,' but on the other hand we know that 'no guts, no glory.'

It would be highly adventurous to put all your savings in one option strategy. It would be like Christopher Columbus going for America or the first astronauts flying to the moon. Both achieved highly significant results, however, with high risk or little protection.

Such bold bets, like the discovery of America, can work, no doubt. And when they do work, they generate a big impact or in trading big money. But we do not recommend them, because they simply are too risky, and too often just don't work.

The opposite of putting all in one stock would be to buy a tiny amount of nearly all stocks in the market. That would of course lead to a bad result, as you would track the market, but suffer the commission cost.

Therefore, a common sense approach has to be taken which lies in between the two. We do not run more than 20 different strategies at any given time. Our research and especially our experience has shown that this is a good number, not making the portfolios too confusing and neither over-diversifying, but still running an acceptable risk.

What this would mean is that we try to have 10-12 sold straddles and the same amount of bought straddles in our portfolio. Ideally we have got over-priced 10 straddles long and 10 under-priced straddles short.

5.5.5   LONG/SHORT STRATEGIES

The long/short strategies explained below, which we use quite frequently, consist of dividing stocks in out-performers and under-performers. Based on that decision, the out-performers are bought, whereas the under-performers are sold.

We recommend to base the division according to performance on technical analysis, best point-and-figure charting. If you are good at fundamental analysis, and you prefer that methodology, that is fine too.

Doing long / short you do not have to be as synchronized as with straddles. If you find a good opportunity for a short or a long, you can set that position up—hedge the market risk with an index future—and wait until you find a good opportunity for an opposite position. You are not obliged to create a long stock, short stock at the very same moment. If you can, that is better, but often you will see that you can't.

Long / short, especially set up with negative gamma, that is by selling options, can imply considerable risks. You have to tackle that problem by diversification, i.e., not to put too much of your money in one such strategy and to define an action plan beforehand that defines stop loss levels, the levels of aggregate loses, where you liquidate.

5.5.5.1   CLASSIC LONG/SHORT WITH OPTIONS

The classic long/short strategy consists of figuring out which stocks will be successful in the future and which one's will not, therefore, not only to pick good stocks, but also bad stocks. The next step follows logically, you buy the good stocks and sell the bad ones.

Buying stocks is easy. Selling them can pose some problems and here is where your broker will be of great help.

But it is actually easier to go synthetically short, by selling a long-term call and buying a long-term put. Remember the options-algebra, that says that the risk of being short a stock equals long put short stock. This is explained in chapter 3.2.

The long position would be established by buying the call and selling the put. You can further enhance the strategy by choosing to do covered calls instead of longs. Or if you have a high risk appetite—like some hedge funds; however, they are not open about it—you can sell naked puts on the stocks you believe are strong. But doing covered calls lets you sleep much better than the naked calls. Refer to chapter 5.3 where we explain both strategies in detail.

To run these types of strategies with options it goes without saying that you have to reduce your stock universe to the optionable stocks, which is a bit more of an issue outside the US markets. But believe us, there are many companies in that universe that have an excellent management, therefore buys, and many that have lousy executives, and are therefore sells.

5.5.5.2 LONG/SHORT STRADDLES

As you must have understood, our preferred strategy. It consists of holding long and short straddles, starting with an equal total premium money paid and premium money received. The straddles are selected according to the methods explained above, preferably the chart approach.

If we aim at setting up a portfolio with a multitude of straddles, we still use the graphical approach; however, we sometimes make our decision rules a bit more aggressive by using the option life (the black ring on the upper and lower lines) as a decision base. We would therefore buy dearer straddles and sell cheaper ones. But as we are diversified, the risk / reward is perfect.

FIGURE 88

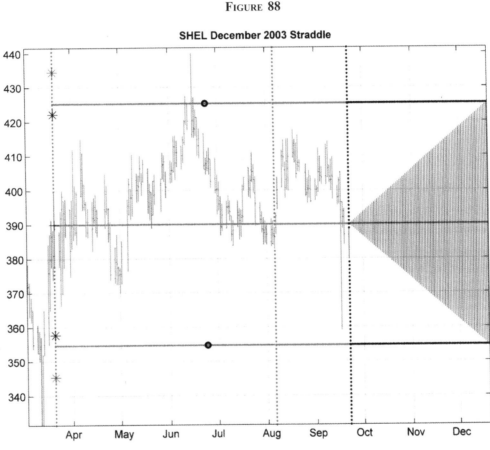

We see on the SHELL (SHEL.L) December straddle chart that the penetration above the break-even line has happened on the left of the full-time marker—the circle. Moreover, the penetration was weak in the sense that it is spread over 3 days only. Therefore, having long straddles in our portfolio, we decided to sell SHEL.L, even though a penetration happened within the double-time but before the full-time. Recall, that if the straddle expires in 30 days, then the double time is 60, the full-time 30 and the half-time 15. The full-time is also the extension of the triangle towards the right side of the graphic, and on the historical time-axis the double-time is marked with the lines towards the left, the full-time with the black-circle and the half-time with the lines towards the right. The vertical black-dotted coincides with the last price. The triangle gives us also a reference towards the future movements the stock has to make in order to be within or without the break-even lines.

199

CHAPTER 6
THE IMPLEMENTATION: THE PRACTICALITIES OF TRADING OPTIONS

6.1 SELECTING A MARKET / UNDERLYING

Starting to trade options is best done where you feel a certain familiarity; therefore, if you already follow some stocks or have a preference for a sector, find the market where the options on those stocks are traded and then start there. You have to start where you feel at home. If you have been investing in BP and Shell, then start to do some straddles on those. It will be easy as you already have a feeling for the price swings in those stocks, you know the price levels, dividend dates and so forth. That should make you comfortable.

It is important that you are open to work on different markets. You know very well that some sectors get hot and others lose interest from the investors. Always keep an eye on the markets that are in the spotlight and experiment with positions in those markets. At the writing of this book the currency markets, especially €/$ and the NASDAQ tech stocks got most of the interest, so we increased our interest towards those markets too.

6.2 SOFTWARE/DATA

6.2.1 SOFTWARE

A good charting package like MetaStock or Updata, or any comparable, is very useful but not strictly required to use the proposed graphical straddle approach. You can simply print a standard chart that you find on many online services and then draw the required lines by hand. Certainly, the use of MetaStock is more efficient and creates charts that are easy to store and manipulate.

If you are already using a charting package, you can probably use it, as long as it allows you to draw horizontal and vertical lines.

If you want to build you own straddle screener—as we did—then the problem starts. We do not know of any software flexible enough. You would probably need to program it yourself. If you have any questions in that respect, don't hesitate to contact us. We have used MatLab to program our software, because its computational results are highly reliable, and we are happy to share some insights and code.

6.2.2 DATA

It is not difficult to get historical data of stocks for free or at a very low price. The things that you have to check are whether the data is adjusted for splits or if there are obvious errors, such as spikes (wrong prices) or missing data.

The bigger issue is the historical data of the options. The problem is the huge amount of options data that is generated each day. One has to have the discipline to collect all the data one is interested in each day. You can also write your own program that does this. The problem is that there are no cheap databases with long term options price history. Some brokers do have the data and are happy to share it with clients. Ask the broker you are working with what he could do in this respect.

Some of the exchanges do also offer options price files. Liffe, for example has quite a good service, which allows you to download daily price files for the last 5 days. That means that you are not lost if you didn't update a certain day, because you have four days remaining to get the data.

A good and price worthy data retrieval program is www.hquotes.com. Other sites that we can recommend for online data are listed under the annex online resources.

6.3   SELECTING A BROKER

The first choice you have to make is whether you want to work online or via telephone. Most likely you will choose the online alternative. Choosing a good broker is crucial and the process merits some time.

There are some magazines, like *Barron's*, that rate brokers, and you have chat rooms where brokers are commented upon. Last but not least you should visit the site of the online broker.

If you are serious with your trading, we recommend that you open accounts with at least two brokers as a mean to reduce the risk of not being able to change a position because your broker has technical difficulties.

We think it is a good idea to test several brokers until you find the one that best suits your needs.

6.4   OUR APPROACH OF TRADING OPTIONS OR HOW WE PUT IT ALL TO WORK

We prefer to trade straddles. We use the graphical method as a decision tool and we follow our checklists.

We try not to have more than 20 different strategies at any one time.

We follow the positions in real-time in order to find opportunities to open new ones or close existing ones during the trading day.

We work through online brokers.

6.5   HOW YOU SHOULD START TO TRADE STRADDLES AND OTHER OPTION STRATEGIES

Find a good broker.

Study the different online services available to get a maximum of information and especially to know where to get information once you need it.

Start small and gather experience.

Work with a small number of strategies at any given time.

Analyze the straddle charts carefully, use our checklists, and don't rush into positions.

6.6   FOR OUR US BASED READERS: IRA ACCOUNTS

6.6.1   ENERGIZING YOUR IRA AND OTHER RETIREMENT ACCOUNTS

One of the major deterrents to annually funding our IRA brokerage account is that IRAs are so boring. To most investors IRA accounts are dull and ultra conservative since they offer very little investment flexibility. This is not only true of IRA accounts, but of most retirement accounts. More retirement accounts only allow the owner to buy stock, bonds, and mutual funds for cash—period! Margin is not allowed. Thus in a strong market, the performance of IRA and retirement accounts falls short of the returns earned on our more aggressively managed accounts which magnify ROI through the use of margin for leverage.

Within the guidelines established by the government and brokerage firms, there are however several exciting things that we can do to put an IRA and other retirement accounts into overdrive. Not all firms allow clients to do all of the following transactions in a retirement account, though. But a quick survey of firms reveal several that will. Brown & Company, a national discount firm offering both broker assisted and internet trading, permit most, and OptionsXpress, a discount Brokerage firm located in Chicago and specializing in stock options, allow all of the following transactions.

Much of this section serves as a review of the basics of stock option strategies. What is important is the slight twists required when they are transacted within a retirement account structure. The other important benefit to consider is that they allow for magnified profits and minimized risks as compared with normal buying of stock for cash.

6.6.1.1   BUY STOCK CHEAPER LATER

If you have cash or Treasury Bills in your retirement account, you can sell naked puts secured by cash or T Bills equal to 100% of the value of the stock that can potentially be sold (put) to you. When you sell a put, you are agreeing to buy 100 shares of the stock at the strike price until the expiration date of the option. For making this commitment, you are paid a premium. For example, let's assume that it is mid February, you like eBay (EBAY), which is selling at 104, and while willing to buy it at 104, would much prefer during the next two months to buy it at 85. You would sell an April 85 put on EBAY and receive a premium of $300 immediately credited to your account. If, prior to the April expiration date, EBay had never traded below 85, you would not be forced to buy the stock and you would have earned $300 for 2 months while also earning interest on the cash credit balance or T Bills in your account. If you did this transaction 6 times yearly, you would earn $300 for 60 days times 6 periods or $1,800 per year. Since you are holding $8,500 in cash or cash equivalent to back your guarantee, you would be earning over 21% in premium income on the $8,500 being held to back the obligation (annual return of $1,800 divided by the investment of $8,500), plus an additional return on the credit balance or T bills (assume 3%) for an annual return of 24%. Alternatively, had you sold the 100 strike puts for one month (March), thus agreeing to buy EBay at 100, the premium would be $600. This would represent a return of 6% on $10,000 for one month or 72% annually plus the 3% yield on the account credit balance or T Bills, for an annual return of 75%.

But what if the stock declined? No big deal! You liked eBay at 104 and were willing to pay 104 for it. Instead you end up buying it in April for $85 a share. That is $19 less than the price the stock was selling in mid February. And since you were paid $300 for the option ($3 per share times 100 shares), you bought the stock at $85 (strike price) less $3 (option premium received) for a true cost of $82. And during the time from mid February until the stock is purchased in April, you earned interest on your credit account balance.

Commissions are ignored in all the examples. But for informational purposes, Brown charges $25 to buy or sell up to 4 options and $19 for up to 5000 shares of stock on option exercises. OptionsXpress charges $14.95 to trade up to 10 option contracts and $12.95 to trade up to 5,000 shares of stock. Thus, if you aggressively shop for a competitive securities broker, use one of these firms, and commissions will not be a significant factor in your return calculations.

A word of caution. Only sell puts on stocks that you believe are strong and ones that you truly want to own. You just might be forced to buy the stock. Should the share price decline below the strike price of the put, and remain below the strike until the option's expiration date, you will be forced to buy 100 shares of stock at the strike price for each and every put sold.

6.6.1.2 SELLING STOCK WELL ABOVE MARKET

You can significantly increase the return on the stock you hold in your IRA account by selling covered calls. Assume it is still mid February and you own 100 shares of International Business Machines (IBM) at 100. You are not willing to sell them at 100, but would be willing to sell the stock at 120 until mid March. In this case, you would sell a March 120 call on IBM and would receive a premium of $500. By selling this call, you are promising and guaranteeing to sell 100 shares of IBM at anytime between now and mid March (equity options always expire on the third Friday of the month) for $120 a share. If the stock never reaches 120, you have earned $500 for one month on a $10,000 investment in IBM, representing a Return on Investment (ROI) for one month of 5%, or 60% annualized return and you still own the IBM shares.

But don't worry if you are forced to sell the 100 shares of IBM stock at 120 in March. It was only worth $10,000 in February. In March you receive $12,000 for the 100 shares of stock on the sale at 120 plus the $500 premium from writing (selling) the covered call. Your total receipt from the sale of the covered call ($500) and the sale of the stock ($12,000) is $12,500. This is equal to selling the stock at 125 a share, and represents a one month gain of $2,500 or 25% return on the $10,000 February value of the IBM stock. That being a one month return, the annualized return is 300%. By writing (selling) the one month covered call with a strike price of 120, any potential stock appreciation for the month above the strike of 120 is lost. Such a monster move in the stock is an unlikely occurrence, though, and one we are willing to forego in exchange for the receipt of a healthy covered call writing premium ($500) and the possibility of capturing stock appreciation from the share price existing at the time of the call sale (100) up to the strike price of the call (120).

A word of caution. Only sell covered calls against stocks you would be willing to sell at a higher price, and ones that you believe either will not move much or will rise. If you believe the stock will drop, sell it today. It is a poor strategy to see the stock drop from 100 to 80 while picking up a 5 point premium. The greatest returns are made in this strategy when the stock is called away (purchased from you at the strike price of the call). When the stock is called away, you earn both stock appreciation and covered call premium income. The selling of covered calls always involves the immediate receipt of the call writing premium. Having the stock called away at the call strike price, a price higher than the share price existing on the date the call was written, is gravy on the transaction, significantly boosting the overall return on the transaction and the overall return on the entire retirement account.

We strongly support a position of selling covered calls against all of the stock in the retirement account. The calls are sold with strike prices higher than current market prices of the underlying shares. They are sold with strikes at high levels which the share prices might reach, but are unlikely to be exceeded by the shares. A consistent strategy of selling covered calls will add much appreciated cash receipts and portfolio yield to the account over and above the returns created by the shares directly. If the portfolio is projected to have an annual return of 10% through normal stock appreciation, a covered call writing program will add a level of additional income to the 10%.

Should some stock be called away (sold) from the portfolio, there is new cash in the account generated from the writing of the covered call and the stock sale. These funds would then logically be employed for the selling of puts to require the sold shares in the future at prices below their selling price, to earn further additional yield on the account, or to acquire other more desirable stocks in the future and at lower than current market prices.

In conclusion, the selling of covered calls against the stock in a retirement account is a win-win situation. Additional income and cash is injected into the portfolio through the writing of the covered calls. Stock, if sold, is sold at higher prices than exist at the time when the covered calls were sold. This adds appreciation income to the account. Sold shares can be reacquired at lower prices in the future through the selling of naked puts.

6.6.1.3   BUY MORE OR SELL EXISTING POSITION

Let's assume that you own 100 shares of Goldman Sachs Group, Inc. (GS) with the stock trading at 100. You like the stock but would prefer to either own 200 shares or closeout the position altogether, since 100 shares is just not significant. In this case you might sell a (one month) March 90 put for $300 and a March 110 call for $400. You are thus committed to buy 100 shares at 90 and sell 100 shares at 110. If the stock trades within the 90 to 110 price range, you make 7% for the month and still own 100 shares of GS. If the stock drops below 90 you are buying the stock at 90 minus the put premium of 3 for an actual cost of 87 and you still have the call premium of $400 as profit. If the stock rises above 110, you sell the stock at 110, with your actual selling price being 114 (110 selling price of the stock plus the call premium of $4 a share). Additionally you have the put premium of $300 as added profit.

Theoretically, due to the volatility of the stock, it is possible to have both the put and the call exercised against you. Since options can be exercised by the buyer at any time prior to their expiration date, the exercise of either could occur. This would happen if during the option life share price fluctuations it carries the price above the call strike price and also below the put strike all prior to the expiration dates of the put and call, and further, put and call option buyers are nimble. This rarely occurs. But if it did happen, it would be a lucky event for the option writer. The retirement account owner who would have sold a covered call on the stock and a naked put on the same company would have bought 100 shares of GS at 87 (90 strike price of the put less the put selling premium of $300) and later sold it at 114 (110 strike price of the covered call less the call selling premium of $400) for a 27 point profit and would still hold the original 100 shares. Alternatively, first the stock price rises and the account sold the 100 share position at 114 and later was forced to buy 100 shares at 87, reestablishing the 100 share position.

As long as you are neutral on the stock at its current price and willing to buy more shares at a lower price or sell the position at a higher price, this is a win-win strategy. Premium is earned immediately through the sale of the naked put and the covered call. If the put is exercised and shares are sold, they are sold at prices higher than the level they traded on the date the call was sold. If the put is exercised and shares are purchased by the account, their buy price is lower than the price at which they traded on the date the put was sold. But remember, if employed in a retirement account, this approach requires margin funds equal to the buy price of the shares on the put being held. The call is covered and is protected by the share position and as such does not require additional margin.

6.6.1.4 *LEVERAGE: AN ALLOWABLE ALTERNATIVE TO MARGIN*

IRA and most other retirement accounts are not allowed to buy stock on margin. Thus, to obtain the benefits of margin and have the use of leverage another technique must be employed; buy call options.

Assume it is currently early February and you love the short-term prospects of 3M Company (MMM) at 160, but hate to utilize $16,000 to buy 100 shares of stock. Alternatively you could buy one call option. A conservative approach would be to purchase a deep in-the-money call option where you are not paying much for time value. For $3,500 you could purchase one April 130 call on MMM. By buying this call option, you have the right (but not the obligation) to buy 100 shares of MMM stock at 130 anytime until mid April. Alternatively, you can resell the option. Buying this option is equivalent to buying 100 shares of stock at 165 (130 strike price of the call plus 35 option premium), which is only 5 points above the current 160 market price of MMM's stock. Owning the call, you benefit from stock price appreciation, yet have only invested 22% of the stock cost. Thus you have leverage.

What can happen? Should MMM split 2 for 1 in late March, your option is adjusted to reflect the split. Your original call for 100 shares at 130 is now 2 calls, each for 100 shares at 65. Options are always adjusted for stock splits. Now, if the split stock rises to 100 (200 pre-split basis), the options are worth at least $3,500 each (100 stock price less the strike price of 65). After the 2 for 1 stock split, you have 2 call options with 65 strike prices. With the split shares trading at 100, you have $7,000 in value for your $3,500 original investment.

You therefore have a 100% profit in 2 months. Had you bought 100 shares of stock for $16,000 (purchased at 160), you would have had $20,000 worth of stock (200 shares trading at 100), generating a profit of $4,000 on an investment of $16,000 for a 25% return. The option has given significant leverage as well as a much higher return on invested capital. There is an added benefit in buying the call rather than the stock: The remainder of the funds ($16,000 cost of the stock less the $3,500 cost of the option or $12,500) are still in the account. These excess funds will earn interest, or alternatively, can be invested in other security or option positions.

If the stock dropped to 75 (150 pre-split), your options would be worth $1,000 each (75 stock price less 65 strike price) times 2, and you would have lost $1,500 ($3,500 cost less $2,000 current value of the 2 long call options). Had you bought the stock at 160, rather than purchasing the call option, the loss would be only $1,000, but you would have invested much more money ($16,000 rather than $3,500).

What would the numbers look like if the shares had declined still further? Assume the stock has dropped to 50 (100 on a pre-split basis). The option buyer has lost his entire investment of $3,500, but the stock investor is out $6,000. It should be noted that the option buyer can never lose more than the premium paid for the option, no matter how low the stock may decline. Thus the option buyer always knows in advance and to the penny the maximum amount of the potential loss.

Had you purchased the MMM call, you could always resell the option at any time, exactly as if it were stock. Alternatively, you could exercise the call option, buying MMM stock at the strike price and holding the stock in the portfolio. If MMM is acquired as a portfolio hold, consider selling covered calls on the stock for added account income.

When you buy a call rather than the stock, you have a number of advantages. You employ less money. You have leverage. You have the opportunity to participate in the price appreciation of the stock, while investing fewer funds. You know to the penny your maximum possible loss. The maximum loss is often less than the loss incurred from the executed stop-loss order. During the option time life, the call buyer need not be concerned with the volatility of the stock (how many times it goes down or how low it may go), but only with the ultimate magnitude of the upside move. MMM could decline 5 times from 160 to 100 during the option period, and even go to 60, and the maximum loss would always only be the premium paid ($3,500). But if MMM ultimately rises to 200 prior to the expiration date, you will have made 100%.

Once again, words of caution. If you can afford to buy 100 shares of a stock in your IRA, buy just one call. Do not employ all of the money buying Calls. If you are wrong, and you only own 1 call for each 100 shares you would normally have purchased, you only lose the premium, a small fraction of the stock price, and you have plenty of money left to try again. MMM could have declined to 100 and you would have lost $3,500. But you could now buy a two month call on MMM with a 70 strike price for $3,500 and try again.

6.6.1.5 LONG-TERM LEVERAGE

The prior strategy dealt with buying relatively short-term options. Short-term options require a more accurate projection of the movement of a security. If you like a certain stock for the long-term and want to avoid the risks of short-term timing and near-term trend predictions, and also want leverage, consider buying LEAPS. LEAPS (Long-Term Equity Anticipation Securities) are simply options that expire on the third Friday of January, one, two or three years in the future. As of September 2003, there are Leaps trading with expiration dates as far out in time as January 2006.

Let's assume you have a very positive long-term outlook for Microsoft (MSFT) when the stock is trading at 29. You could buy 100 shares for $2,900, or buy a January 2006 LEAP call with a 20 strike price for $980. The call costs $980 - less than half the $2,900 cost of 100 shares of stock. Owning the 2006 Leap call with the 20 strike price allows the holder to participate in any price appreciation in Microsoft for the next two years. The only money cost for the time factor is $80 (20 strike price of the option plus the option cost of $980 (9.8) less the current market price of 29 times 100 shares of stock).

The purchase of a call creates leverage without margin. The leap call buyer of the MSFT 20 strike call for 2006 is spending only $980 to control 100 shares of stock for 2 years. There is no margin loan, no debit balance in the account, no margin interest, and no chance of a margin call. And the only real cost of the option is the amount spent for the time value ($80) Even if margin was allowed in a retirement account, which it is not, the investment in the stock would have been 50% of the stock purchase cost (50% of $2,900 or $1,450, there would be a $1,450 margin loan bearing interest, and there would always be the possibility of having margin calls.

Margin is not permitted in an IRA. Buying a call is allowed. The call offers similar results as buying stock on margin, and is often more favorable than margin. Remember, when buying a call rather than purchasing stock, there is leverage without margin. There can never be a margin call, and there is never any interest charge on the debit balance created by margin buying.

When an at-the money call is purchased, the leverage is greatest. The offset is that the break-even point for an at-the-money call is much higher than for a deep-in-the-money call. The premium cost of a 2006 MFST 30 call would be $360 making its break-even 33.60 (strike price of 30 plus the premium cost of 3.60 to buy the call). The 2006 call with a 20 strike cost $980 making its break-even only 29.80 (20 strike price of the call plus the call premium of 9.80). A minimal price advance would make the 20 strike price leap call profitable, while a much larger price rise of the shares is required to make a profit on the 30 strike leap. Yet in the case of both the 20 and the 30 strike leap calls, the options have over 2 years of time remaining for the move to occur.

6.6.1.6   BUYING CALLS AND SELLING COVERED CALLS AGAINST THEM: A COMBINATION APPROACH

There is a logical manner of combining the leverage benefits of owning calls in the retirement account with the income generating features of selling covered calls.

Deep-in-the-money leaps are purchased in the IRA account. These calls provide leverage without the negative aspects of margin. They also represent the only method of obtaining leverage in the restrictive structure of retirement account guidelines and law. By being deep-in-the-money, they have low break-even levels and as such act similarly to common stock.

Having secured the leap call position, a call can be written (sold) against the leap. If the short call position (the call being written) has a strike price above the strike price of the leap, it is considered covered. If covered, no margin funds are required. The premium received from writing (selling) the covered call is added cash and income for the IRA account, and as such, lowers the net cost of the purchased leap.

Consider the following scenario. A Microsoft (MSFT) 2006 call with a 20 strike is sold for $980 when MSFT is trading at 29 in September 2003. The break-even is 29.80 (20 strike price plus the 9.80 premium). A one month (October) call on MSFT with a 30 strike is sold for .50 ($50). The premium obtained (.50) is cash immediately received into the account. It will be profit. It also lowers the cost of the leap (9.80 premium cost of the leap less the premium (.50) received from the sale of the covered call). The leap now has a net cost of only 9.30. The resulting break-even point for the leap is now only 29.30 (20 strike price plus the adjusted premium of 9.30).

Should the price of MSFT rise above 30, the October covered call could be repurchased, removing the obligation to deliver stock. A new, longer maturity date (November) and a higher lever strike call (32.50) could now be written as a covered call against the leap. The premium received from the sale of the newer, later maturity, higher strike priced covered call would closely match the cost of buying back the covered call with its lower strike price and earlier maturity date. With Microsoft trading at 30, the leap would have become profitable. Should the shares reach the 32.50 strike price of the November covered call, the buying back of the 32.50 call and the selling of a December 35 call would be the strategically correct move. As the stock moves even higher, the leap gains in value and profitability. If the stock fails to rise to the strike price of the covered call, the covered call expires worthless and a new covered call is written. In this process additional premium cash receipts are generated for the retirement account.

6.6.1.7 *SUMMARY*

Although stock options are not for everyone, their use in an IRA account can add leverage, increase returns, and even reduce risk. They can convert a boring IRA into a market sensitive and super-charged investment vehicle that is fun and intellectually challenging to manage.

Always consider maintaining your retirement account with a major options specialist brokerage firm. In the selection process consider and seek a firm offering:

* Low stock commission structure
* Low option commission charges
* Low option exercise fees
* Permitting the sale of naked puts
* Allowing the purchase of calls
* Approving the purchasing of puts
* Permitting the sale of calls covered by long calls held in the account
* Allowing the sale of calls covered by long stock positions

Ideally in a retirement account stock is acquired in the future at lower prices through the sale of naked puts. The shares purchased through the exercise of puts are liquidated at higher prices through the sale of covered calls. Leaps are purchased for leverage. Calls are written covered by the leaps.

When options become an integral part of the investment philosophy of the retirement account, the account has a lower risk while simultaneously generating higher returns. The logical employment of options super-charges the profitability of the account, makes it fun to manage, and provides intellectual stimulation, while the stability of the risk versus return ratio is maintained.

We would never consider funding a retirement account void of an option component. So why should you?

GREAT NEWS FOR YOU FROM TRADERS PRESS...
A FREE COPY OF OUR LATEST BOOK RESERVED JUST FOR YOU!

Traders Press, publisher and distributor of educational materials for traders and investors, has just published a new 40 page E-book by trading coach (and trader herself), Ruth Roosevelt: *Keeping a Cool Head in a Hot Market.* We are reserving a FREE COPY just for you. All you have to do is go to the following link to register for and print out your own copy:

http://www.traderspress.org/3800.asp

Learn how to keep a cool head in a hot market....When a "hot" market situation develops, you have an exceptional opportunity to make extraordinary profits...but also, an emotionally draining environment in which it is easy to make mistakes in judgment which can not only lose the opportunity to profit, but can also destroy your trading account. It is vitally important to keep your wits about you when you become involved in such a situation. Veteran trading coach Ruth Roosevelt shows you in her usual no-nonsense, right to the point style, how to maximize the benefits and avoid the land mines encountered in a "hot market."

Be sure to get your own FREE copy now...while it is fresh on your mind. Just go to this link: http://www.traderspress.org/3800.asp

Published by Traders Press, Inc.®

ID#	ISBN#	TITLE	LIST PRICE
1840	0934380740	12 Habitudes of Highly Successful Traders by Ruth B Roosevelt	19.95
301	093438018X	A Comparison of 12 Technical Trading Systems by Lukac & Brorsen	25.00
38	0934380589	A Complete Guide to Trading Profits by Alexander Paris	19.95
1394	093438049X	A Professional Look at S&P Day Trading by Don Trivette	29.00
2100	0934380651	A Treasury of Wall Street Wisdom by Schultz and Coslow	24.95
1494	0934380511	Ask Mr. Easy Language by Sam Tennis	49.00
263	0934380317	Astro-Cycles: The Trader's Viewpoint by Larry Pesavento	49.00
1116	0934380376	Beginners Guide to Computer-Assisted Trading by Peter Alexander	29.95
1401	0934380503	Channels and Cycles: A Tribute to J M Hurst by Brian Millard	45.00
889	0934380287	Chart Reading for Professional Traders by Michael Jenkins	75.00
1722	0934380635	Charting Commodity Market Price Behavior by L Dee Belveal	34.95
1500	0934380562	Cyclic Analysis: A Dynamic Approach to Tech. Analysis by JM Hurst	19.95
2700	093438083X	Dynamic Trading by Robert Miner	97.00
3150	0934380937	Essentials of Trading by Pesavento & Jouflas	35.00
1470	0934380546	Exceptional Trading: The Mind Game by Ruth B Roosevelt	39.95
1098	0934380368	Fibonacci Ratios with Pattern Recognition by Larry Pesavento	49.00
1300	0934380481	Futures Spread Trading: The Complete Guide by Courtney Smith	49.95
888	0934380279	Geometry of Stock Market Profits by Michael Jenkins	50.00
390	0934380333	Harmonic Vibrations by Larry Pesavento	49.00
277-B	0934380759	How to Trade in Stocks by Jesse Livermore/Richard Smitten	29.95
962-A	0934380643	Investing by the Stars by Henry Weingarten	29.95
3600	093438097X	Investor Skills Training by Rob Ronin	24.95
2250	0934380864	It's Your Option by Marvin Zelkin	29.95
3800	0934380996	Keeping a Cool Head in a Hot Market by Ruth B Roosevelt	10.00
1287	0934380430	Magic of Moving Averages by Scot Lowry	29.95
3450	0934380953	Market Beaters by Art Collins	40.00
1700	0934380619	Market Rap by Art Collins	24.95
329-S	0934380538	Mind Over Markets: Power Trdg with Mkt Generated Info by J.Dalton	29.95
3500	0934380961	Option Strategies for Sophisticated Traders by Mitch Crask	34.95
3050	0934380910	Overcoming 7 Deadly Sins of Trading by Ruth B Roosevelt	24.95
1514	093438052X	Pit Trading: Do You Have the Right Stuff by Hoffman & Bacetti	39.95
336	0934380325	Planetary Harmonics of Speculative Markets by Larry Pesavento	49.00
538-A	0934380309	Point and Figure Charting: The Complete Guide by Carroll Aby	35.00
1162	0934380384	Point and Figure Commodity & Stock Trading Techniques by K.Zieg	35.00
3400	0934380945	Precision Trdg with Stevenson Price & Time Targets by JR Stevenson	49.00
2500	0934380813	Private Thoughts from a Trader's Diary by Pesavento & MacKay	40.00
72-S	0934380260	Professional Commodity Traders by Stanley Kroll	19.95
32	093438004X	Profitable Grain Trading by Ralph Ainsworth	25.00
77-A	0934380627	Profit Magic of Stock Transaction Timing by JM Hurst	25.00
1388	0934380473	Profitable Patterns for Stock Trading by Larry Pesavento	49.00
3000	0934380856	Roadmap to the Markets by Tom Busby	24.95
3200	0934380880	RSI: The Complete Guide by John Hayden	34.95
1600	0934380600	Short Term Trading with Price Patterns by Michael Harris	69.95

1208	0934380414	Stock Patterns for Day Trading by Barry Rudd	95.00
2000	0934380686	Stock Trading Techniques Based on Price Patterns by Michael Harris	95.00
2900	0934380848	Taming Complexity by Dennis McNicholl	29.95
914	0934380457	Technical Trading Systems for Commodities & Stocks By C. Patel	50.00
1115	0934380392	Technically Speaking by Chris Wilkinson	39.00
1524	0934380597	The Amazing Life of Jesse Livermore by Richard Smitten	29.95
3700	0934380716	The Complete Guide to Non-Directional Trading by Weber/Zieg	39.95
551	0934380236	The Crowd/Extraordinary Popular Delusions by Lebon & MacKay	19.95
3100	0934380872	The Handbook of Global Securities Operations by Jerry O'Connell	65.00
800	0934380708	The Opening Price Principle by Larry Pesavento	29.95
195-A	0934380244	The Taylor Trading Technique by Douglas Taylor	25.00
5	0934380031	The Trading Rule That Can Make You Rich* by Edward Dobson	29.95
1165	0934380406	Trading Secrets of the Inner Circle by Andrew Goodwin	49.00
580	0934380252	Understanding Bollinger Bands by Edward Dobson	8.00
3300	0934380902	Understanding E-Minis by Jerry Williams	24.95
43-A	0934380082	Understanding Fibonacci Numbers by Edward Dobson	5.00
174	0934380139	Wall St. Ventures and Adventures thru 40 Years by Richard Wyckoff	24.95
2400	0934380767	When Supertraders Meet Kryptonite by Art Collins	35.00
2800	0934380821	Winning Edge 4 by Adrien Toghraie	69.00
175	0934380120	Winning Market Systems: 83 Ways to Beat the Mkt by Gerald Appel	39.95

Wholesale Discount Schedule

1-9 copies	30% discount
10-25 copies	44% discount
26-50 copies	48% discount
51-100 copies	55% discount
101 plus copies	60% discount

Traders Press Inc.®
PO Box 6206
Greenville, SC 29606

Phone: 800-927-8222 or 864-298-0222
Fax: 864-298-0221
http://www.traderspress.com